LA PREM DE LA PREM

A CELEBRATION OF 30 YEARS OF PREMIER LEAGUE FOOTBALL

WRITTEN BY

STEVE MARSH, KEITH MARSH & BEN KNAPMAN

ILLUSTRATED BY **CHRIS KNAPMAN**

LA PREM DE LA PREM

FIRST PUBLISHED IN GREAT BRITAIN AS A SOFTBACK ORIGINAL IN 2022

COPYRIGHT © CHRIS KNAPMAN, STEVE MARSH, KEITH MARSH AND BEN KNAPMAN

EDITING, TYPESETTING AND PUBLISHING BY UK BOOK PUBLISHING

WWW.UKBOOKPUBLISHING.COM

ISBN: 978-1-915338-43-3

CONTENTS

INTRODUCTION

This book is both a celebration and critique of the footballers – the personalities – who have starred in arguably the world's most compelling league over the last three decades. As the Premier League's 30th anniversary is now upon us, what better time to celebrate its colourful history?

We have extracted accurate statistical data to enable us to write a balanced and engaging critique of the characters concerned. We have used a combination of football writing and caricature to engage the reader's interest.

We hope you enjoy reading it as much as we enjoyed creating it.

ACKNOWLEDGEMENTS

This book has been written by four avid football fans, who have followed the progress of the Premier League since its inception 30 years ago. We have tapped into our memory banks for much of the detail, but we would like to acknowledge a variety of information sources from which we have extracted statistical data, quotes etc. These include The Premier League website, PL club websites, newspaper articles, players' autobiographies and many more.

It has been a privilege for us to profile the players included in these chapters. We apologise if any of your favourite players have not been included, but with such a plethora of talent available, it would have been impossible to cover them all. We hope you have derived as much pleasure from reading about the players herein as we did from writing about them.

THE
CREATIVE
TEAM

CHRIS KNAPMAN

Chris is a Freelance Caricaturist of over 20 years' experience. He trained in 'Fine Art and Graphic Design' prior to completing a degree in 'Illustration' at West Hertfordshire College. He earns a crust drawing at live events such as wedding receptions and corporate functions. Chris also undertakes highly

detailed commissions from photographs and is available for talks, demonstrations and tuition on caricature. He is a Blackpool F.C. supporter. Back in late 2010, when his team were flying high in The Premier League, Chris first approached Steve about creating a book about the characters that made the global powerhouse it is today.

STEVE MARSH

Steve is a graduate in English Literature attained at The University of Leeds. He has excellent writing skills, research experience and an in-depth knowledge of football, having followed the game all his life. He enjoyed playing the game at amateur level for a number of years. He has followed his local team Blackburn Rovers through good times and bad. In his spare time he dabbles in writing poetry.

BEN KNAPMAN

Ben is 20 years old and is a university student at UCLAN in Preston, where he is undertaking a degree in Football Studies. He supports Fleetwood Town and has a weekly column in the local paper, The Blackpool Evening Gazette, where he has his take on his club's performances. Ben has also featured on Sky Sports, BBC platforms and EFL platforms too. He also has his own YouTube Channel, Cods Vlogs, which covers Fleetwood Town and Division 1 in general. Ben has always loved football at all levels and watches it as much as he can.

KEITH MARSH

Keith is the elder statesman of the team. Now retired, he worked as a marketing executive mainly in the motor industry. In his younger days he also turned out for a number of local amateur teams. A lifelong supporter of Blackburn Rovers, he still lives in hope that his team will one day make it back into the Premier League.

PROLOGUE

Even the most cursory of backward glances into the annals of Premier League history will reveal a seismic shift in the nature of top-flight English football since its inception. Whether it be stadia, attendances, media coverage, financial matters or the players themselves, our game is, on many levels, wholly unrecognisable from its long-suffering predecessor, the old First Division.

In the late 80s and early 90s, English football was fraught with difficulties. Crumbling stadia – many of which comprised old-style terracing deemed unsafe and outlawed by the 1990 *Taylor Report* in the wake of the 1989 Hillsborough disaster – had to be adapted and made safe by becoming all-seater, with clubs having to shoulder the financial burden.

The game in this country was also blighted by hooliganism, which had plagued English football since the late 1960s, worsened year upon year, culminating in the cataclysmic events of the Heysel Stadium tragedy. English clubs were subsequently banned from competing in European competition and there is strong evidence that this was to the detriment of player development, with the First Division falling behind Serie A, La Liga and the Bundesliga in terms of both quality of play and spectator appeal. Indeed, when English clubs were permitted to end their six-year exile from European competition, it was immediately apparent that there was now a sizeable difference in class between top English teams and their continental counterparts.

Chris Knapman '13

During the death throes of the First Division, one team stood out in particular: George Graham's indomitable Arsenal. In 1991, the Gunners cantered to the title with a seven-point margin over their nearest rivals Liverpool – and it would've been nine but for a pitch-side brawl against Manchester United, which resulted in the FA docking them two points. With just 18 goals conceded in a season which saw them lose just one game, they appeared to be well-equipped to spearhead England's assault upon its continental foes when English clubs were readmitted to European competition in the 91-92 season – or so we thought. This quickly proved to be a fallacy. This was not the Europe of old; not the Europe of the late 70s and early 80s, when the European Cup remained firmly on English soil for six successive seasons. The game on mainland Europe had moved on apace and this was ably demonstrated by a Benfica team who, superior in skill, technique and tactical knowhow, simply swept the English champions aside in the second round of the European Cup. After a 1-1 draw in Portugal, they came to Highbury and delivered a master-class. Arsenal's seemingly impenetrable phalanx of Dixon, Bould, Adams and Winterburn simply couldn't cope with the one-touch passing and movement of the rampant Portuguese. For me, this was a pivotal moment in the evolution of the English game. As an island nation, our blinkered view of the game we spawned was worsened by the absence of European competition – as was our ability to compete.

No longer could we look at our football through the prism of nostalgia and patriotism – *'This royal throne of kings, this scepter'd isle... this blessed plot, this earth, this realm, this England, This nurse, this teeming womb of royal kings, Fear'd by their breed and famous by their birth, renowned for their deeds as far from home... Dear for her reputation through the world, Is now leased out... Whose rocky shore beats back the envious siege...'* – it was high time to open our borders.

So the delusional beliefs about the quality of our league had been shattered by Benfica and many of their contemporaries. We patently needed to add guile and sophistication to our play; we needed footballers of superior technical ability. Our assiduous, high-tempo pressing game was not enough; sometimes you need to be able to absorb pressure and counter-attack swiftly and decisively – à la Benfica et al.

It was time for change and, boy, did we see it.

Over the next few seasons we saw momentous changes in the recruitment of players and, at a slightly slower rate, managerial and coaching staff. Foreign footballers flooded over English shores exponentially. Cynics have argued that this was nothing to do with trying to play the so-called 'beautiful game' and everything to do with circumventing the spiralling cost of both signing and paying home-grown talent; however, when one delves into the annals of Premier League history, they'll find an abundance of wheat, which more than makes up for the chaff. The roll call of overseas players who've lit up our league is incandescent and simply breathtaking. Zola, Bergkamp, Cantona, Suarez, Aguero, Silva, Henry – the list goes on, and on...

Whilst the emergence of ball-playing magicians from afar hasn't exactly sounded the death-knell of the 'long ball game', some will say they've certainly heard a few distant peals. Another change in the game, its introduction coinciding with the league's birth (1992), was FIFA's Law 12 – prohibiting goalkeepers from handling backpasses. Devised in the wake of a mind-bendingly dull Italia '90, it was designed to discourage overly defensive play and time-wasting; a good example being when keepers dribbled the ball around their penalty-area needlessly – only to pick it up the second an opponent bore down on them. This was extended to include throw-ins in 1997. These rulings sat nicely with the growing phenomenon of continental defenders and midfielders who are comfortable on the ball and have the poise to pick a pass. With goalkeepers only able to clear a backpass with their feet, some of us expected to see more instances of defenders panicked into hastily hoofing the ball down the other end of the field. This didn't really happen as often as we might have expected – we'd imported players who could calmly turn on the ball and carefully feed it through the midfield; a refreshing sight to say the least.

Although overseas stars and a shift towards a 'passing game' will titillate the purists, their ramifications for the nurturing of English talent – and ultimately – the national team are obvious. The bar has been raised; players who would've played in the top division in bygone eras have found themselves being sold to Football League sides when, at a whim, managers at cash-rich clubs have replaced them with a Croatian who just happened to have shone quite brightly at the last World Cup. This adds a new meaning to the term 'throw-away society'! In 2014, approximately just one third of Premier League regulars were English, fuelling the argument that the fortunes of young English players, together with that of the national team, can only improve with the introduction of minimum quotas. Indeed Michael Woods, signed by José Mourinho for £5 million at 16, but subsequently playing for Hartlepool United at 24, would certainly endorse this argument. Younger English players are often lost in the depths of the enormous squads that clubs competing on three – if not four – fronts, perhaps earning the odd rare outing in the League Cup.

Transfer fees are widely regarded as being disproportionate to ability and players simply go to the highest bidder. In 1994, Blackburn Rovers broke the British transfer record when they paid Norwich City £5 million for Chris Sutton. By the autumn of 2014, this record stood at the £59.7 million Manchester United were prepared to pay for Real Madrid's Angel di Maria – a player who's hardly been the lustrous presence we all anticipated. Where will it end?!

One of the most salient features of the Premier League is its global appeal. Despite an explosion in media coverage, attendances are markedly better than those in the latter years of First Division history. People have flocked to watch players like Alan Shearer, Cristiano Ronaldo and Alexis Sanchez in unprecedented numbers; and media coverage itself has meant that, in the true spirit of Benthamism, we've all been able to enjoy the cornucopia of multinational footballing talent. When the old First Division resigned from the Football League in 1992, it was then empowered to negotiate its own broadcasting and sponsorship deals; the corollary of this freedom was the establishment of a now long-standing relationship with BSkyB. Far, far more top-flight games are shown live per season than pre-Premier League inception – both in the UK and to a growing global audience.

Television revenue has had far-reaching implications for club performance. Teams in the upper echelons of the league enjoy the additional bonus of revenue from live coverage of Champions League and Europa League games, as well as domestic fixtures. This led to the dominance of a super-affluent 'big four' in the 2000s: Manchester United, Arsenal, Chelsea and Liverpool. (Though since 2011 Manchester City have disrupted this with six league titles.)

The burgeoning wealth of teams in the top-flight has attracted much criticism – the main bone of contention being the yawning financial gap between clubs in the Premier League and their Football League counterparts. Firstly, teams who are promoted are frequently relegated at the end of their first season. Secondly, there's evidence of a 'bouncebackability' factor. When clubs established long enough in the Premier League to put them on strong financial footing are actually relegated, they dwarf their Championship rivals in terms of spending power, and simply 'buy' their way straight back up. The likelihood of a relegated club returning to the Premier League at the first time of asking is further increased by 'parachute payments', designed to compensate clubs for a loss of television revenue. (On average, the annual television revenue of a Premier League club is approximately 27 times that of a Championship club.)

In 2007, the Premier League was declared to be 'officially' the best in the world. Using performance statistics from European competition as a yardstick, the Premier League ended La Liga's eight-year reign at the top of the table. In achieving this success, the game in England has co-existed with the real world in some sort of parallel monetary universe. In 2014, Manchester United were paying Radamel Falcao – a player with four goals in 29 games, who was unable to gain a regular foothold in the first team – £265,000 a week. Worryingly, such incredulous wages have become the rule, rather than the exception. In 1991, Paul Gascoigne became the first player in our highest division to earn £2000 a week. The relationship between the average weekly wage in the UK and the dizzying sums of money paid to Premier League footballers is alarmingly hyperbolic. And fans of Premier League sides, already aghast at such statistics, are further embittered by being asked to pay increasingly extortionate ticket prices. At the start of the 2014-15 season, the average price of the cheapest Premier League season ticket was £467.95. This denoted a rise of 8.7% since 2012-13 at a time when salary freezes and cuts abound. Although watching the Premier League live remains ever-popular (despite prohibitive ticket pricing and an ever widening televisual menu), the proportion of away fans per game is much lower than in the old First Division. Perhaps fans, already stretched in forking out for season tickets, balk at the prospect of paying to see away games as well?

The financial disjunction between club and fan is aggravated by what they often perceive to be attacks upon their club's identity. Recent examples include Cardiff City owner Vincent Tan's insistence that the Bluebirds switch to a red home strip for commercial reasons. Of course, most of their supporters still defiantly watch their games in traditional blue. Hull City's Egyptian owner, Assem Allam, has taken steps towards renaming the club 'Hull Tigers'. He clearly perceives them as a brand, as opposed to an integral part of the community's infrastructure; pursuit of filthy lucre is all that seems to matter. There is no xenophobia here – but these examples beg the question as to whether foreign owners are oblivious to the cultural history of their new acquisitions, or whether it's simply a case of riding roughshod over tradition to maximise the return on their investment? The naming or renaming of stadia also disconnects clubs from their locality and the community they ought to serve. Surely the link between a stadium's name and its geographical location should be sacrosanct, because it helps preserve a club's cultural identity? Names like the Emirates Stadium, the Etihad Stadium, the Kingpower Stadium, and so on, tell us little about a place, a club and its community.

Since football has become a slave to fiscal market forces, preserving one's status has become paramount – for all owners per se. A knock-on effect of this mentality is that owners and directors, when faced with a string of poor results on the pitch, envisage the monstrous spectre of relegation and all its financial horrors to boot, then act quickly by sacking the team manager. Clubs are coming under increasing criticism because the 'life-expectancy' in the job of a Premier League manager is becoming ever-shorter. This hair-trigger approach to the tenure of managers almost makes Albert Pierrepoint look complacent and lackadaisical. Economic pressures and a subsequent unwillingness to give managers time to assess, recruit, train, coach and, erm, manage, has seen people with hitherto shining reputations shown the door all too hastily. The game is venal to its very core.

Another moot point is behaviour. All too often we see referees encircled and vainly harangued by a glowering throng of irate players. (When do officials ever bow to player pressure?) To make matters worse, replays then show the players' chagrin to be entirely misplaced. This renders the whole Premier League debate somewhat depressingly cyclical – as we then remind ourselves that the mendacious superstars who apoplectically demand phantom penalties, or hit the turf like a knight downed by a bowman at *Agincourt*, are the same people that earn in a week what many fans earn in nigh on a decade.

A hackneyed debate, yes – but one which will rumble on as long players are overpaid and fans are asked to pay a relative fortune to watch them.

Discontent with the distribution of wealth in the game on all levels is a perennial bugbear of fans' forums, meetings and pressure groups, and this looks set to fester for the foreseeable future. Yet, despite the growing resentment, fans are – to some critics inexplicably so – prepared to part with ticket money and Sky subscriptions despite exercising their right to grumble at every opportunity. Proponents of the Premier League and televisual brands won't care a jot for this curious ambivalence as long as fans ultimately take the plunge and invest their meagre disposable income in celebrating the best football on offer. Some will argue that watching the cream of football is now a bourgeois dalliance, with 'working class' supporters (once the lifeblood of the English game) being priced out of top-flight stadia. But that's yet another debate...

Maybe we should dwell on what lures supporters and their wallets back time and again? It could be Alex Ferguson and Manchester United's 'Class of '92' – the backbone of a team which claimed an unparalleled 13 Premier League crowns; it could be Arsène Wenger's Arsenal 'Invincibles', whose totally unbeaten run in 2002-3 swept the Gunners to the title. It could be a moment of eye-watering brilliance from Bergkamp, Cantona, Suarez, Fowler or Giggs. It could be the joyous pandemonium of Sergio Aguero's injury-time title-clincher in the final moments of 2011-12 – after Manchester City had overhauled their city rival's eight-point lead. Or it might be Beckham, Alonso or Adam scoring audaciously from inside their own half; a look through the archives never disappoints. My favourite moment is my beloved Rovers clinging on to the title at Anfield, as Manchester United's Andy Cole decisively struck the post in the dying seconds at Upton Park, squandering the chance to deny us at the last. We can all draw upon a rich seam of cherished Premier League moments; the prospect of more to come keeps us all well and truly hooked.

MAIN
PLAYER
PROFILES

ALAN SHEARER

"You have to accept whatever comes and the only important thing is that you meet it with courage and with the best that you have to give"

(Eleanor Roosevelt)

Alan Shearer's debut for Blackburn in 1992 is etched in the memory of every Rovers fan. Bathed in late summer sunshine, Selhurst Park saw this old-school Geordie centre-forward serve notice of what was to come. (Despite his obvious potential at his first club, Southampton, one might argue that a return of 23 goals from 118 top-flight games for the Saints, was a slightly disappointing return for a forward who had made the world sit-up with a scorching debut hat-trick as a seventeen-year-old against Arsenal.) With his new club trailing 2-1 just inside the second half, Britain's costliest player controlled a Mike Newell knockdown on his chest before sending a ferocious right-foot volley whistling over Nigel Martyn's flailing arms into the roof of the Palace net from nigh on twenty-five yards. Minutes later, in a truly irrepressible display, Shearer neatly controlled a low pass on the left-hand touchline before ushering the ball past his marker into the midfield with his right foot, before sending what, in the vernacular, can only be described as a 'pile-driver' curling into the bottom right-hand corner of Martyn's goal from approaching thirty yards this time.

The raw power of his debut Rovers goals were Alan Shearer's trademark; his sledgehammer of a right boot left goal-keepers redundant time and time again. Allied to this were a stocky build and rambunctious style, enabling this burgeoning talent to outmuscle defenders then race away to finish with typically unerring poise. Television punditry routinely (and quite correctly) invites us to focus the mindset of footballers – 'confidence' is as frequently-used a word in coverage as most. Well, Alan Shearer had self-confidence by the bucket-load, which best explains why he was able to play the game with such energy, persistence and ebullience – again traits which enabled him to bag more goals than many of his more sublimely skilful contemporaries. A mere footnote by comparison, but add to all that a mention that he hardly lacked pace in his Blackburn days, and you'll understand why Rovers fans go misty-eyed at the mention of his name and rightly anoint this awesome centre-forward as the greatest-ever player to step out in the famous blue and white halves.

Recognising Shearer's qualities, manager Kenny Dalglish was quick to employ two wingers, Stuart Ripley and Jason Wilcox, to get early crosses in to Shearer as often as possible – as he knew his now talismanic striker could keep opponents at bay and then pretty much do the rest himself. This plan worked well-enough in his first two seasons, but it really came to fruition when Chris Sutton arrived from Norwich in his third. Dubbed 'the SAS', this duo functioned brilliantly together, with Sutton contributing 15 goals himself, as well as providing the ideal foil for Shearer – the 'senior' partner in the relationship. With Shearer's contribution that year an impressive 34, the 'SAS's 49-goal haul fired Blackburn Rovers to their first post-war title (pipping Manchester United on a tumultuous final day of the season). 'The SAS', in fact, plundered an impressive 58 goals in all competitions. The Premier League title represented Alan Shearer's one and only honour in senior football. For a footballer of Shearer's ability and standing (one of the greatest strikers in modern times), this is a truly lamentable anomaly and perhaps the most startling statistic on his extensive and wholly impressive CV.

Resuscitated by the then prodigious funds of local steel tycoon Jack Walker, Rovers had languished outside the top division for the previous 26 seasons. A plethora of six-figure signings saw the team's stock rise immeasurably – as did the belief of the long-tormented supporters – but, in truth, it was the presence of Shearer, the unrivalled England number 9, which propelled the fans' confidence way up into the stratosphere. Having previously trudged into Ewood Park contemplating a win against Barnsley, Millwall and Walsall et al as a 'realistic possibility', I distinctly recall breezing into the ground one September afternoon believing that victory over Liverpool, the most illustrious club in British football, was almost 'a given'. It seemed somewhat surreal, but that is how it felt. This sense of club superiority was, however, interrupted by a fleeting moment of self-censure, during which I remember telling myself that it was rather naïve and tantamount to sheer hubris to think that we might quell the mighty 'pool – after all, they were four-times European champions.

We brushed them aside, 5-2. Without Alan Shearer, no Blackburn Rovers supporter would have ever entered a stadium harbouring such inflated and 'preposterous' ideas: he was the conduit for our newfound faith.

It was around this time that Mr Shearer revealed the hitherto arcane secret behind his uncanny knack for goal-poaching. "Chicken and beans, always chicken and beans before a match", came the terse reply to the Lancashire Evening Telegraph reporter who enquired as to how he readied himself for games. Well, they did keep talking about 'a wind of change' blowing through Ewood at the time! No pretentions around food science here then, so I doubt Jackie Milburn would've thought him a prima donna or 'fancy dan' – he even informed the BBC that he celebrated winning the Premier League title by creosoting his garden fence. As a modern footballer, festooned with riches, surely, he could've asked one of his underlings to delegate this prosaic task to one of the gardening staff. Maybe he found the stultifying process of daubing on the black stuff grounding after lifting his only silverware in the heady maelstrom of Anfield.

When Shearer left Ewood Park with his solitary medal, he ironically passed-up opportunities to join both Manchester United and Barcelona – and no doubt collect countless honours in either city. He even agreed terms with United and got as far as looking for a house in the area, only to capitulate at the eleventh hour when Newcastle boss Kevin Keegan renewed his interest and left him one final voicemail, imploring him to join his hometown club. The visceral need to walk out at St. James' Park in black and white stripes eventually proved too much and the chance to win more honours had gone; but that's easy for us to say with the illumination of hindsight. An idealist might argue that the clamour, the ardour, of his Newcastle public, would render financial gain an irrelevance.

No less effusive in their praise of Shearer are his fans on Tyneside. Numerous stellar performances for Blackburn and 112 goals in just 138 league starts (despite his four seasons there being badly interrupted by knee injury) persuaded Newcastle to part with an unprecedented 15 million pounds in the summer of '96. Seen by many as the heir-apparent to the throne of the long-departed Jackie Milburn, Shearer was expected to be the saviour of Tyneside.

It would be remiss of me not to single-out one of his many unforgettable goals for the Magpies (so many jaw-droppers and show-stoppers to choose from!), but I finally settled upon a volley that probably makes the hairs on Geordie necks stand on end to this day. It's December 2002 and Newcastle are a goal down to Everton at St. James' Park. Laurent Robert's speculative punt from the halfway line is nodded across the edge of penalty area by Shola Ameobi to the arriving Shearer. Not wishing to encumber himself with the more trifling aspects of the coaching manual (such as chest or thigh control, yawn...) he hits a thunderous, right-foot volley, first-time, which simply burns its way into the Everton net from over twenty yards. His only goal in blue and white to rival this for unadulterated ferocity came in a 4-0 romp over QPR in Rovers' title-winning season. Picking up the ball at much the same distance, Shearer unleashed a drive that was as unexpected as it was powerful; so much so, that it had crashed in off the Rangers cross-bar before some cameramen were able to adjust. But, for me, his goal against Everton is the best example of his ability to strike from distance.

Over his 10 seasons at St James' Park, Shearer lost a little pace, but his predatory instincts and rapacity for goals did not desert him one iota. His 303 Premier League games there yielded a further 148 goals. It is no coincidence that just like at Blackburn, he thrived on the sterling service of two wingers – this time Nolberto Solano and the mercurially talented David Ginola.

'Big Al', as he was affectionately-known on Tyneside (and beyond), finished his top-flight career with statistics to back-up his towering reputation: 283 goals in 559 Premier League games. He also finished his Newcastle career as the club's all-time leading scorer, six ahead of the legendary Jackie Milburn. To this day he is still the Premier League's all-time leading goalscorer. Whilst fans and pundits alike are agog at the sophisticated play and superior technique of the ever-growing number of foreign imports, Alan Shearer, cast from the die labelled 'swashbuckling target-man', of the same ilk as Nat Lofthouse and Milburn himself, demonstrated that the old-fashioned British centre-forward still has as much to offer as anyone else.

I don't think 'Wor Jackie' would've been disappointed, do you?

DAVID BECKHAM

'If a man loves the labour of his trade, apart from any question of success or fame, the gods have called him.'

(Robert Louis Stevenson)

In describing social, cultural and economic change, 'globalisation' has undoubtedly become one of the watchwords – indeed key concepts – of the late twentieth and early twenty-first century; and football is no exception to this unifying process. The advent of the Premier League and its lucrative synergy with BskyB, has seen top-flight English football beamed not just across a nation, but across the globe; which has, of course, enabled Premier League clubs to develop an international fanbase, rather than rely on denizens of their locality. In doing so, football has been subsumed (but not consumed) by popular culture. Celebrity became the lifeblood of popular culture – so football needed a popstar with worldwide appeal: enter one David Beckham.

Born in Leytonstone, east London, Beckham enjoyed a happy – if fairly unremarkable – working-class upbringing: his mother a hairdresser and father a kitchen fitter. His introduction to football came when he played for local junior sides, Ridgeway Rovers and Brimsdown Rovers. Although he had trials with local club Leyton Orient, Norwich City and Tottenham Hotspur, he was seemingly always destined to join Manchester United. His parents are avid United supporters and, together with young David, would frequently head north to watch games at Old Trafford. Beckham also attended a Bobby Charlton football school and even won a talent competition, for which the prize was the chance to train with Barcelona. So, perhaps inevitably, he signed associate schoolboy forms for Manchester United on his fourteenth birthday.

Beckham enjoyed some early success at Old Trafford with the youth team, whom he helped win the FA Youth Cup in 1992 – an experience with which he was to become very well-acquainted. Under the experienced stewardship of manager Alex Ferguson, Beckham was allowed to develop at a natural pace and only progress through the youth ranks when ready: thrust headlong into the cauldron of Old Trafford as a raw stripling he certainly wasn't. Ferguson, as has increasingly become the norm amongst bigger clubs, decided to blood Beckham in the humbler surroundings of Preston North End's Deepdale. Although he only made five appearances (scoring twice), he made an instant impression on North End fans - most notably scoring directly from a corner-kick. Even though he played merely a cameo role in their season, many PNE supporters were trumpeting the emergence of an exceptional talent.

David Beckham finally made his senior United bow in April 1995 (a month shy of his twentieth birthday) in a goalless draw with Leeds United; and it soon became apparent what he could and couldn't do. Quite frankly, anyone who cared to list what was missing from his armoury, would've paused and wondered why he wasn't following his father's footsteps into the kitchen world and a life of formica, false promises and flooring; however, with the benefit of hindsight, it's difficult to imagine 'Becks' the style icon and international talisman hard at it with a rawl plug between his teeth and a pencil behind his ear, as he awaits his next mug of builder's tea. Unable to unnerve opponents with a thrust of the afterburners, unlikely to bamboozle defenders with a Cruyff turn (or trickery of any kind really) and unlikely to give Frank Lampard sleepless nights over the goalscoring midfielder's record, Beckham was, nonetheless, simply indispensable to the England national team, whilst his club career at Manchester United saw him become one of the most opulently decorated footballers in the world.

Although David Beckham didn't boast the same array of skills as, say, Paul Gascoigne, his right foot posed the gravest of danger for opponents. Able to pass or cross the ball from deep on the right of midfield – even his own half – Beckham's whipped right-foot deliveries bore the deadly accuracy of a heat-seeking missile; opponents knew what was coming, but were powerless to do anything to stifle the threat. At his best, Beckham's killer balls were no more playable than Shane Warne's fabled delivery to Mike Gatting at Old Trafford's cricket ground in 1993.

Clearly a much-needed asset to a team in transition (in the wake of Ince, Hughes and Kanchelskis departing), the most lauded of the new breed, or 'Fergie's Fledglings', enjoyed immediate success. In his first full season as a regular starter, he was pivotal in United winning the Premier League – memorably overhauling Newcastle United who'd raced ten points clear, in a stirring second half to the season. United then completed a league and FA Cup double, with Beckham setting-up Eric Cantona's winner at Wembley.

The sight of a United striker converting a Beckham cross with consummate ease and alacrity – due to its pin-point accuracy – became gleefully familiar to United fans; however, what was not so expected was what occurred playing away to Wimbledon on August 17th, 1996. With the cricket season still in full-swing, a summery, sun-kissed Selhurst Park witnessed something genuinely breathtaking. Seizing upon a loose ball just inside his own half, the young midfielder saw Wimbledon keeper Neil Sullivan enjoying a carefree wander from his goal line. With Beckham some sixty yards away on the halfway line, the Dons' keeper could be forgiven for not foreseeing any immediate peril to his goal – but he hadn't reckoned on him taking a glance upwards and launching an extraordinary lob from the chalk of the halfway line. Vainly back-pedalling, there was nothing Sullivan could do as the ball sailed over his head and to the right, nestling triumphantly in the back of his unguarded net. Had this missile hit ground amongst those thronged behind the goal, or even made a souvenir for a passer-by in the streets of South Norwood, we would've dismissed it as the hubris of youth; but Beckham's audacity was not misplaced and provided an early illustration of a self-confidence which threaded his whole career.

Heralded as one of the nation's brightest emerging talents, the fashion-conscious, 'man-about-town' fiancé of Spice Girl Victoria Adams could seemingly do no wrong in the eyes of the press or public. The French World Cup of 1998 saw Beckham's public image badly tarnished, if not irreparably damaged. His petulant retaliation, to being pole-axed by Argentina's Diego Simeone, was perceived by many as the main reason for England's chastening penalties exit at the hands of the South Americans. The ensuing episode provided a perfect example of just how fickle the media can be. No longer the handsome beau of English football – the British press adjourned their gushing, sycophantic courting of Beckham – instead, he was confronted by a phalanx of angry journalists, baying for his blood – the very same people who'd recently seen fit to lionize him. All was not lost for Beckham – a battery of very effective performances on the right of England's midfield saw this rancour dissipated; and his stock rose once again and again – and again.

The process of forgiving was finally complete in October 2001. When England hosted Greece in their final qualifying match for the 2002 World Cup, only victory could ensure automatic qualification and spare them the harrowing ordeal of the play-offs. With just seconds remaining, and the visitors 2-1 ahead, England were awarded a penalty twenty-five yards from goal. Perhaps emboldened by recent good form – not to mention a decisive free-kick against Columbia at France '98 – Beckham took responsibility for England's last chance. With a nation on tenterhooks, up stepped the Manchester United man. Bending his run-up from the left, he struck the sweetest of right-foot shots; the ball flew slightly to the right as it cleared the Greek wall, before arcing into the top left-hand corner. The goalkeeper remained motionless and stunned as pandemonium coursed through Old Trafford and beyond; as for Beckham – his homecoming and beatification were now complete.

David Beckham's career medal haul is one of the most impressive in Premier League history – indeed modern European football as a whole – and it goes like this: six Premier League titles, two FA Cups, two Community Shields, one FA Youth Cup, one UEFA Champions League and one Intercontinental Cup – all achieved during his time in Manchester. Not finished there, he went on to win the Spanish title and Supercopa de Espana with Real Madrid, followed by the French title with Paris Saint-Germain. And he's also won a raft of titles with LA Galaxy in the MLS. Individually, Beckham's collection of awards is huge and multifarious; stand-out accolades include PFA Young Player of the Year (1997), Ballon d'Or Runner-up (1999), BBC Sports Personality of the Year (2001) and Real Madrid Player of the Year (2006).

His move to Real Madrid – or departure from Manchester United – was mired in controversy, as rumours circulated in the media suggesting discord between Beckham and the seemingly omnipotent Alex Ferguson. His unveiling at Real Madrid attracted gold-plated, A-list celebrity attention. In front of more than 500 journalists from 25 different countries, Beckham was handed the iconic white shirt by Real legend Alfredo Di Stefano. This scene said so much about his elevation in status. It's also important to note that the acquisition of Beckham – who fell short of being a genuinely world class player for most people – was as much about commercial gain as it was about football. Already brimming with world class players, such as Zidane and Figo, Real Madrid hardly needed to add David Beckham; but he was integral to their marketing strategy. It was hardly a surprise when, with Beckham now amongst their ranks, the club embarked on an extensive pre-season tour of Asia – presenting a huge merchandising opportunity; and 'Brand Beckham' made it all the more lucrative.

2007 saw Beckham cross the Atlantic and play for LA Galaxy in the MLS. Again, this was commercially important for the club in question – but Beckham was also there to augment the profile of football in the USA and Canada. His time with Galaxy saw him loaned to AC Milan during the American close season of 2009 and again the following season. His finally called time on his career in 2013 – but not without a final flourish. He returned to Europe once more, when he signed for Paris Saint-Germain in the January transfer window. In his final professional season, he made 10 appearances as PSG went on to lift the French title.

Beckham is quite simply a megastar – his ubiquitous presence transcending mere football. From endorsing mobile phone networks to marketing his own toiletries, this man seems to have a finger in every money-making pie. The subject of a film eulogy, **Bend It Like Beckham**, his folkloric status seems rather disproportionate to his footballing ability. But with money in the coffers, neither The Premier League nor any of his former employers are complaining. And, much to Beckham's credit, he made the most of the ability he *did* have.

TONY ADAMS

"Prosperity doth best discover vice, but adversity doth best discover virtue"

(Francis Bacon)

The professional and personal life of Tony Adams, MBE, is not so much a story, but more of an odyssey. His hapless performances for England at Euro '88 rendered him the butt of derision at stadia the length and breadth of the country. Well into the Premier League era, Adams, dubbed 'The Donkey', was roundly jeered by opposing fans – usually subjecting him to cacophonous cries of "ee-yore, ee-yore".

Although the teenage starlet's shaky start to his senior career owed much to inexperience – he was only 21 at Euro '88 and had debuted for Arsenal at barely 17 – it was the burgeoning vice of alcoholism that affected the performances of a clearly talented centre-half and, by his own admission, contributed to some dreadful, error-strewn displays.

Despite his affliction, Adams managed 672 appearances for the Gunners – 290 of which were in the Premier League. Standing at six feet and three inches, he was imposing in the air at set-pieces and clocked up 48 goals in the red and white too. In fact, an Adams goal marks one of the most iconic moments in modern Arsenal history, occurring on the final day of the 1998 season. Put through on goal by Steve Bould, Adams rifles the ball into the corner before celebrating in front of his adoring fans on a jubilant North Bank, as Arsenal seals the title.

Signed as a schoolboy at 14, Adams rose up through the ranks and was already an integral part of Arsenal's 'Famous Four' (forming a formidable rearguard with Dixon, Bould and Winterburn) by the time the Premier League came into being. The 'Famous Four', led by Adams, were the unyielding bulwark upon which Arsenal built their success. They were breached on so few occasions, that one goal was often adequate to secure all three points. They deployed the 'offside trap' with a lightning efficiency that'd shame any police armed response unit. And it was this discipline that enabled them to quell sortie after sortie, with Adams taking the role of commander-in-chief. Having already won the old first division twice, the England international further decorated his curriculum vitae with two Premier League winners' medals in 1998 and 2002 – both FA Cup double-winning years for a team which had reigned supreme in the capital for more than a decade.

Known on Highbury's North Bank as 'Mr Arsenal', George Graham called him "my colossus" – high praise from a somewhat old-school and exacting manager.

The identikit old-fashioned English centre-half, Adams was aerially supreme and no stranger to a full-blooded tackle. He was also a natural leader; the image of Adams clenching his fist, teeth bared, as he rallies his team-mates to match his spirit and tenacity is an enduring one. This 'never-say-die' attitude and ability to communicate on the field helped land him the England captaincy just before Euro '96. His only notable flaw was a slight susceptibility to pace – though his superb reading of the game went some way to compensating for this. Once in possession, without ever caressing and distributing the ball with quite the composure and finesse of Franz Beckenbauer, Adams did develop this side of his game thanks to Don Howe and Arsène Wenger. He eventually became a more complete player.

Since his retirement, Adams has been inducted into the English Football Hall of Fame – such was his impact – and in 2008 came third in a '50 Greatest Gunners poll' on the club's website. In 2011 the club itself paid him the rarefied – arguably ultimate – tribute of erecting a statue of him outside the Emirates Stadium, in the exalted company of 'Thierry Henry' and 'Herbert Chapman'.

Although Adams ended his career in triumph, his path to this success was as rocky as they come. Before Arsenal's French revolution in the mid-nineties, and the arrival of Arsène Wenger and his salubrious, ultra-professional regime, many of Arsenal's senior players were, not too unsurprisingly, immersed in drinking culture; affluence exceeded maturity and the upshot was a hedonism unbefitting of a professional footballer. But whilst most of the other players would only imbibe heavily with their colleagues, Adams held an additional, solitary, drinking club all of his own. His critically acclaimed 1998 autobiography, *Addicted*, lays bare the extent of his alcohol problem. Team-mates would give him showers to try and sober him up ahead of training, in a bid to keep the problem beneath the radar of the austere George Graham. On one occasion, he even played a competitive match still inebriated from the night before. His lowest point came in 1990, when he drunkenly ploughed his Ford Sierra into a garden wall in Southend-on-Sea. Upon being breathalysed, he blew more than four times the legal drink-drive limit and was imprisoned for four months, but was freed after serving half his sentence. This didn't, however, prompt an immediate quest for salvation, as Adams continued to struggle with his addiction. After one binge, he fell down stairs whilst intoxicated and needed 29 stitches to repair a head wound. On a night out with midfielder Ray Parlour, fans of rival clubs mocked his drunken demeanour in Hornchurch Pizza Hut – to which he responded with all the decorum of a cornered skunk, by setting off fire extinguishers and firing a flare gun into the disabled lavatory.

Eventually, in September 1996, Adams confessed to the public that he was an alcoholic. Following a successful programme of treatment, the Highbury hero re-emerged as a rejuvenated and somewhat changed character. Demonstrating a cerebral, sensitive side to his nature, Adams embarked on a sports science degree at Brunel University, developed a taste for classical literature, and started taking piano lessons. Though admirable, his attempts to better himself post-booze, post-playing aren't what he'll be remembered for off the field. And it certainly won't be for his fruitless bid to manage/coach with Portsmouth, Wycombe and two Dutch clubs. Aside from serving Arsenal with a loyalty seldom found in the modern game (he was a one-club man), he will leave a lasting legacy in the work he has done to support other sportsmen and women who've also been hampered by addiction to drink, drugs and gambling et cetera. As a result of his own harrowing experiences, Adams set up the Sporting Chance Clinic to provide treatment, counselling and support for fellow sufferers. Patrons include Kate Hoey MP, Elton John and former Premier League footballer Alex Rae. Another patron is former team-mate Paul Merson – himself a recovering alcoholic. Adams is also a patron for NACOA – a charity which supports people affected by their parents' drinking.

It's no coincidence that the form of the promising young defender dipped dramatically when his addiction took a stranglehold. Commenting on the drink issue, then new Arsenal boss Arsène Wenger once remarked that Adams had played to only 70 percent of his capacity for a huge swathe of his career. But remembered by Gunners fans as a towering presence in the Arsenal back four, not to mention captain of England, it's also no coincidence that Tony Adams prospered enormously once he'd given up alcohol. As the silverware flooded into Highbury under the auspices of the Frenchman, a clean and focused Adams enjoyed something of an Indian summer, playing arguably the best football of his career.

A telling footnote to the tale of this tumultuous, epic career concerns the supporters. As Adams started to answer his critics, Arsenal fans could be seen sporting huge plastic donkey's ears in a bizarre, ironic tribute to their hero. My, how things can come full-circle.

Tony Adams was a loyal servant to both club and country, a top-class centre-half and an inspiration both on and off the field. A true personification of what can be born out of adversity, when the vision and determination lie within.

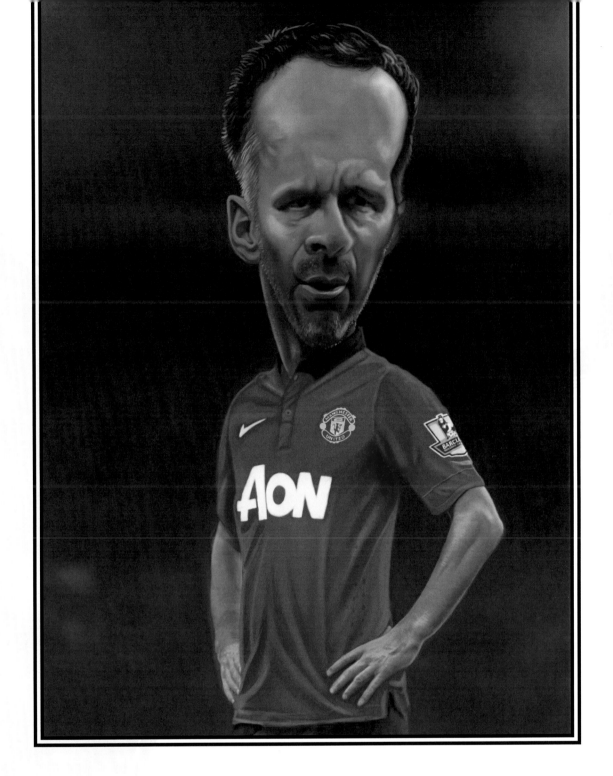

RYAN GIGGS

"Mediocrity knows nothing higher than itself, but talent easily recognizes genius"

(Sir Arthur Conan Doyle)

No story of the Premier League would be quite complete without a chapter documenting the heroics of one Ryan Joseph Giggs OBE. The mercurial Welshman graced the Premier League with his presence for a staggering 22 consecutive seasons from its inception – no other player has matched this achievement. For his entire professional career spanning 23 years, he wore the red shirt of Manchester United and was never sent off in a domestic match. He became the most decorated player in the history of the Premier League.

The son of a Welsh rugby player, he was born in Cardiff, but at the age of six his family moved to Manchester when his father switched from rugby union to rugby league and joined Swinton RLFC. He began his career with Manchester City after being recommended by Dennis Schofield, the coach of his local team Deans, who also happened to be on City's scouting staff. After joining City's School of Excellence, he continued to play for Salford Boys, with whom he enjoyed success as captain of the side which won the Granada Schools Cup in 1987, picking up the Man of the Match award after their triumph over Blackburn.

Throughout his time at Deans and Salford Boys, Giggs's progress was being closely monitored by Manchester United steward Harold Wood, who spoke directly to United Manager Alex Ferguson and recommended the youngster to the Old Trafford boss. Later on, Ferguson was able to view the young Welshman's talent at close range when Salford Boys played in a trial match against the United Under-15s side at United's then training ground, The Cliff. Giggs knocked in a hat-trick as Ferguson watched the game through his office window. That was enough to convince Fergie, and he subsequently turned up at the boy's house and signed him on schoolboy forms on his 14th birthday, and what a birthday present that turned out to be!

Giggs had the distinction of captaining England at schoolboy level, playing against Germany in 1989 at Wembley. At the time he played under his father's surname of Wilson, but subsequently changed his name to Giggs after his mother remarried. He also later pledged his international allegiance to Wales and represented the country of his birth more than 60 times, as we shall hear in due course.

He made his professional debut for United in 1991 and spent the rest of his 23 years there as a fixture in the Reds' first team. He was the only player to have scored in every Premier League season in which he was involved. His extensive list of achievements is testimony to his supreme skill, fitness and dedication to the sport he loved – but more of that later.

When Giggs turned pro on his 17th birthday, United were in their fourth season of the Ferguson era and had lifted their first trophy, the FA Cup, under the Scot's stewardship. However, United were still living in the shadow of Liverpool and Arsenal, but the feeling was that they were beginning to gain ground and that they would soon threaten the dominance of the aforementioned. Ferguson had been looking for a left winger to fill the void created by the departure of the popular Jesper Olsen. Ex-Saints winger Danny Wallace looked to be the solution, but he was unable to produce the promise he had shown at Southampton. As a natural left winger, Giggs initially competed with Lee Sharpe for the left wing berth.

His League debut eventually came against Everton in March '91 as a substitute for the injured left back, Denis Irwin. His first full start came in the 1991 Manchester derby in which he was credited with his first league goal. Replays showed that it was more likely a Colin Hendry own goal but no matter, Giggs was up-and-running and hungry for more. The 1991-92 season saw Giggs become a first team regular at United, and as Ferguson began to put his faith in youth, other notable names began to appear in the ranks – Butt, Scholes, Beckham, the Neville brothers, and thus the 'Class of '92' began to evolve.

Giggs was part of the team that finished runners-up to Leeds United in the final year of the old First division. He collected his first piece of silverware in April

1992 as United defeated Forest in the League Cup Final, and later that season he had the distinction of being voted the PFA Young Player of the Year, following in the footsteps of team-mate Lee Sharpe, who had won it the previous year.

The 1992-93 season saw Giggs claim the left-wing position ahead of Lee Sharpe, as he helped United claim the Premier League title in its inaugural season. The emergence of Giggs, along with the arrival from Leeds of the enigmatic Frenchman Eric Cantona, heralded a period of Premier League dominance for the Old Trafford club.

Off the pitch Ferguson was very protective of his young star and kept him out of the spotlight as much as possible – only granting him his first TV interview at the age of 20 with BBC's Des Lynam. However, as the media warmed to this emerging superstar, it became clear that the demands on him would increase and his public persona was about to change to a pop-star-like status. A TV show, Ryan Giggs' Soccer Skills, soon followed, as well as multiple appearances on the covers of soccer magazines. Parallels with George Best began to enhance his popularity.

Meanwhile, Manchester United's dominance of English football continued as they achieved a League and cup double in 1993-94 and Giggs became the first player to claim consecutive PFA Young Player of the Year awards, a feat later equalled by Robbie Fowler and club mate Wayne Rooney.

Giggs' career continued to prosper at United, wowing the fans with numerous spectacular goals as his confidence grew. The list is truly endless, but the stand-out Giggs goal which is etched into the memories of most football watchers came in the 1999 FA Cup semi-final replay against the mighty Arsenal.

In a match full of incident, an early goal by David Beckham was cancelled out by a Bergkamp deflected equaliser. At one apiece, things looked decidedly bad for United when, firstly, Roy Keane was dismissed for a second yellow following a reckless tackle on Overmars, and secondly, Arsenal were awarded a late penalty after Phil Neville clumsily floored Ray Parlour in the box. The normally reliable Bergkamp stepped up to take the spot kick, which to Arsenal's utter dismay, was saved by Peter Schmeichel.

As the game went into extra time, mounting Arsenal pressure had 10-man United on the brink, when suddenly a misplaced pass by Patrick Viera was picked up by Giggs deep in his own half. The mercurial Welshman raced towards the opposition goal and proceeded to slice through the Arsenal rearguard like a knife through butter. Leaving five defenders in his wake, he burst into the Arsenal box and unleashed an unstoppable drive past Seaman, which had the net bulging as if hit by a cannonball. What a goal and what a memorable celebration as Giggs ripped off his shirt, displaying the now famous hairy chest, and ran back to his ecstatic team-mates, twirling the displaced garment in a flamboyant manner, reminiscent of former Southampton favourite Mick Channon. United were in the final thanks to Giggs' solo effort and later went on to lift the trophy after beating Newcastle United.

In the following campaign, injury restricted Giggs' appearances to fewer than 30 with only one League goal to show for his efforts, and United were disappointingly pipped to the League title by Blackburn Rovers on the final day of a trophy-less season for the Reds. A couple of goals against FK Goteborg in the opening Champions League fixture and an FA Cup goal against Wrexham saw his tally reach four in what was an indifferent season for him.

The 1995-96 season saw a return to form and fitness for the Welshman, as he helped United achieve their second double. In the Premier League, United were trailing in the wake of a resurgent Newcastle managed by Kevin Keegan, and on December 23rd were an alarming ten points adrift of the Magpies. However, the lead was overhauled by mid-March as the United juggernaut pressed on to take the League title. Giggs played in the Cup Final win over

Liverpool, in which a solitary Eric Cantona goal sealed the double for the Manchester boys.

The following season, Giggs played a big part in helping United to reach the semi-final of the Champions League, but their hopes of success were dashed when they lost 2-0 on aggregate to Borussia Dortmund.

The 1997-98 season saw United pipped to the League title by Arsenal, and the Old Trafford trophy cabinet remained undisturbed for only the second time since 1989. Giggs had an injury-hampered season but still managed the earlier-mentioned FA Cup semi-final winner that sank Arsenal, as well as a 90th minute equaliser in the home leg of the Champions League semi-final against Juventus.

The following season saw United achieve a stunning treble, when they won the Premier League title, FA Cup and Champions League Final. Giggs had featured prominently in the latter success, providing the assist for Sheringham to score the equalising goal. Later in the year, Giggs was named Man of the Match when United claimed victory in the Intercontinental Cup against Brazilian side Palmeiras.

Giggs was rewarded with a new five-year contract in April 2001 and, following the departure of Denis Irwin in May 2002, he became United's longest serving player. In August of the same year, he reached a further milestone when he notched up his 100th career goal.

The 2002-03 season as a whole, however, became his 'Annus Horribilis' with a significant drop in form for the beleaguered Welshman. His faltering performances started to irritate a section of the United faithful and, on one occasion, led to him being booed off the pitch after a woeful match against Blackburn Rovers in the League Cup semi-final. Mutterings in the Press about dressing room spats began to surface, but the possibility of him being sold were quickly discounted by chief executive Peter Kenyon. Ironically, the day after Kenyon's statement, Giggs turned in a stunning performance in a Champions League tie with Juventus. After coming on as an early substitute for Diego Forlan, he scored two goals in a thrilling 3-0 victory over the Italian giants, including a thumping left foot drive into the roof of the net from a difficult angle. This went some way to endearing him to the fans once more.

As speculation about his possible departure continued, he declared his intention to stay at Old Trafford and in May 2004 he collected his fourth FA Cup winners' medal. In September of the same year he completed his 600th game for the club, only the third player to reach this milestone after Bobby Charlton and Bill Foulkes. 2005 saw him inducted into the English Football Hall of Fame in recognition of his contribution to the English game.

Although now well into his thirties, Giggs continued to be an ever-present in the United team, as the goals and assists still flourished over the next few seasons. One notable goal came in a Champions League game against Lille in 2007, when the Welshman scored the winner with a quickly taken free-kick, whilst Lille were still assembling their defensive wall. Mortified by the referee's decision to allow the goal, the Lille players walked off the pitch in protest.

They eventually returned and United held on for a 1-0 win. Well, I suppose it makes a change from air traffic controllers going on strike!

United clinched the Premier title in 2007, giving Giggs a record-breaking ninth league winners' medal. The following season he played fewer games as Ferguson opted for a more rotational policy with team selection. Nevertheless, in December 2007 he scored his 100th league goal in a 4-1 victory against Derby. He achieved a second century in February 2008, with his 100th Champions League appearance against Lille. A further landmark came in May when he broke Bobby Charlton's record of 758 appearances for United, when he came on as a sub in the Champions League final against Chelsea. United triumphed in a penalty shoot-out, with Giggs clinching victory when he converted the winning penalty in sudden death.

The 2008-09 season saw Giggs deployed in a midfield role. Inevitably, the advancing years had reduced the blistering pace of his heyday but even at the tender age of 35, he still played a key role in Ferguson's eyes. Around this time he had begun to look to the future by starting to take his coaching badges.

Over the next five seasons until his retirement in May 2014, the twilight of his marathon career, he continued to add to his many achievements. Worthy of mention are:

- April 2009 - PFA Player of the Year and 800th appearance for Man U
- May 2009 - 11th Premier League Title
- Sept 2009 – 700th start for Man U & 150th goal for the club
- Nov 2009 - 100th Premier League goal
- Dec 2009 – Passes Gary Speed's outfield record of 535 PL appearances
- Named Manchester United Player of the Decade
- Jan 2011 – 600th league appearance
- March 2011 – Passes Bobby Charlton's appearance record with his 607th game
- Feb 2012 – 900th League appearance
- June 2014 – 1000th competitive appearance

On the international front, Giggs made his debut in in 1991 against Germany at the tender age of 17. He made a total of 64 appearances for his country, scoring 12 goals, and captained the side on several occasions during his 16-year career. One might think such a long international career would have produced more caps, but Giggs restricted his outings for Wales mainly to competitive matches to preserve his fitness. He missed a total of 18 consecutive friendly games before playing his first friendly against Finland in March 2003. He received some criticism for limiting his appearances for Wales, but his response to this was, as outlined in his autobiography, "whenever I played two games in one week I always seemed to pick up an injury".

After a friendly against Brazil in 2006, Brazil coach Dunga paid Giggs the ultimate compliment by saying the Welshman would not look out of place playing for the five-times world champions alongside the likes of Kaka and Ronaldinho.

Giggs also represented Great Britain in the 2012 Summer Olympics and was subsequently appointed as team captain. He bowed out of international football after a Euro 2008 qualifier against the Czech Republic, receiving the Man of the Match award in a 0-0 draw.

In July 2014 he ventured into football management as player coach at Man United and later became assistant manager to Louis van Gaal during the Dutchman's tenure at Old Trafford. Although tipped as a potential successor to van Gaal, the job went to José Mourinho and, with heavy heart after such a long association with the club, Giggs announced his departure from Old Trafford in July 2016.

In January 2018 he was appointed manager of the Wales national team, succeeding Chris Coleman, who had left to return to club football with Sunderland after a successful tenure as Welsh manager. Giggs later led Wales to qualify for Euro 2020 (postponed to 2021).

In 2014 he joined forces with ex-United stars Scholes, Butt and the Neville brothers in a deal to purchase Salford City football club. Under their stewardship the club has progressed from non-league to League 2 status and, who knows? Perhaps another Giggs could emerge from their ranks in years to come.

NEVILLE SOUTHALL

*"A diligent hawker today, can be
a great tycoon tomorrow"*

(Ernest Agyemang Yeboah)

We're all too aware of the striking differences between the old First Division and the Premier League, as it closes in on 30 years since inception: the broadcasting and sponsorship deals, an exponential growth in the wealth of the biggest clubs (usually owned and bankrolled by business moguls from around the globe), the huge influx of foreign players and the ever-widening gap between a handful of elite clubs and even the rest of the Premier League. Many fans and media observers habitually compartmentalise the former First Division and the Premier League as two distinct eras; and this is something we frequently do with players. Neville Southall, though, doesn't allow us to do that.

Back in 1981, Southall wasn't lining up against Shearer, Viera or Ginola, and it was before Andy Gray breezed into town and set pulses racing as a refreshed, resurgent Everton stormed to the title. No, Everton were mediocre and a dreary watch.

But the ordinariness of early 80s Everton was nothing compared to Southall's humble origins as a footballer. Compared to his roots in the game, Everton circa '82 were positively enthralling. When a teenage Southall (just 15 in fact) debuted for Llandudno Town in the early 1970s, it's rather unlikely that he envisaged sharing a pitch with exotic talents from afar: Juninho, Bergkamp, Desailly and myriad others. As he stood in goal, no doubt enchanted by a growing number of superstars from across the globe, one wonders whether he reflected on the painfully circuitous route he had taken to the big-time.

After fruitless trials with Wrexham, Crewe Alexandra and Bolton Wanderers, Southall left Llandudno to join Bangor City in the Northern Premier League. Now a semi-professional, he was paid £10 a week by Bangor. Even in the mid 1970s, this was a paltry sum and very obviously not enough to sustain an existence. Southall was forced to seek employment elsewhere, running concurrently with his stuttering start to football life. In his early days as a footballer, he looked destined to be a journeyman at best – and his career off pitch also befitted 'journeyman' as a description; spells as a binman, waiter and hod carrier helped the young goalkeeper make ends meet.

It was at Bangor that Southall began to draw attention. Everton were his principal suitors and they asked the Welsh side's manager, Dave Elliot, for permission to take their goalkeeper on trial. He could hardly refuse really, could he!?... Unfortunately for Southall, Elliot left the club before any firm arrangements could be made.

With Bangor running into serious financial trouble, Southall was forced to move to Conwy United. After missing out on a trip to Goodison Park, the level of his despondency must've been incalculable – especially as Conwy paid him an infinitesimal – and in the 21st century incomprehensible – £3 per week ! Next stop was the Cheshire County League with Winsford United. This meant that Southall was still playing at a lower level than when he was at Bangor – so the start to his career couldn't have been more inauspicious. There was absolutely no indication of the heady days and unbridled success that lay ahead.

Southall didn't let his misfortune affect him on the pitch and continued to excel at Conwy. He then took his Bangor and Conwy form over the Welsh-English border upon joining Winsford. Wigan Athletic and Bury competed for his signature and the latter won out. Maybe he'd a preference for black pudding over pies! His transfer fee of £6,000 (rising to £25,000 when he moved on) would've looked a pittance even then (with the £1,000,000 transfer barrier breached for the first time in 1979); but to a club of Winsford United's tiny stature, it would've been considerable. Everyone benefited: Bury got their man, Southall got the overdue professional break that he'd craved for some time – leaving the Cheshire side to luxuriate in their newfound affluence.

With his days in refuse collection behind him, the man who also aspired to be a postman as a youth could now afford to entertain more elevated ideas; and he didn't have to wait long. One superlative season was enough to persuade Everton manager Howard Kendall to take Southall to Merseyside for £150,000.

If Southall wasn't harbouring any towering ambitions, a more diffident outlook would've been understandable after such a laboured passage to the promised land. And in the summer of 1981, few people saw Everton as league champions in the making. Howard Kendall, though, was slowly assembling a very capable team, consisting of young players who were coming of age and some very shrewd purchases.

Beginning with the FA Cup in 1984, Southall and Everton were very much amongst the honours in the mid-80s. A 2-0 victory over Watford at Wembley might've had club officials scratching around for the key to the trophy cabinet, having failed to win any silverware of any kind in 14 years. The middle years of the decade were the club's most bounteous since the 1930s and certainly marked the acme for Southall. Having struggled down in English football's basement – even sub-basement – leagues, success must've been sweetened by a sense of how abject mediocrity and failure actually feels. Two First Division titles, three FA Charity Shields and the European Cup Winners' Cup were a very healthy return for a goalkeeper and a team at the height of their powers.

At the end of the 1984-85 season, the first of the club's two title triumphs during this period, the Welsh international was named the Football Writers' Association Footballer of the Year. Scooping this award was a magnificent achievement – as it's extremely rare that the award goes to a goalkeeper; it's a prize almost invariably won by an outfield player. In the 72 seasons since Stanley Matthews took the inaugural prize, it's only been awarded to a keeper on four occasions: the other winners being Bert Trautmann, Gordon Banks and Pat Jennings. Journalists are known for being utterly savage at times, and notoriously difficult to please. The fact that they deemed Southall worthy of joining this illustrious club tells you everything you need to know about how he was playing at this time. Two years later, Everton were again league champions. But it was the following season, 1987-88, that stands out. In 40 league games, Everton and Southall conceded a mere 27 goals, setting a new club record in the process.

Southall's story is arguably defined by the heady days of the 1980s; what was to follow wasn't simply an insignificant postscript to a career on the wane. In fact, Southall hadn't read the script at all. What did follow was a glorious addendum to an already illustrious career. Rather than quietly fade back into the lower leagues, Southall was to play at the highest level well beyond the advent of the Premier League. At the inception of English football's new league, Everton's greatest ever stopper was already afforded legendary status in the minds of the supporters. When the Premier League kicked off in August 1992, Southall was just short of his 34th birthday. Even then, few would've predicted how the rest of his career would pan out – rather expecting it to peter out.

Neville Southall was to represent Everton Football Club for another five years. He, remarkably, added 207 Premier League appearances to the 300-plus appearances in the First Division. He'd already served the club with distinction for 11 years – a figure that he was to extend to 16. His last appearances for the Toffees came in November 1997 – by which time he'd turned 39.

Anyone tasked with placing Southall's finest saves in rank order – or indeed narrowing it down to a 'top ten' – would be facing a practically impossible undertaking. The candidates for such a category are innumerable. It would be akin to reading all 37 of Shakespeare's plays and attempting to come up with his ten most telling and insightful quotes. Returning to Southall, there are, however, a few that would surely occupy the upper reaches of any such list. In 1985, with the Toffees closing in on their first title since 1970, Everton's redoubtable goalkeeper makes a truly memorable save from Tottenham's Marc Falco. In the April of that season, it was a critical moment in the title run-in. A ball whipped in from the left flank reached its apex at the midpoint to the goal. Five yards out, Falco was perfectly placed to head home. Falco did nothing wrong and his connection was a solid one. Planting a firm header to Southall's right and slightly above him, spectators and Falco himself must've thought he had done enough to see the Everton net bulge. Not so; miraculously not so. Such was Falco's nearness to the goal, Big Nev had, frankly, no time at all to judge the flight of the ball, as a keeper would, for example, a strike from distance. Diving to his right, Southall's reactions were absolute lightning and he somehow managed to push the ball over the crossbar: pure and unadulterated instinct. Eulogies abounded – including one from *The Daily Mail's* Jeff Powell, who wrote:

'the most astonishing save since Gordon Banks left Pele dumbfounded in Mexico'.

Another outstanding performance came in the 1995 FA Cup Final, when Everton and Paul Rideout edged out Manchester United 1-0. The performance of Southall, now 36 years-old, was critical on the day – not least when he made a memorable double save from United's Paul Scholes. This triumph made 'Big Nev' the most decorated player in Everton history.

The ageing keeper showed no signs of relenting. He continued to be a rather more than adequate last line of defence. This proficiency ensured that he remained Everton's first choice goalkeeper for the first five seasons of the Premier League. The only time that Southall's place was in doubt was in the summer of 1995, with the club now under the stewardship of Joe Royle; the new manager made an unsuccessful attempt to sign Nigel Martyn from Crystal Palace, whilst aiming to sell Southall to Wolverhampton Wanderers. A problem then arose when Southall's touted successor, Paul Gerrard, suffered a loss of form during the pre-season. Royle reacted by aborting Southall's move to the midlands and duly doubled his wages to £6,000 a week. Nowadays many players earn far more even at Championship level. But to a man who, once upon a time, toiled for an impossibly meagre £3 a week, he must've felt like John D. Rockefeller, or the Duke of Westminster!

When Southall was replaced by Thomas Myhre during the 1997-98 season, he did finally return to the lower leagues, playing for brief stints at various clubs.

One of the most notable episodes of his playing career beyond Everton came when he made a brief return to the Premier League as 'player-coach' at Bradford City for the 1999-2000 season. Though registered as a player, he was expected to fulfil his coaching role, rather than take to the field himself. But, when all three senior Bradford keepers were injured, manager Paul Jewell had little option but to play Southall against Leeds United at Valley Parade. At the age of 41 years and 178 days, he became the fourth oldest player in Premier League history, behind John Burridge, Alec Chamberlain and Steve Ogrizovic – all of whom were also goalkeepers.

Whilst 1995 was a remunerative one for Southall, it was also rewarding in other ways. The club granted him a testimonial – which is arguably as much about recognition and kudos as it is about financial gain. I think his pay rise had taken care of any concerns about how he'd manage in his dotage. Perhaps the highlight of the year came when Southall was awarded an MBE. During the presentation ceremony, the Queen asked him a rather pertinent question:

"What will you do now that you're retired?"

Well, Neville Southall has done plenty. Firstly, he's tried his hand as a manager, at non-league level, but not with much success – being sacked on more than one occasion. Those who excel on the pitch aren't necessarily suited to management – take Bobby Charlton.

He's also spent time coaching young players from deprived backgrounds and worked in the special educational sector. He now works as a teaching assistant at a pupil referral unit in South Wales. Additionally, he's the international officer for his branch of UNISON.

Unusually, but to his credit, Southall has handed over his Twitter account to be used as a platform for various charitable causes and give a voice to marginalised social groups. These include members of the LGBT community, a drugs helpline, a suicide bereavement charity and a sex workers' collective. Whilst it's not unusual for high-profile figures in football to endorse charities, Southall's post-retirement activities have more of a philanthropic bent than most.

Also, Southall is affectionately remembered for his innate and therefore inescapable scruffiness. This is exemplified by his appearance at PFA award dinners. Sporting their tuxedos, his contemporaries looked smart and refined – sartorially impeccable. Neville Southall, on the other hand, looked like he'd been whipped up in a blender and poured into his. With a face like the proverbial unmade bed, Southall faced an uphill and ultimately impossible task in his attempts to cultivate an air of style and culture. He was essentially deconstructed homo sapiens reconstructed by a chimpanzee with cataracts. Southall was playing on Merseyside during the early 1980s, amid soaring unemployment. When Alan Bleasdale and Michael Wearing wrote and produced *Boys from the Blackstuff*, surely they made a sizeable mistake in failing to cast Neville Southall in a lead role? He could definitely have cut a shabby, disenfranchised unemployed docker rather convincingly. And he seems to be deeply pervaded by the mien of refuge collection – a feature which may never leave him! Once a binman...

If you look hard enough, there's a humorous dimension to the lives and careers of most footballers. But if he'd not left a real imprint on English football's top flight, we wouldn't even discuss him – let alone joke about some of his characteristics. The jokes are borne out of a fondness in how we remember one of our league's finest ever goalkeepers. And Southall himself showed an appetite for self-deprecating humour, when he titled his autobiography *The Binman Chronicles*!

We obviously don't just remember him for jocular reasons, we remember him for things like his dazzling shot-stopping ability; we remember him for his knack of darting off his line at speed – to intimidate and unnerve onrushing forwards (he read numerous books about the technical aspects of golf and boxing, in order to improve his balance and spring – something which clearly worked!); and we most certainly remember him for his impressive longevity. On that point, unwilling to quietly vanish from sight, Southall was Torquay United's Player of the Year at the tender age of 40.

The Neville Southall story also illustrates something about football by comparison to some other sports. With some, the colour of your, or your father's, school tie might well influence whether you 'get on' in your chosen sport; but this isn't so in football. In football, it doesn't matter who you are or where you come from – you can make it to the very apex of the game – if you have the gift and you bolster that gift with the necessary application. 'Big Nev's' long career demonstrates this very well. His unwavering dedication and dogged pursuit of the career he yearned for, saw him rise from the lowliest of the lowly to being recognised as one of the best goalkeepers in the land and probably the world. He was named in the PFA Team of the Year four times: quite simply, not many players can do that, not many at all.

MATTHEW LE TISSIER

"Men of lofty genius when they are doing the least work are most active."

(Leonardo da Vinci)

Matt Le Tissier, an unforgettable name and an unforgettable footballer. Le Tissier translates from French as 'The Weaver'. An absolutely appropriate 'nom de guerre' for a player who weaved his way and his magic through so many seemingly resolute Premier League defences, captivating the Southampton faithful and opposition fans alike, who were privileged to witness his silky skills.

Le Tissier was a one-club player, whose 16-year career for The Saints was blessed with many memorable performances. He was the club's second highest scorer behind Mick Channon – but mere statistics barely do justice to his undoubted footballing prowess. He has often been described not as a great goalscorer, but as a scorer of great goals. How true is that! He was surely the most gifted player never to have won a major honour in the game.

Just for the record, Matthew Le Tissier scored 162 Premier League goals in 443 appearances for Southampton – not a bad record when you consider he played from midfield for a club whose top-flight life was spent mainly in intensive care. Statistics, however, are the argumentative crutch upon which an international manager leans, when he feels compelled to select a prolific striker whose game extends little beyond six-yard tap-ins. In the case of 'Le Tiss,' there's no need to rely on these figures – impressive though they are – for this technically gifted, two-footed Channel Islander, will be long-remembered for moments of scintillating skill and a raft of audacious goals to keep the south coast club's Plimsoll line visible far longer than it would otherwise have been.

There's no denying that Le Tissier's game was hugely deficient in some areas – bordering on the portly, alarmingly bereft of pace for a top-class player and oblivious to defensive duty – he sauntered around the pitch like he'd just unleashed his Red Setter on a deserted beach in his native Guernsey, one indolent Sunday morning. Le Tissier's shortcomings, his languid style of play, belied the fact that he was a player of sumptuous skill whose trademark was a penchant for attempting the outlandish and pulling it off more often than most. Deft flicks carved open hitherto steely defences; ludicrous attempts on goal at the expense of an obvious pass seemed to work for this man – too often to be merely fortunate.

Le Tissier's portfolio of league goals alone is still the frisson of many an internet chatroom, as fans way beyond Southampton work up many a hot dactyl in homage to the man dubbed 'Le God'. I'm not going to join in the 'top 10' debate', but I will pick out some (even that was agonising) of the leading contenders.

During the 1994-95 season, The Saints came up against a high-flying Blackburn Rovers side at Ewood Park. (Rovers were destined to be crowned Premier League champions at the end of the season.) Picking up a pass just over the halfway line, he sped deep into the opposition half, side-stepping three bemused Rovers defenders in the process. He then proceeded to chip the ball from 30 yards over a startled goalkeeper and former Southampton team-mate, Tim Flowers. Time seemed to stand still as the ball floated unerringly into the top left corner of the net. The commentator's words "Only Matt Le Tissier can score goals like that !" summed up a sublime piece of skill, which was rightly awarded the BBC 'Goal of the Season' that year.

Norwich City were the visitors for a memorable match during the 1989-90 season. 'The Weaver' had a couple of early goal efforts thwarted by Norwich keeper Bryan Gunn, as The Saints dominated the initial proceedings. However, Norwich somehow managed to score the opening goal through Dale Gordon – much against the run of play. Le Tiss pulled a goal back from close range, after a neat turn in the six-yard box.

His second goal bore the genuine Le Tissier hallmark. Picking up the ball on the edge of the centre circle, he strode to the edge of the Norwich box, leaving three defenders in his wake and unleashed a 'daisy-cutter', which clipped the keeper's right hand post on its way in. A third Southampton goal was scored by Kevin Moore with a long-range volley of which Le Tiss himself would have been proud.

The pièce de résistance was to follow when he picked up a defensive clearance on the left and arrogantly shrugged off a challenge from the right back. As he darted to the corner of the Norwich box, he saw Gunn advancing towards him and nonchalantly floated the ball over the keeper's head from all of 30 yards. A stunning goal to complete a memorable hat-trick!

With no shortage of contenders, choosing Matt Le Tissier's finest ever strike is obviously subjective and extremely onerous. One of the strongest candidates came against Newcastle United at The Dell in the winter of 1993. Disappointingly, only 13,804 were in the ground to witness it live; fortunately for connoisseurs of the 'beautiful game', it was beamed live nationwide – courtesy of Sky Sports and its burgeoning empire – and, therefore, archived for posterity. A speculative ball was launched up field towards centre-forward Iain Dowie. Dowie then attempts to nod the ball into Le Tissier's path. Unfortunately, the Northern Ireland international misdirects his header and it bounces slightly behind him. 'Le God', unfazed by this minor inconvenience, remedies the situation with a flash of improvised ingenuity. With the bouncing ball on the rise, he shows great agility to alter his body shape, arching his foot backwards and cleverly hooking it into his path. Problem number two: Barry Venison is purposefully bearing down on him. Without letting the ball bounce after his first touch, he makes nonsense of the art of defending by tapping it past the defender and effortlessly drifting past him. Next, he lets the ball bounce the once, before lobbing it over the head of the other centre-half, Kevin Scott. Before Scott's worked out what has happened, he strokes the ball home to the right of goalkeeper Mike Hooper from about level with the penalty spot. When asked about this goal, Le Tissier referred to the importance of playing with a 'free mind' – as opposed to a preordained plan – thus allowing instinct to take over. That being the case, if this goal is a barometer of his skill and natural ability, then it must surely have left the glass well and truly shattered.

Revered German physicist Albert Einstein told us that "time is an illusion"; well, in scoring this goal, Le Tissier didn't have time to do what he did – yet he did it. Though he tells us that it was largely down to instinct, one might suspect that the lightning mind of a brilliant footballer played some part in the goal: enterprising, mesmerising and absolutely capital.

Try to compile a list of players who can score a goal like that one – the most notable thing about it will be its brevity.

Whilst the wizardry behind many of Le Tissier's goals from open play dominates our febrile attentions, his penalty-taking was also a tour de force in itself. Scoring 48 out of a possible 49 penalties, Matt Le Tissier remains the unrivalled king from 12 yards. To which this record owes most – his outstanding technique or dress-down Friday temperament – it is difficult to say.

The one blot on his career, however, is a failure to gain much international recognition. A meagre eight England caps might surprise fans from other footballing cultures, but in a country where work-rate is everything, an idle midfielder who rarely tackled was always going to be up against it – even if he could adroitly turn a defence inside-out and score from seemingly nothing. Quantity, not quality? – interchange as you see fit. Personally, I think there is a certain allure about a player who can be listless for 89 minutes and then suddenly lash in one of the best goals you've ever seen.

Whether it be due to his lack of industry, playing football for a club without real kudos, or the fact that England had already assigned the 'maverick spot' in the squad to Gazza, surely Le Tissier's talent was criminally neglected at international level.

An interesting detail of Le Tissier's retirement years to date is his relationship with Channel 4's long running quiz show, Countdown, which tests vocabulary and mental arithmetic. He's made a total of 10 appearances – six as assistant to the programme's lexicographer, Susie Dent, and four as an actual contestant – entering by exactly the same process as any other member of public. He debuted impressively, leaving his opponent for dead and winning by a yawning 57 points. Another couple of convincing victories saw 'Le Tiss' complete his hat-trick, before bowing out gracefully – to eventual finalist John Hardie. By way of a tribute, 'LETISSIER' has twice been the end-of-show conundrum teaser. Footballers are often mocked – harshly in my view – for a perceived lack of intellectual ability. Whilst nobody is suggesting that Le Tissier is an academic genius, a paragon of erudition, the way he acquitted himself on Countdown reminds us that there are footballers who are comfortably above average intelligence – as he clearly is. Cerebrally, he's a lot more to offer than telling us that he's 'sick as a parrot' or 'over the moon' and so on. He remains only the third person, after Damian Eadie and Mark Nyman, to appear as both guest celebrity and contestant in the show's 38-year history. And, in case you were wondering where he sits in the pantheon of professional footballers to compete on Countdown, former Burnley defender Clark Carlisle also won a trio of matches, whilst ex-Notts County midfielder Neil MacKenzie won an impressive five matches, before losing in the quarter-finals.

Returning to Matthew Le Tissier the footballer – as opposed to the wordsmith and mathematician! – we mortals can wax lyrical all day long about his élan for the spectacular etc, but surely the most cogent tribute to his ability comes, fittingly, from a doyen of the beautiful game. Writing in his recent book, Barcelona great Xavi tells us that LeTiss was one of his boyhood idols and inspiration for his own career: "He could simply dribble past seven or eight players but without speed – he just walked past them. For me he was sensational."

Eight England caps, really?? Case well and truly rested.

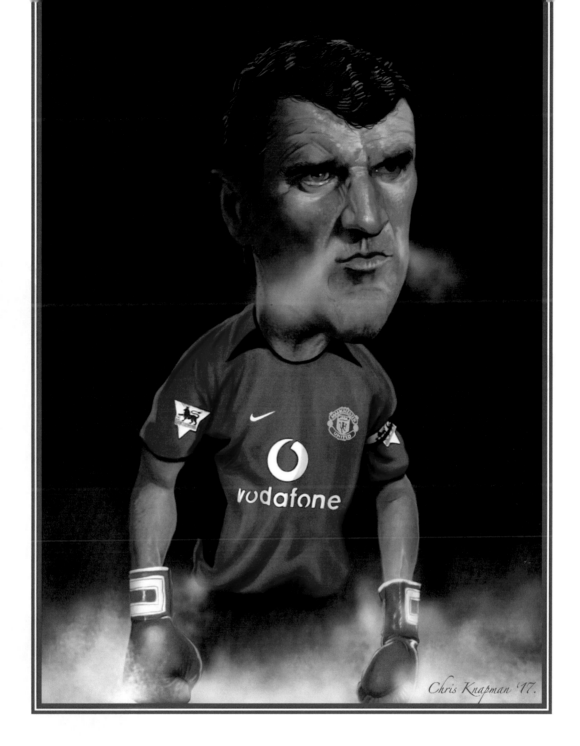

ROY KEANE

"If I had an argument with a player we would sit down for twenty minutes, talk about it and then decide I was right"

Brian Clough

Two fiery characters and no mistake! There is no doubt Roy Keane had plenty of arguments with Cloughie in the early days of his career. I'm sure he gave as good as he got.

Lee Dixon never looked entirely comfortable perched on the ITV Champions League sofa next to Roy Keane – but, then again, who would? For even in retirement, the opinionated Irishman from County Cork still exuded an air of disquieting menace. Before it became clear that a football career beckoned, Keane spent much of his time boxing, winning all four of his amateur bouts as a youth. 'Feared' and 'fiery' are amongst the watchwords of his career – so maybe the boxing was an augury to his modus operandi as a footballer?

Roy Keane's football career got off to a rather inauspicious start. Firstly, he was rejected by Ireland Schoolboys, having failed a trial in Dublin. Ireland schools' coach deemed the 14 year-old "just too small" to make the grade. Further disappointment followed when he was rejected by a raft of English clubs – in some cases, he wasn't even offered a trial.

Keane eventually managed to persuade the semi-professional Cobh Ramblers to give him a much-needed break. Initially, he played for both the youth and first teams, playing twice every week. By the time he was 19, he was an established star of the Irish non-league scene and this drew the attention of Nottingham Forest scout Noel McCabe. An impressive trial prompted Forest manager Brian Clough to part with the paltry sum of £47,000 to bring Keane to the City Ground. Initially, Keane struggled to cope with life in England and often yearned to be back in his native Eire. Brian Clough, realising that he'd got a player of vast potential in his midst, was prepared to afford him special treatment – magnanimously agreeing to frequent trips back home to Cork.

Keane soon displaced England international Steve Hodge and scored three goals as Forest marched to the 1991 FA Cup final. This early success was, however, marred by his first major faux pas. Forest beat Crystal Palace in the third round at the second time of asking – with a Keane error leading to the Palace goal that necessitated a replay. To say that Brian Clough was underwhelmed by Keane conceding possession, allowing Palace to score, might be regarded as an understatement. On returning to the dressing room a livid Cloughie punched his young midfielder squarely in the face, knocking him to the floor. He didn't, though, bear any resentment towards his manager, instead stating that he understood the pressures of management and sympathized with his boss. Perhaps this was another omen – namely Keane taking the view that, in certain situations, aggression – even unadulterated violence – can be justified?

After losing the FA and League Cup finals to Spurs and Manchester United respectively, Keane knew that he'd probably have to look elsewhere for the success that he craved. Blackburn Rovers were the first club to court him. Bizarrely, the Lancashire club saw their bid to sign Keane stymied by a somewhat unprofessional administrative error. Rovers and Forest had agreed a £4 million fee and Keane had also agreed personal terms; however, late on a Friday afternoon, Rovers manager Kenny Dalglish realised that he didn't have the correct paperwork to complete the deal. Unfortunately for Kenny, the club offices had closed for the weekend, meaning that the deal would have to be completed the following Monday. This delay proved to be a 'sliding doors' moment in time for Roy Keane and probably for Blackburn Rovers too. Over the weekend, Manchester United manager Alex Ferguson intervened and persuaded him to sign for the Red Devils instead. Fergie and United showed the required diligence and attention to admin detail and he signed for the club for a British record £3.75 million.

With Bryan Robson's fitness starting to fail him, the early to mid-nineties saw Keane cement his place in the midfield. He made the best possible start – scoring a brace on his home debut, as United beat Sheffield United. Additionally, grabbing the winning goal in the Manchester derby, as the Reds overturned a 2-0 reverse to win 3-2 at Maine Road, did much to endear him to the Old Trafford hardcore. He was also pivotal in United winning their first English title for 26 years in 1993, as again when they retained it in 1994. There was no Premier League winner's medal in the spring of 1995 though – as Blackburn Rovers pipped the Manchester club to the title on a heart-stopping final day. Perhaps it's no coincidence that Keane missed 17 games through injury and suspension? He spent three games wallowing in the stands (plus a £5000 fine to boot) after stamping on Crystal Palace's Gareth Southgate. This incident proved to be portentous; for the pugnacious, combustible Irishman was to go on to rack up 11 red cards and innumerable yellows. This blight of character was undoubtedly the one issue to be a hindrance to a career which, otherwise, bobbed along swimmingly.

The following season saw some of the old guard jettisoned and the emergence of new talent, namely Beckham, Butt and Scholes – leaving Keane as the most seasoned head in midfield. He took to this challenge with aplomb as United chalked up their second Premier League and FA Cup double in three years. United retained the title in 1997 – despite injury limiting Keane to 21 league games. The following season, however, further injury problems restricted him to just nine league games; this time his sheer length of absence proved too much, and the very same silverware won by United a year earlier was now headed for Arsenal's Highbury. Whilst Keane was sidelined, United actually frittered away an 11-point lead over the Gunners – and many fans pointed to what was critically missing: the energy, drive and midfield authority of one Roy Keane. Keane was now club captain and clearly a true leader.

If the 97-98 season was Keane's 'annus horribilis', then the following season emphatically made up for it. Now fully fit, he played a vital role in a resurgent United side who took on all comers and clinically dispatched them – often with alarming ease. The spring of 1999 saw the culmination of 12 years of hard work on the part of Alex Ferguson; his team – inspired by the 'Class of '92', led by the fearless, imperious Corkman, played their way to an unforgettable treble: the Premier League title, the FA Cup and the Champions League.

It's widely agreed that United's stunning Champions League semi-final comeback against Juventus saw Keane give his finest performance in Manchester red.

Unable to play in the breathtaking, last-gasp final victory over Bayern Munich, due to suspension, the semi-final second leg in Turin was to be the thrilling apogee to a capital career. Having drawn 1-1 at Old Trafford, the plight of Keane and company looked grave when two early Filippo Inzaghi strikes put the Bianconeri 2-0 in front after just 11 minutes. Manchester United's driven, irrepressible captain didn't think the tie was beyond them. This is Roy Keane we're talking about: a hard-running box-to-box midfielder who could ride a tackle and then play in the team's more creative forces and occasionally pitch in with a vital goal – as he did in the face of Turin adversity. From a left-hand side corner, Keane made his run with pristine timing, before rising perfectly to place a glancing header just inside the right-hand post. But his performance was about much more than the goal that gave United the platform to go and clinch the match 3-2 (4-3 on aggregate) and go through. Noted as a steely defensive midfielder, Keane won tackle after tackle and out-passed Juve with a fluency more readily associated with his colleagues. Alex Ferguson, known for his incredibly high standards, could not fail to be moved by Keane's efforts that night:

'It was the most emphatic display of selflessness I have ever seen on a football field. Pounding over blade of grass, competing as if he would rather die of exhaustion than lose, he inspired all around him. I felt it was an honour to be associated with such a player.'

In a footballing context, Keane's booking for tripping Zinedine Zidane – ruling him out of the final – seemed a real travesty after such a hypnotic, spellbinding display.

The following season, for most onlookers, was to be Keane's finest. Despite missing nine league games through injury or suspension, fans saw wave-after-wave of gnarly, gritty, barnstorming performances, as United breezed to a second successive title – leaving Arsenal trailing haplessly 18 points in their wake. It was of little surprise when Keane was named PFA Players' Player of the Year, with the Football Writers' Association following suit.

PATRICK VIERA

"Out of difficulties grow miracles."

(Jean de la Bruyere)

Across all continents – including the colonially subjugated Africa – we have seen two things happen. Internationally, we've seen African football emerge from obscurity and become a relevant feature of world football; only the hand of Luis Suarez prevented Ghana reaching the World Cup semi-final in 2010. Secondly, African footballers prosper in the stronger European leagues of Italy, Spain, Germany and, of course, the Premier League. An abundance of black African players (and Caribbean) have gushed into Premier League football. Some have helped deliver trophies; some have helped keep their club in the division.

There is possibly no finer example of what Africa has gifted English football than Patrick Viera. Senegalese by birth, but an adopted French national, he strode into the midst of the Premier League like he already owned it. His development as a player is impressive when one takes a glance at his upbringing. His parents divorced when he was very young, he was uprooted and moved to France at the age of eight, and he was never to see his father again. Some youngsters would've buckled under this morass of uncertainty; not young Patrick. Tall, rangy and the embodiment of athleticism, he could get from one box to another in the time it takes me to butter my toast in the morning. He was physically robust and strong enough to go toe-to-toe with thuggery. Even Manchester United's Roy Keane held no fears for Viera. Their notorious – often toxic – relationship sometimes showed them in a bad light, whilst at other times it helped cultivate the legendary reputations of both players and soup up the rivalry between their respective clubs. Viera had stamina, strength and was proficient in the air. Allied to this was a canny ability to anticipate what the opposition were about to do, subsequently breaking up their moves with usually well-timed tackles. (He occasionally misjudged tackles and incurred the wrath of the referee!) In addition to his ability to do battle with the midfield ruffians of the Premier League, the man from Senegal was well-acquainted with the finer side of the game. He was technically immaculate and had the vision to make a telling pass. Yes, he could mix it with the bovver boys – but he could also be delicate and graceful; he covered the whole gamut of footballing attributes. Not every player has immense skill as well as a real physical presence. Viera was a rare exception in this sense; few players are so aggressive and competitive – yet equally blessed with oodles of finesse. He had all the attributes a manager seeks in a captain, and fulfilled this role from 2002 until his departure in 2005.

An impressive debut season for Cannes in Ligue 1 soon had scouts making a beeline to watch him perform for the French side. Still a teenager, his potential was deemed to be vast. In 1995 he signed for AC Milan. Ostensibly, it was a wonderful move – Milan had swept the continent aside to claim the UEFA Champions League. Unfortunately, the competition for a first team berth proved to be too stiff and he spent most of his time in the reserve team. His time on Italian soil was somewhat transient. Arsenal manager Arsène Wenger spotted that a considerable talent was being neglected and took him to Highbury for £3.5 million in 1996. Viera clearly wanted to play Premier League football – but he was also drawn by the opportunity to play for a manager to whom he could speak French. Although Pat Rice gave him his senior bow, it's widely believed that Arsène Wenger actually orchestrated it before being officially unveiled as Arsenal boss.

Having just dismissed Bruce Rioch, Arsenal appointed Pat Rice as caretaker manager, with Stewart Houston assisting. Trailing Sheffield Wednesday 1-0, Rice needed to avert a shock defeat and he needed to replace the injured Ray Parlour. Viera came off the bench and immediately began to dominate. This continued after the break, David Platt struck the equalizer and Ian Wright bagged a hat-trick – but it was The Gunners' Gallic recruit who ran the game for 60 minutes and made their stirring recovery possible. The game is also of interest to those of a statistical bent – Owls' forward David Hirst smashed the most powerfully struck shot in Premier League history – a searing 114 mph; however, to his dismay it came back off the crossbar!

Once described by *The Times* newspaper as "a thinking man's Carlton Palmer … who, at last, gives the Arsenal midfield some variety", I don't think this description does him justice. Clearly *The Times* weren't anticipating what was to come! Fans noted that he was the club's first genuine playmaker since Paul Davis helped them to the title in 1991. Davis himself noted that the Arsenal team struggled if he was side-lined.

After narrowly missing out on a Champions League place in his first season (1996-97), it was the following season that things really started to gain momentum. Paired with French international team-mate, Emmanuel Petit, in central midfield, this relationship blossomed quickly. Club, country – no matter – their ability to work in tandem effectively was pivotal.

Viera opened his goalscoring account with a strike in a 3-2 victory over the club rapidly becoming their nemesis, Manchester United. After spells out through injury and suspension, Viera returned to help the team erode the lead of their Manchester rivals. He ended an epic first season in England with a Premier League winner's medal and likewise for the FA Cup.

In 98-99, Viera was buoyant after winning the World Cup with France and enjoyed another excellent season. And, although The Gunners failed to retain their Premier League crown, his continued great form earned him a place in the PFA Team of the Year; unsurprisingly alongside Petit.

The following season was an annus horribilis for both player and club. In October 1999 he was disciplined for spitting at Neil Ruddock and subsequently handed down a six-match ban and fined a record £45,000. As for Arsenal – they finished second – but just the 18 points behind Manchester United! The UEFA Cup ultimately failed to provide any solace either. Arsenal lost the final on penalties to Galatasaray; Viera's spot-kick struck a post. The season's zenith came on international duty, as France and Viera were crowned champions of Europe, courtesy of David Trezeguet's 'golden goal' in Rotterdam.

The following season forced Viera to cross uncharted waters – his side-kick and foil, Emmanuel Petit, had moved to Barcelona, along with Marc Overmars. It was at this juncture that he showed real maturity as a player.

Although Viera was – in terms of his own performance—approaching his peak, much of his and Arsenal's success hinged upon how he dovetailed with his midfield partner. This was always a key factor during his time in the Premier League. Early on, he was alongside Ray Parlour, whose stamina and physicality seemed to complement the Frenchman very well. He also enjoyed some good games alongside the dynamic David Platt, who had an eye for goal, plus van Bronckhorst briefly too. In November 1997, The Gunners recorded a memorable 3-2 victory over Manchester United, with both Viera and Platt both on the score-sheet. The same can be said of Emmanuel Petit. They seemed to be cut from the same cloth in some respects; both oozed boundless energy, could tackle ferociously and pick an incisive pass. Not many players have that balance between skill and the physical aspects of midfield play. Also crucial to their relationship was an understanding that appeared almost telepathic at times. I can only surmise that they discussed their tactics extensively between matches; one simply knew when they needed to hold a deep defensive position, as the other was venturing forward – and vice-versa. How many midfield duos have anchored both European Championship and World Cup winning teams...

Viera was also an integral part of Arsène Wenger's 'Invincibles' – who romped to the title without losing a single game in 2003-04. This unprecedented success followed a troubling start to the campaign, when he was sent-off against their main foe, Manchester United. His protestation and refusal to take the shameful walk to the tunnel resulted in a £20,000 fine and an additional one-match ban. With Petit long gone, his ability to gel with his midfield partner still remained vital to the team's success. Now it was Brazilian midfielder Gilberto Silva. Joining Viera and compatriot Edu, Silva was an inspired signing. Whilst he possessed a stellar all-round game, he was a naturally defensive midfield player. As he provided 'backbone' – extra defensive shield – this gave the boy who had emerged from the French Riviera carte blanche to stride deep into opposition territory. Viera, with his telescopic legs, had the freedom to make endless ebullient runs – creating a cornucopia of scoring opportunities. At the end of the season Viera was – unsurprisingly – named in the PFA Team of the Year. And for Wenger, the fans and the player himself – this accomplishment was all the more sweeter as it came on the back of the club and player fending off strong interest from Manchester United, Chelsea and Real Madrid. For sure, a vision that will be etched into the Arsenal psyche is Silva babysitting the defence (not that they were by any means inept!), as the gazelle-like Frenchman swept masterfully into the heart of their opposition. The fact that it was his sixth inclusion is an accurate testament to what he has contributed to Premier League football. We are privileged to have hosted his finest years. Commentators have, in recent times, focused on the emergence of a 'new breed' of footballer – meaning the complete athlete; frequently bought on the back of an impressive World Cup or African Cup of Nations. What we still pejoratively refer to as the 'sub-continent' has brought us a host of supremely fit and exceptionally talented footballers – as have the Americas – and Viera epitomises this evolution. There is nothing 'sub' or sub-standard about Patrick Viera. I can't imagine him and the 'new breed' travelling to a match on the number 12 bus and preparing for a game with egg, chips and two pints of best; but some of his Arsenal forebears did just that!

The following 2004-05 season proved to be Viera's last in north London. Surprisingly left trailing in the title race by Mourinho's Chelsea, The Gunners fell foul of Manchester United in the League Cup quarter-finals; the latter competition being notoriously hard to assess, as the bigger clubs frequently take the opportunity to blood young players in experimental line-ups. Everyone associated with the club was, however, fixated on winning that most elusive of prizes – the Champions League. It's a natural extension of, or progression from, winning the Premier League title. Wenger, Viera, his colleagues and the supporters had craved it for years. This yearning was undoubtedly magnified by the fact they'd looked on as arch-rivals Manchester United paraded it through their own city in 1999. Sadly for Viera, a couple of quarter-finals in 2001 and 2004 were as near as he got. He did also collect a UEFA Cup runners-up medal when Arsenal succumbed to Galatasaray. After the game and extra-time failed to produce any goals, the Turkish champions ran out winners on penalties – with Viera amongst the Arsenal men who failed to convert.

Returning to the subject of Viera's Arsenal swansong and relationship with silverware, it wasn't all doom and gloom. He was never a European champion, but he didn't sign off empty-handed. Cardiff's Millennium Stadium saw the London side overcome nemesis Manchester United on penalties after 120 goalless minutes – and this time the Frenchman made no mistake from 12 yards.

Whilst there are clearly some gaps in Viera's haul of honours, if one shifts the focus to 'acts' from 'omissions', he has a collection that must engender considerable envy amongst other players. One way (by no means the only method!) to assess a player's achievements in the game is to simply reflect upon what they've won. Here goes with the most salient of Viera's successes: four Premier League titles, four FA Cup Winner's medals (three with Arsenal and one with Manchester City), three FA Community Shield triumphs. In addition to team honours, he also had a number of individual honours bestowed upon him. Not content with making the PFA Team of the Year a dozen times, he had an unforgettable 2001. He was named in the UEFA Team of the Year and as French Player of the Year. He also played a crucial role in France winning the FIFA Confederations Cup, picking up the FIFA Confederations Cup Silver Ball in the process! Domestically, he'd already been crowned Premier League Player of the Season. Internationally, he was a vital cog in the French midfield, as France hosted and won the 1998 World Cup. And nobody reeled in shock when David Trezeguet's 'golden goal' put paid to Italy in the final of Euro 2000. Viera remained an integral part of the Gallic midfield, emerging as one of the leading luminaries at the Benelux tournament. His splendid performances in the Low Countries earned him a deserved place in the UEFA European Championship Team of the Tournament 2000.

When he finally departed the Premier League for Italy, success followed him. After briefly stopping off in Turin with Juventus, he decided to undertake a new challenge with Inter Milan, and – you guessed it – he seized the opportunity to augment his already impressive haul of honours. In his stint with *I Nerazzurri* (The Black and Blues), or *La Beneamata* (The Cherished One), or if you really prefer, *Il Biscione* (The Big Grass Snake!), he won four Serie A titles and twice the Supercoppa Italiana. What have I missed? Well, 2006 saw him named in the FIFA World Cup All-star Team and he twice made the Premier League Overseas Team of the Decade. Furthermore, he was twice selected for the Premier League Overall Team of the Decade.

No Champions League glory – granted; but many footballers would sacrifice almost anything for such an impressively decorated career; but his many feats in the game simply mirror – indeed fairly reflect – the size of his talent: enormous. Viera's combative style brought him his share of bookings and dismissals – yet he was still one of the game's highest achievers. France (for whom he enjoyed a couple of spells as captain) used him sparingly in his latter years; however, they regarded him highly enough to cap him 107 times no less.

Manchester United manager Alex Ferguson couldn't lure him to Old Trafford and Real Madrid's autocratic president, Florentino Perez, was unable to entice him to the Spanish capital. No, it was fellow Frenchman, Arsène Wenger, who spotted his potential during his salad days in AC Milan's reserves.

How many better overseas signings has the Premier League seen? The case for Viera being inducted into any Premier League hall of fame, as we have seen, is simply overwhelming. His many qualities grossly override his lack of goals. His myriad abilities enabled his colleagues to bag them. Finally, you don't play for a strong footballing nation like France 107 times if you're not occupying the highest echelons of talent. A World Cup winner in 1998, plus a European champion two years later: both accolades very much in sync with his ability.

Viera's influence wasn't restricted to the field. He and Petit are credited with helping end a somewhat corrosive drinking culture, which had grown to be endemic at Highbury. Sometimes, however, his opinions angered the footballing hierarchy. In 2003, he was racially abused playing away to Valencia. He criticized UEFA for not doing enough to counter racism; they duly fined him £2,300.

Despite locking horns with Manchester United time and again, perhaps he'll be best remembered for a rare strike in a ding-dong North London derby in November 2004 – which the Gunners won 5-4.

After his cup-winning cameo with Manchester City, he retired and gave the club's academy youngsters the benefit of his experience. Then after a brief period managing New York City, he returned to France to manage OGC Nice.

How long will it be before we again see such an intense, vivacious presence adorn the English game?

SOL CAMPBELL

"It was as if he was indestructible, such a power spread from him"

(Arsène Wenger)

Sulzeer Jeremiah Campbell was the youngest of 12 siblings and grew up in a rough eighties neighbourhood where crime was endemic. The fact that he veered away from a life of crime himself owes much to the strictness of his parents – an understandable approach when so heavily outnumbered by your offspring. Campbell has attributed his success to how he learnt to cope in such an overcrowded and stifling household:

"I became a recluse in my own house. I became insular because at home there was no space to grow or evolve, everything was tight and there was no room to breathe. People don't realise how that affects you as a kid. I wasn't allowed to speak, so my expression was football."

Debuting for Tottenham at 18 in 1992, Sol Campbell went on to make 255 league appearances, scoring 10 goals. He was a natural leader, with the spirit to rally those around him and he captained the club to League Cup success in 1999. The most impressive feature of his game was perhaps his confounding pace for a man of his physical stature: 6ft 2in tall and weighing more than 14 stone, he was still able to go toe-to-toe with practically any opposing forward. Data amassed by the Castrol Football Index over the 07-08 and 08-09 seasons indicates that Campbell, with a maximum speed of 22.5 miles per hour, was the second quickest player in the Premier League over that period – second only to Theo Walcott. Also a strong tackler with aerial supremacy over most forwards, he was a good all-round centre half. His reading of the game and positional sense were rarely found wanting either.

For all Campbell's star quality as an individual, football is first and foremost a team game and, as Campbell grew in stature, a procession of stellar names from home and abroad passed through the club showing no more than glimpses of their true talent. The upshot of playing for a club in perennial flux (both on the pitch and in the dugout) was that Champions League football was eluding him. During his nine seasons at White Hart Lane, the club never finished higher than seventh. A move was inevitable for a player harbouring aspirations of competing amongst the game's elite.

But nobody quite reckoned for the move that was to come.

Whilst the prawn-munching gentrified class of supporter hopes that raw, tribal antipathy amongst fans is confined to an unruly few, Sol Campbell's transfer to arch-rivals Arsenal showed that testosterone-fuelled hostility lurks just beneath the surface for many. Having publicly vowed to Spurs fans that he would never cross North London, this highly controversial deal sparked an intense war of words. Online fans' forums were the site of many a pitched battle between the Arsenal and Spurs fans – sometimes debating notions of loyalty and integrity – and sometimes descending into scurrilous slanging matches. Tottenham fans were quick to label their departed idol 'Judas' and this disparaging moniker is still bandied about to this day.

Campbell's departure from Spurs to Arsenal on a free transfer was first and foremost a career move. He had, however, felt let down by the Spurs hierarchy over an incident when he had been accused of breaking a steward's arm in a match at Derby County. The club's advice involved Campbell admitting to some responsibility for the offence in exchange for the case being bound over. Adamant that he was innocent, he conducted his own defence and the case was later dismissed. But the damage was done!

These mitigating circumstances cut no ice with the Spurs faithful. He had committed the mortal sin and there was no room for redemption. However, with hindsight, even the most begrudging Spurs fan would have to admit that Campbell's decision to move to Arsenal catapulted his career to a level that he would never have reached at Tottenham. His signing was a great coup for Arsenal manager Arsène Wenger, who described him as "indestructible". He debuted for Arsenal at the start of the 2001-02 season in a 4-0 victory away to Middlesbrough. On his first return visit to Spurs he was, as expected, bombarded by insults from the opposition fans but, undaunted, he played well in the one-all draw.

Campbell enjoyed immediate success with Arsenal. In his first season they won the Premier League and FA Cup – not a bad start and, metaphorically speaking, a suitable two-fingered salute to the White Hart Lane contingent, and there was plenty more success to come.

He was an integral part of the so-called 'Invincibles' side of 2003-04, who sailed through the season without a single Premier League defeat. The following season saw him collect a second FA Cup winners' medal and in 2005-06 he came close to adding a Champions League medal to his collection, only to lose to Barcelona in the final, having contributed to the Spurs goal with a powerful header.

After five successful years at the Gunners, he joined Portsmouth on a free transfer and, during a three-year spell at Pompey, captained them to FA Cup success in 2008, for only the second time in the club's history.

Campbell's international career was no less distinguished than his club career. Capped 73 times by England, he represented his country in six consecutive major tournaments. His England debut came at the tender age of 21 and in May 98 he wore the captain's armband at the age of 23 years and 248 days, making him the second youngest to do so after the legendary Bobby Moore. During Terry Venables' tenure as National Coach, he was a fixture at the heart of the defence alongside Gareth Southgate and Tony Adams.

After bowing out as a player, he flirted briefly with the management side, initially as assistant manager to the Trinidad and Tobago national side. In November 2008 he became manager of Macclesfield Town, who at the time were bottom of League Two and five points adrift of safety. Under his stewardship the club avoided relegation, having finished three points above the drop-zone following a 1-1 draw with Cambridge United on the last day of the campaign.

In 2015 Campbell put his name forward as a Tory candidate for the role of London Mayor but was not selected. The then incumbent Boris Johnson was re-elected for a second term. He has never shied away from controversy and has always been vocal in supporting the game's black players. He has on occasions accused the FA of "Institutional Racism", notably when they failed to make him a full England captain during his international career. His three appearances as captain were all in friendly matches.

Controversy aside, Campbell has been admired by most as a great player and leader throughout his football career. A true Colossus of the Premier League and a great servant to professional football.

ERIC CANTONA

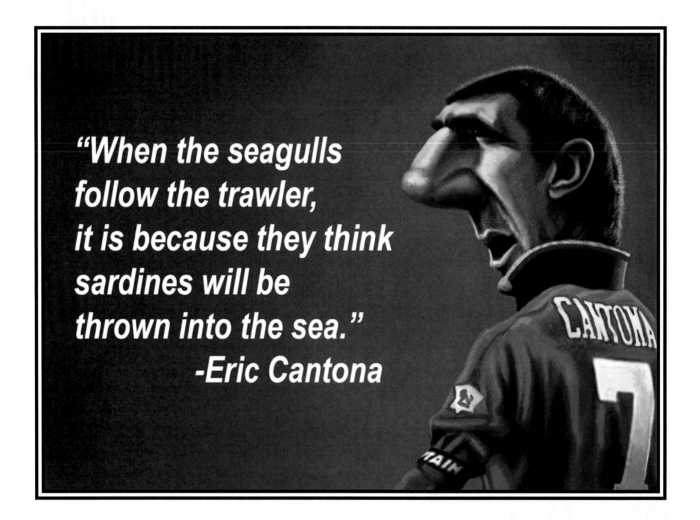

"When the seagulls follow the trawler, it is because they think sardines will be thrown into the sea."
-Eric Cantona

"To err is human, to forgive divine."

(Alexander Pope)

It's March 1996. A series of well-worked passes culminate in Eric Cantona's sweetly volleyed finish on the edge of the six-yard box from Phil Neville's leftwing cross to give Manchester United a telling 1-0 victory over Newcastle United.

Though not Cantona's most startling strike, it was surely the most critical of all. Firstly, it saw the Geordies' lead, which had been 12 points at one stage, whittled down to just one. Secondly, it crowned a remarkable renaissance in the career of the enigmatic Eric Cantona. When, just 14 months earlier, the Marseille-born forward reacted atrociously to dismissal, it seemed unlikely that his career could be revived at all. One January night in 1995, Cantona was dispatched to the dressing room for kicking Crystal Palace's Richard Shaw. As he trudged towards the tunnel he was taunted by the Palace supporters. Incensed by this, he proceeded to launch a sanguine assault on Palace fan Matthew Simmons. A kick which belonged to the martial arts, followed by a flurry of punches, saw the Gallic superstar land himself in the deepest of hot water. It was an incident which appalled the entire football world and it resulted in Cantona receiving an eight-month worldwide ban, a £20,000 fine and a two-week prison sentence – reduced to community service on appeal. Perhaps reports of him hurling his boots in the face of a team-mate in his native France and the verbal abuse of a French FA disciplinary panel should have made English clubs balk at the prospect of signing him; either way, few could have expected such extremity of behaviour.

So, his glorious return, which saw him at the heart of United's successful tilt at the double with 19 goals and numerous assists, marked the unlikeliest comeback the Premier League has ever seen. This was recognised by the press who made him Football Writers' Association Footballer of the Year 1996. (He'd already been PFA Players' Player of the Year in 1994.)

The turnaround in Cantona's fortunes is interesting – as it contrasts sharply with the treatment of football managers in recent times – yet both can be attributed to the fickle, transient nature of the sport. A manager can be the toast of the town one season, only to be hastily dismissed just a handful of fixtures into the next – with memories of his none too distant triumphs obliterated by cash consciousness amid fears of relegation.

For Cantona, however, the short memory span of the footballing fraternity was a positive thing. How else could he have ended 95-96 steeped in glory and cast as the hero? Football forgets quickly and it is this facet of the game that often makes or breaks a career; a caveat to the man in the dugout, but the saving grace of 'King Eric'. One could, however, argue that it's easy to forgive the sublimely gifted.

When all is said and done, the pardoning of Cantona by Alex Ferguson, the club's hierarchy and the fans, proved to be a truly momentous decision. He was at the epicentre of Manchester United's re-emergence as the top flight's dominant force. And this forgiveness spread to the wider footballing public too.

No football fan in the country can make a backward nostalgic glance without recalling Cantona's moments of genius. Cantona arrived in England having played intermittently well for six French clubs in an eight-year spell dotted with moments of ill-discipline. His debut season saw him win the league with Leeds United. Though three goals in 15 appearances sounds as though Cantona (destined for a cinematic career) was playing little more than a cameo role, his ability to provide assists for fellow striker Lee Chapman proved decisive in helping the Yorkshiremen win the title.

His good form continued into the following season, averaging a goal every two games, and Alex Ferguson took what appeared to be a gamble in luring the capricious Frenchman to Old Trafford. Subsequent years have seen Ferguson make some astute signings, but at this juncture, Cantona appeared to be a risk.

Whilst rather more than a journeyman, his wayward nature meant that he'd yet to truly settle at any club. Ferguson, however, had clearly recognised his potential and was determined to bring a halt to his nomadic existence and it's a testament to his man-management skills that he largely did so. What he'd seen was a player with strength, a brilliant touch, balance, the keenest of eyes for a defence-splitting pass and the ability to finish – often from distance – with deadly poise. Time and again he was United's match-winner, popping up with a visionary pass or cheeky finish, when they were running out of time, fruitlessly toiling against a stubborn defence.

Playing with collar turned up to protect him from the cold, Cantona quickly established himself as a talismanic figure and a cult hero among fans. The turning up of the collar was often mistaken as being indicative of his undoubted arrogance, but Cantona claims it was to protect him from the biting northern gales! We can give him the benefit of the doubt on that matter – but the same cannot be said for the way he strutted around the pitch imperiously puffing out his chest with a deep sense of self-importance.

Playing his part in United's first title triumph for 26 years, he ended his fairly brief Manchester United career with four Premier League winners' medals, plus two in the FA Cup. It may surprise some readers that Cantona only figured in the Premier League for United on 144 occasions, though he did tot up an impressive 64 goals in the process – not to mention providing countless assists.

It was these vital assists that prompted manager Sir Alex Ferguson to pay him the following compliment:

"Of all the many qualities a good team must possess, the supreme essential for me is penetration. And Eric brought the can-opener."

During his reign at Old Trafford, King Eric adorned this grand arena with some fittingly majestic strikes – one of which came against Sunderland in December 1996. Flanked by two opponents just inside the Maccams' half, Cantona gave us an object-lesson in close control and the maximization of limited space. Keeping the ball on the end of his toes, he jinked smartly aside both markers before accelerating away on the turn. A one-two at a canter with Brian McClair saw him bypass two more hapless defenders, before showing typical Cantona sangfroid to send a delicate chip sailing into the top left-hand corner from the edge of the area.

Bramhall Lane was the scene of another of Cantona's finest moments in 1996. Capping a sweeping four-man counter-attack which left Sheffield United trailing, a galloping Cantona took Ryan Giggs's low pass from the left in his stride and, having the awareness to spot the keeper off his line, beat him with an almost effortless chip, with scarcely any back lift. A terrific team move deliciously rounded off by United's finest import; trademark audacity really.

Eric Cantona hardly conformed to any stereotype of the professional footballer. Abundantly charismatic, this arcane and unpredictable talent was often portrayed as part of the footballing intelligentsia – though one might point out that the game is far from replete with intellectuals. His association with wisdom stems from his best known quotation, given at a press conference, which appears to metaphorically allude to the media's monitoring of his conduct. In a slow and rather pensive manner he told us, "When the seagulls follow the trawler, it's because they think sardines will be thrown into the sea." Clearly Cantona felt that the press pursued him in anticipation of trouble or scandal.

Another dimension to the man is his interest in the arts. His film career was already underway even before he finished playing – his most notable credits being 1998's *Elizabeth*, starring alongside Cate Blanchett, and the semi-biographical *Looking for Eric* in 2009. One wonders whether he perceived his "nice to see it go in" and "obviously we're all sick as parrots like" team-mates as a touch gauche, a little bit crass... That said, if Graeme Le Saux leafing through *The Guardian* on the Chelsea team bus can result in a homosexual slur, then it's entirely possible that Cantona's penchant for film and philosophical ramblings might have cast him as a latter-day Sartre in the eyes of United players. Those up-to-speed, existentially speaking.

On one level, the temperamental Frenchman's career was characterised by a litany of indiscretions and clashes with authority which rendered him unemployable to some managers. He'd once went on record describing French national coach Henri Michel as a "sac a merdi" – "a shitbag"! Even the battle-hardened, savvy Graeme Souness passed up the opportunity to take him to Liverpool in 1991, for fear that he might ruffle a few feathers in the dressing room and possibly the boardroom too. If you add to the inglorious disciplinary record his sadly premature retirement at 30, you don't get the prettiest of pictures. But if one reflects upon what he achieved in a short space of time – the rare beauty of his touch, passing and finishing – one might conclude that he decorated the Premier League in a way no other player ever has done. I sincerely hope such memories override the acrimony.

Halley's Comet is a long time in coming, its presence is fleeting when it finally does – but it illuminates and dazzles us like nothing else can. Much the same can be said of those five heady years we spent in the presence of King Eric Cantona.

A legend of the modern game and never to be forgotten.

DENNIS WISE

*'It is better to be violent, if there is violence
in our hearts, than to put on the cloak
of nonviolence to cover impotence.'*

(Mohandas Gandhi)

'What's in a name?' people often ask. British fans of imported hit American cop series *The Wire* will be familiar with the character Dennis 'Cutty' Wise. Dennis 'Cutty' Wise is a reformed criminal who sets up a boxing gym for young men in his impoverished inner-city neighbourhood. Furthermore, the character gets his name from a real-life Baltimore contract killer who's currently in prison serving a life sentence. Whilst our Dennis, the Kensington-born central midfielder, has never quite made blood curdle or been caged by the judiciary (certainly not at the time this went to press), one may be forgiven for spotting a theme. Known for his explosive temper and often gratuitous levels of aggression, Wise both hampered his career and sullied his reputation with episodes of unnecessary belligerence – both on and off the field.

Wise began his career as he meant to go on by clashing with well-respected boss Lawrie McMenemy at Southampton, where he served his apprenticeship. Kicked out by the wily Geordie, his next stop was Wimbledon, where he began to make his name both as a player and as a member of 'The Crazy Gang'. This group, featuring John Fashanu and the infamous Vinnie Jones, were known for their philistine approach to the game – long, aimless balls and a brutal approach to tackling. Between matches, they were known for playing rather extreme practical jokes of a mentality a la *Jackass.* In all, hardly the place for Wise to quell the temperamental excess he displayed at The Dell. In actual fact, it was here that Wise honed his savage tackling skills, before going on to decorate his curriculum vitae with 65 yellow cards (plus five reds) in the Premier League alone. Not quite in the Lee Bowyer class (when one peruses the statistics), but certainly a heavyweight in this aspect of the game. Whereas Paul Scholes was clumsily late in the tackle, Wise was simply unsociable – deliberately so – often appearing as though he intended to incapacitate or even possibly maim his opponent.

Like Bowyer, the ever-fractious Wise was versatile in terms of where he was capable of causing mayhem. Not content with clobbering opponents amidst the white heat of competition, Wise contrived to assault one of his Leicester team-mates in the comparatively anodyne atmosphere of a training session. His vicious attack on Callum Davidson saw the Foxes' left-back hospitalised with a broken nose and jaw. And the unfortunate Davidson had merely been trying to act as peacemaker in a spat between Wise and another of his colleagues. Wise was sacked by the club, but reinstated by The Football League Disciplinary Commission. This decision was then overturned by the club's successful appeal.

Wise also courted conflict off the field and one notorious incident came in 1995 when, whilst Chelsea's club captain, he was convicted of assaulting a London taxi driver. This unsavoury incident saw him meted out a three-month prison sentence, later overturned on appeal. His Chelsea boss Glen Hoddle, the diametric opposite to Wise in temperament and – to a large extent – style of play as well, stripped him of the captaincy. Another manager to show disdain for Wise was Alex Ferguson, who once quipped that Wise could "start a fight in an empty house".

Despite his well-documented volatility, Wise – unforgiven by most for his assault on Callum Davidson – did have some redeeming qualities. After starring in the Wimbledon side that won the 1988 FA Cup, he spent a decade at Chelsea, amassing 445 appearances and notching up 76 goals. His tenacious approach to midfield duty garnered him 21 England caps and a trip to Euro 2000. It might surprise one or two people, on reflection, that an exponent of football's vulgarities should win so many caps, but it should not be forgotten that Wise's knack of tackling and harrying opponents into mistakes was coupled with his ability to pass the ball sensibly and often decisively – as he did in the 1988 FA Cup final for Lawrie Sanchez to famously nod home.

There is no doubt that a lack of self-control stymied his progress, but it is equally fair to say that Dennis Wise did very well for a player whose natural flair fell well short of that of his Chelsea manager Glen Hoddle. A Champions League equaliser in the San Siro against AC Milan saw the confrontational cockney nuzzle up with glee to an immovable glass ceiling. But more England caps than Rodney Marsh and Matthew Le Tissier combined are a testament to that fact that some managers held Wise in high esteem. A raft of honours including three FA Cups and a Cup Winners' Cup are quite an achievement for a good, but never sparkling, midfield player. Despite what almost looked like crude attempts to sabotage his own progress, Wise achieved more than many of his more able countrymen.

Since stepping down from the tumult of the top-flight, Wise has dabbled in management. He was player-manager at Millwall (leading them to an FA Cup final) as well spells in the dugout at Southampton (fleetingly), Swindon and Leeds. His most curious move was to Newcastle to be their Director of Football – much to the annoyance of Toon God and manager Kevin Keegan. Substandard foreign imports were drafted to the north-east at the behest of Wise – exasperating Keegan and fans alike. Keegan departed in protest in the autumn of 2008 and Wise likewise in the spring, when Alan Shearer took temporary charge. Since this exit, Wise has kept a low profile. His most recent credit is a television appearance, in which host Andrew Flintoff invites him to bobsleigh somewhere in Scandinavia. Like fellow retired sportsman Phil Tufnell, he has the alacrity, boundless energy and charisma to make a big impact in 'reality' television. Good luck, Dennis…

I rather suspect that, as a schoolboy, Dennis saw detention as routine and an occupational hazard. Intuition suggests that Dennis's schooldays were characterized by a catalogue of misdemeanours, foolish pranks and geography lessons stood outside the chip shop when he should've been studiously imbibing key facts about active transfer, the Jacobite Rebellion or the Patagonian Desert. Being kept behind until the last bus to Bermondsey both desensitized and prepared the snappy midfielder for what was to come. How often did Chelsea have to reshape their midfield when their little dynamo was 'in detention'?

Teachers tell naughty boys that they'll never make anything. But this one didn't do too badly, did he?

COLIN HENDRY

"It is not the strength of the body that counts, but the strength of the spirit."

(J.R.R. Tolkein)

In his early days at Ewood Park, a fanzine run by arch-rivals Burnley once likened Colin Hendry to a llama – due to his straggly blond locks and slightly ungainly playing style. Granted, he didn't quite have the coolness and composure of Bobby Moore, nor the technical prowess and passing ability of Franco Baresi. He did, however, have SOMETHING. And, as his career soared, the comments made in the Clarets' fanzine were made to look increasingly foolish. The man from the Scottish Highlands displayed a whole raft of other vital attributes, even if pure finesse wasn't amongst them.

Hendry played junior football for Islavale FC, before getting his first taste of the senior game in the Scottish Highland League with hometown club Keith FC. He turned professional in 1983, having been spotted by Scottish Premier League Dundee – for whom he made 41 appearances. Although he played chiefly as a striker, his time there only yielded two goals. Upon joining Blackburn Rovers for a bargain £30,000 in 1987, he soon converted to centre-half.

Although Hendry switched to a defensive role, it was at the other end of the field that his mutual love-affair with the Ewood Park faithful began. Despite playing in the final of the much-maligned and now defunct Full Members' Cup in 1987, a club starved of success for several decades were keen to get their palms on any silverware available. So when the new signing popped up to sweep home a late winner against Charlton Athletic at Wembley, sending 30,000 travelling Rovers fans into delirium, a special and enduring relationship was born.

After 102 largely impressive games in the old Second Division, Hendry seized the opportunity of top-flight football with Manchester City in 1989. He was the club's player of the year in 1990, but fell out-of-favour when Peter Reid took the reins in November of that year. Barely a year later, he was returned to Ewood Park by new manager Kenny Dalglish, as the Jack Walker revolution began to gain momentum. It really was akin to the 'return of the prodigal son', with a strong sense amongst supporters that 'Big Col' was back where he belonged.

When Hendry first played in England nobody doubted his spirit and endeavour – however, his game was also marked by moments of rashness and the naivety of youth. He was still a little raw. Under the stewardship of Dalglish and astute coach Ray Harford, the rough edges to his game were soon smoothed over. He also garnered a great deal of knowhow under the tutelage of central-defensive partner and former Manchester United star Kevin Moran – with the Irish World Cup player himself enjoying an Indian summer to his career.

Playing 235 games in his second spell at the club, Hendry will always be synonymous with the 'Braveheart' tag. Clichéd it may be, but certainly a richly-deserved epithet for a player whose game was defined by courage and commitment. His all-action performances and countless goal-saving, timely tackles rendered him a folk-hero at Ewood Park. Like all good defenders, he was prepared to put his body on the line. And although no longer a striker, this swashbuckling centre-half was still partial to the odd rampaging sortie up field – especially when his team desperately needed a late goal.

The pinnacle of Hendry's career came in 1994-95, when Blackburn Rovers were crowned champions of England. Whilst those of a statistical bent will point to the goals of Alan Shearer and Chris Sutton, it should not be forgotten that, without Hendry's stirring defensive displays (he played 40 league games that season), the title would've surely eluded the club. He was deservedly named in the PFA Premier League XI at the end of that season.

Hendry continued to star for Rovers until 1998, when Rangers took the Scottish international to Ibrox, leaving the club's fans crestfallen. Despite winning the domestic treble in his first season, he was dropped by manager Dick Advocaat, who declared that Hendry was "not his type of player" – despite having signed him in the first place! His career then petered out with spells at Coventry, Bolton Wanderers (twice), Preston North End and Blackpool.

Post-career, Hendry managed Blackpool for 17 months, but was dismissed after a string of poor results in November 2005. After nine months as assistant manager at Boston United, the Highlander headed back to Scotland to manage Clyde. After just seven months at the helm, he resigned in January 2008.

Colin Hendry's life outside football was also becoming somewhat turbulent and traumatic in the extreme. In 2009 he tragically lost his wife, Denise, aged 42, who died from an infection following botched cosmetic surgery. Further misery was to follow for the father of four when, in 2010, Blackpool County Court formally declared him bankrupt. Amongst his creditors were the betting company SpreadEx – amid rumours that he had a gambling addiction. He also owed £85,000 to a now former friend, who unsuccessfully tried to have him prosecuted on the grounds that he borrowed the money in full knowledge that he couldn't repay it. The police, however, deemed it to be a civil matter.

Despite his harrowing personal experiences, Hendry was to return to Blackburn one more time – this time as first team coach in June 2012. He later became assistant boss of the club's under-21 team. With the club in disarray under new owners Venkys (India) Limited, resentment grew amongst supporters – some of them tarring Hendry with the same brush as the hapless Indian regime. His reputation wasn't helped by stories in the media about his debt issues. He eventually left the club in June 2014.

Whilst some supporters may remember him for his forgettable final stint at the club, most fans, happily, prefer to remember the pivotal role he played in the halcyon days of the 1990s. Arguably the best defender ever to wear blue and white halves. What he lacked in grace, he more than compensated for with fearless and sanguine displays, marauding up-and-down the field week-after-week-after-week.

He is also remembered with affection for his bizarre pre-match ritual, which marked a significant departure from the usual superstitions found amongst players. During the warm-up at home games, a chorus of "Colin, Colin, show us your arse !" would always ring out from the home fans. The Scot, right on cue, would then turn his back on the home end, bend over and drop his shorts. Thankfully, for those of a sensitive disposition, he didn't neglect to don his undergarments before taking the field. Quite how this ritual was born remains a mystery to this day – but it was considered a prerequisite at home games and just as sacrosanct as the halftime spud pie! All rather strange, but indicative of his popularity.

A very British centre-half, who made the very most of what he had – to great effect.

PETER SCHMEICHEL

"To make our way, we must have firm resolve, persistence, tenacity. We must gear ourselves to work hard all the way. We can never let up."

(Ralph Bunche)

'Schmeichel' has practically become a byword for excellence and his truly commanding displays for both club and country are the yardstick by which subsequent Premier League goalkeepers are measured.

It may surprise some that Peter Schmeichel played for seven professional clubs, but is most noted and fondly remembered for his eight years at Manchester United, for whom he figured on 292 occasions in the Premier League. His years at Old Trafford were undoubtedly his finest, and during this era he was twice voted 'World's Best Goalkeeper', in 1992 and 1993.

Born in Gladsaxe, Denmark, to a Polish father and Danish mother, he held Polish citizenship until 1970, when he, his father and his siblings assumed Danish citizenship.

Having progressed through the junior football ranks with distinction, Schmeichel's first taste of senior football came with Gladsaxe-Hero. Already condemned to relegation to the Danish third tier, the club saw their three remaining games as an opportunity to blood seven players from their youth ranks. Schmeichel was singled out for praise in the local media and went on to represent the club for two more seasons. In his second season, the club found themselves in the position of needing a point from their final game to avoid relegation. Helping beat opponents Stubbekobing, he played one of his finest games ever. At the end of the game the coach's daughter, Bente, raced across the pitch to embrace the heroic stopper – and they eventually went on to get married.

At this stage of his career, Schmeichel was playing as a mere amateur. After a three-year spell with Hvidovre (during which he debuted for the Danish national team still very much an amateur), his first professional contract came when he signed for leading Danish club Brondby in 1987.

Before eking out a living from the game, he held a number of positions in order to make ends meet. His first job was in the dyeing department at a textile factory – but he left because he felt that the company's application of health and safety directives were somewhat less than robust. He spent the next 12 months beavering away as a cleaner at a retirement home, before taking up a post in the office of the World Wildlife Fund. He initially just served in the organisation's shops, but three weeks into his role the store manager quit and Schmeichel was promoted to sales manager. This was shortly followed by a four-week stint of compulsory military service. Next came a spell with his father-in-law's flooring firm – but he soon found that his knees were unable to support his considerable 15 stone frame for eight hours a day! His final non-footballing vocation was to be with an advertising firm owned by Hvidovre's chairman, which came to an end when he was recruited by Brondby. Given Schmeichel's varied employment before professional football – menial, artisan, blue collar, white collar – and the fact that he was probably 30 before he earned any 'serious' money, he should have a compelling appreciation of what it's like to lead a comparatively modest, humble life to the footballers of the noughties and beyond; often signed before puberty and on the same salary as a headteacher whilst playing in the reserves at 16. He was in his late twenties by the time he joined United, so he wasn't indulged until well into his career. Financially speaking, maybe his generation were the last to breathe the same air as the common fan, before the birth of the footballing millionaire?

His Brondby career met with immediate success and the club won the Danish title in his first season. His form at Brondby saw him gain selection for Denmark's Euro '88 squad, where he became first-choice goalkeeper. In his time at Brondby, Schmeichel won four titles in five happy seasons and reached the semi-finals of the 1991 UEFA Cup.

His next move was quite an elevation from the second-rate Danish league football – when none other than Manchester United came calling. His career in Manchester was a glittering one. After eight seasons, and 393 appearances in all completions, he'd collected five Premier League titles, three FA Cups and a League Cup, before signing off following the Nou Camp crescendo, when United scooped the UEFA Champions League. (United also claimed the Premier League title and FA Cup that same year.) The first Premier League success came in only his second season, when the Danish number one's 22 clean sheets were highly instrumental in United bringing the league title back to Old Trafford for the first time in 26 years.

For all Schmeichel's success, his time at Old Trafford almost came to a premature end in early 1994. He fell out with manager Alex Ferguson after the team had frittered away a three-goal lead to draw with Liverpool. Words of some vitriol were exchanged in the dressing-room and Schmeichel was promptly sacked by the fiery Scot. Just days later, Ferguson eavesdropped on the keeper apologising for the spat to his team-mates and subsequently reinstated him.

The 1996-97 season again saw the man affectionately nicknamed the 'Great Dane' at the heart of controversy, when he was twice accused by Arsenal's Ian Wright of making racist remarks. A police inquiry was launched, but no action was taken. Interestingly, the FA and PFA seized the opportunity to portray him as 'converted' and use him to front their 'Kick Racism out of Football' campaign.

Upon examining Schmeichel's attributes, it's difficult – nigh on impossible – to find an obvious weakness. Whether it be shots from distance, reflex saves at close quarters, the imposing blond had it all. Despite his bulky 6ft 4in frame, he had remarkable agility and was able to spring up to claw balls from the top corner. His physique and strength were also great assets when it came to commanding his penalty area in dealing with corners and crosses. An abiding memory is that of Schmeichel gobbling up high balls under aerial duress and quickly bowling the ball more than fifty yards to an attacking player. Numerous United goals stemmed from his quickness to spot a player in space and Goliath throwing ability. Another undoubted strength of the hulking Scandinavian was charisma; keen to marshal his defence, he could often be seen barking out orders to his back four – for whom sloppy defensive play invariably met with a bellowing rebuke.

Schmeichel also deserves special mention for his frequent up-field sorties. It's become increasingly common to see keepers racing up to the opposing end of the field to further the quest for a last-minute equalizer. Once upon a time this was considered rash, madcap behaviour; but boasting 10 career goals, the big Dane would argue that his appearances in the other team's penalty area were not so foolhardy or eccentric after all.

His post-United career was, unsurprisingly, less remarkable. He played briefly for Sporting Lisbon (winning one Portuguese title), Aston Villa and Manchester City. Despite playing for both Manchester clubs, he never finished on the losing side in any of their derby games – with City taking four points off United in his one season there. That season, 2003-04, was to be his last.

Since discarding his gloves, Schmeichel has enjoyed a fulfilling and industrious 'retirement'. A regular on both *Match of the Day* and football broadcasts in his homeland, he's become well-respected as a football pundit. His other television credits include his appearance as a contestant on the BBC programmes *Strictly Come Dancing* and *The Weakest Link* – where a dismal performance on the latter saw him jettisoned at the end of the first round!

Although he will be remembered fondly for years, there is another 'Schmeichel' making a name for himself between the goalposts – his son Kasper, who's currently in the Championship with Leicester City. If he proves to be half as good as his father, he'll have done very well for himself.

Schmeichel may never have been taken for granted by his colleagues or the fans, but the passage of time has heightened our awareness of just how exemplary a goalkeeper he was. Alex Ferguson was frustrated by a succession of poor imitators: Bosnich, Taibi, Barthez, Howard and Carroll. It wasn't until he signed Edwin van der Sar that he had a keeper close to being worthy of comparison with the 'Great Dane'.

Without a chink in his armour, Peter Schmeichel is arguably the best goalkeeper ever to play in the Premier League to date. It is often said that his ilk are worth an extra ten or eleven points a season: surely this figure does him a huge disservice?

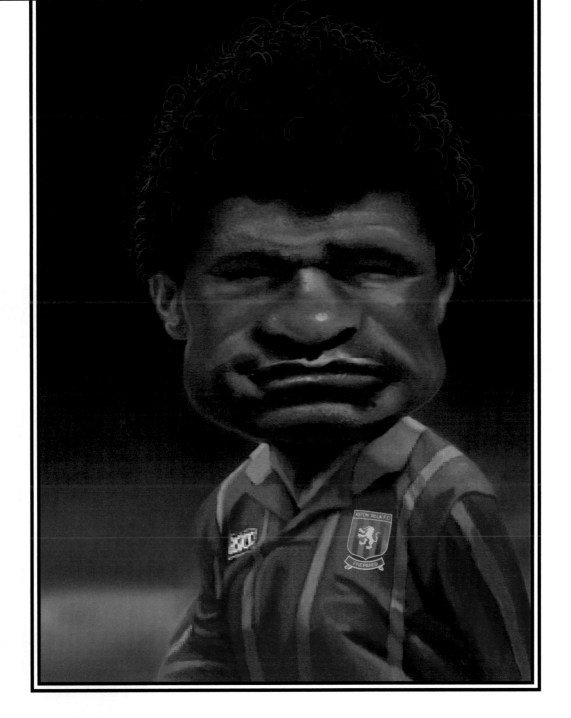

PAUL MCGRATH

"As a camel beareth labour, and heat, and hunger, and thirst, through deserts of sand, and fainteth not; so the fortitude of a man shall sustain him through all perils."

(King Akhenaten of Egypt)

Despite a career blighted by recurrent knee problems (he underwent a total of eight operations during his playing days alone) and the effects of alcoholism, 'The Black Pearl of Inchicore' (as he was affectionately known at his first professional club, St Patrick's Athletic) both enjoyed and suffered a remarkable career.

His start in life was not the best (which, to be fair, can be said of many individuals who made their ascension through football). Born to an Irish mother and a Nigerian father who vanished before he was born, McGrath was given up for adoption by his mother who feared that a child out of wedlock in an interracial relationship would bring shame to the family and incite castigation from her father. Although his mother eventually re-established contact with her son, Paul Nwoblio, as he was then known, had spent his childhood being passed from one Dublin orphanage to another. And with enough to contend with, he lost his only sister, too.

Imperious in the air and robust in the challenge, McGrath was, in the words of Villa team-mate Shaun Teale, "like a piece of old teak", adding "I don't think people realised how hard he could be if riled". Tough certainly – but he also seemed to play the game with consummate ease – something which owed greatly to his ability to read the game so very well. His shrewd defensive judgement was a vital component of his game as it largely, if not entirely, compensated for the fact that he was not particularly nimble over distance.

After working as an apprentice metal worker and security guard, 'St Pats' of Dublin gave McGrath his first professional contract. It was here that Manchester United scout Billy Behan homed in on this emerging talent. But Behan's early hopes were never fully realised in red. Although he showed the depth of this ability in patches, McGrath's time at Old Trafford saw him stagger from one hiatus to another. Sometimes at the mercy of his legendary knees, but often stymied by his malevolent relationship with the booze, a succession of setbacks prevented him from developing into the player that fans of Aston Villa and the

Republic of Ireland alike hold in such high esteem. Whilst McGrath's physical problems were, to a large degree, beyond his control, his battle with alcohol was seen by manager Alex Ferguson as a flaw and gave rise to discord between the pair. McGrath frequently missed training sessions due to his prodigious drinking and, by his own admission, even played the odd game still under the influence, holding his breath to prevent opposing strikers smelling the liquor. He recounts one particular occasion when he came up against the potent aerial threat of Duncan Ferguson. When his co-rival arrogantly claimed that he would win every single header, McGrath, who still had plenty of Dutch courage coursing through his bloodstream from a binge the night before, declared that it was he who would prevail. He proceeded to win practically every header, but conceded that his confidence was enhanced greatly by drink! Profoundly affected by excess alcohol, McGrath reportedly attempted suicide on four occasions. His repeated failure to address the issue (compounded by concerns over his endless injury problems) led to United letting him go to Villa in 1989 for just £400,000, after a disappointing 163 league appearances in seven seasons.

In a top-flight career spanning 14 seasons, it's considered almost a physiological miracle that McGrath and his troublesome knees endured so long into the Premier League era – let alone scoop the PFA Players' Player of the Year award in 1993, well after his career had become plagued with physical and psychological difficulties. The familiar sight of McGrath's recumbent, war-wasted hulk on the Villa treatment table must've felt like 'groundhog day' to their physio team – yet they returned the centre-half to battle time after time and he clocked up 252 league appearances and became a cult-hero amongst fans.

Time and again, McGrath had the measure of fearsome opponents. One of his most inspiring displays came in the emerald of Eire when he spiflicated the great Roberto Baggio as the Irish overcame Italy in the heat of New York at USA '94. The Juventus talisman didn't get a kick all afternoon in the aptly-named 'Giants Stadium' – so befitting of the big man's performance. It was also in the first half of this decade that Villa benefited from the best football of his career. In his first season in the Black Country, McGrath's stirring defensive displays were hugely significant as the Villains ran Liverpool close for the title. In 1992-93, he enjoyed another outstanding season as Villa again finished runners-up, this time to Manchester United. But the old warhorse ended the season on a high when his contemporaries deservedly voted him as their player of the year.

Nicknamed 'God' in one half of Birmingham, McGrath left Villa in 1996, before retiring in 1998 after a handful of games for Derby County and Sheffield United. Since the end of his playing days, he's written an autobiography, *Back from the Brink*, which is now the best-selling sports book in Irish history. He's also briefly dabbled in the running of a club, with Waterford United, as director of football. McGrath has also turned his hand to making music, releasing his debut album in late 2011. Marked by his startlingly tender vocals, this album of covers brings us McGrath's interpretation of tracks by artists such as Christy Moore and Elvis Costello, with all proceeds being donated to charity.

But we'll all remember Paul McGrath as one of the best defenders ever to grace the Premier League. His command seemed effortless as he played with a coolness reminiscent of Bobby Moore. On the field at least, he remained stoic in the face of adversity.

It may well be that Alex Ferguson regrets his decision to jettison the Irish stalwart when he did; then again, perhaps this was the very making of this Aston Villa legend. What is certain is that Ferguson had the good grace to acknowledge his attributes: "He was an exceptionally skilful and stylish defender, with marvellous innate athleticism, a man whose abilities stood comparison with any central defender in the game."

Another moot point, again broached by Ferguson and others, is the question of what McGrath might have achieved had he remained free of injury and personal demons? Certainly one of the best central defenders in living memory, perhaps he should have been up there with Moore himself? Anyhow, let's remember this trojan with affection and positivity: however dystopian his personal life, he largely vanquished his physical problems and will be remembered as a hero in the West Midlands; Villa fans will genuflect with ease in homage – even if the big man can't!

ANDREW COLE

"Teamwork – a few harmless flakes working together can unleash an avalanche of destruction."

(Larry Kersten)

"Narky, sullen and unapproachable" – that's Andrew 'don't call me Andy' Cole's own assessment of his own character. One-time strike partner at Manchester United, Teddy Sheringham, might be inclined to agree. Despite spearheading the United attack together, the pair never spoke at all off the field. This resentment of Sheringham stems from Cole's first outing for England in 1995 against Uruguay. Making way for substitute Cole, the then Spurs forward appeared to snub the debutant by actively avoiding the customary handshake. Whilst his view of Sheringham remains rancorous to this day, he was still able to focus, play with him and maintain his reputation as one of the most feared marksmen in the land.

Perhaps grateful for a second chance at top-level football, Cole served his apprenticeship in the Football League. Having been overlooked by Arsenal (a solitary league outing for the Gunners is somewhat perplexing), he arrived at Bristol City via an uneventful loan spell at Fulham. Twenty goals in 41 games for the Ashton Gate club led to him being courted by a string of Premier League clubs; and it was Newcastle United and Kevin Keegan who took the plunge by parting with a club record £1.75 million in the winter of 1993.

Players who don't hit the Premier League ground running, as it were, are usually permitted to shelter beneath the canopy of mitigation for a time, amid a flood of excuses bestowed by fans, media and managers alike: "he's still only young"; "he's got to adapt to the pace of the league"; "it'll take time to develop an understanding with the other players" – to name but a few.

Not Andrew Cole.

There was no hiding or cowering from this man, no craven excuses – he burst onto the scene to terrorize Premier League defences from day one, blasting 12 goals in as many games and looking as though he'd been doing it for years. 'Cole the Goal', however, was merely serving notice of what was to come.

The following campaign, 93-94, saw him team up in attack with the lively, creative talent that was Peter Beardsley – and this clearly galvanised Cole. In his first full season in the North-east, the boy from Nottingham rattled in an improbable 41 goals in just 46 games, with 34 of them coming in the league – breaking Hughie Gallacher's club scoring record, which had stood for nearly 70 years. At the season's end Cole briefly supplanted Shearer as the deadliest marksman in the country and it was of little surprise when he was named PFA Young Player of the Year for 1994. It was a memorable nine months for Cole and his adoring fans won't forget his hat-trick as they crushed Liverpool 3-0 at St. James' Park, nor his outstanding treble against Coventry City. At the end of their best season for decades, Newcastle finished third, qualifying for the UEFA Cup in the process.

Quite simply, markers left Cole unattended at their peril. Fleet of foot, always lurking, Cole had a knack of being on hand to punish defensive errors and surely undeserving of the criticism laid at his door by then England manager Glen Hoddle. Hoddle's claim that he needed six or seven chances to score one goal is hardly borne out by the record books. Second only to the great Alan Shearer, Cole was sufficiently clinical to trouble the scorers on no fewer than 189 Premier League occasions – with a career haul of 271 goals across all competitions. It's also worthy of mention that 50 of Shearer's league goals came from the penalty-spot, whereas all of Cole's goals came from open-play, bar one.

Cole had opened 94-95 with a steady nine goals in 18 matches when Manchester United came calling. After striking 64 times in 84 appearances, he left for Old Trafford for a then British transfer record of £7 million, causing widespread dismay throughout Tyneside; his departure deemed a catastrophe, an Armageddon – not truly assuaged until the introduction of 24-hour licensing laws reached the city.

Cole fitted seamlessly into Alex Ferguson's team of rising stars and ended the season with 12 United goals in 18 games; 27 in 36 for both clubs in total. His season, however, ended in dismay when his two glaring misses at West Ham, in the closing minutes of the season, presented the title to Blackburn. The following season proved problematic for Cole, as the team was built around the triumphantly returning Eric Cantona. Manager Alex Ferguson even remarked that "Cole thought he was the best centre-forward in the world" – his ego slightly deflated by the presence of the imperious Frenchman at his side. The 95-96 and 96-97 seasons were hardly the most fruitful for the man who'd made his name with a rash of Newcastle goals – just 21 in 70 league and cup appearances. His cause was not helped when, early in the season, a malicious Neil Ruddock tackle left him with two broken legs. Recovering by mid-season though, he finished the season with some vigour, scoring vital goals both in the league and in Europe. But the piece de resistance to a season which had begun so catastrophically was his title-winning goal away to Liverpool, which did nothing to mollify the club's mutually held vitriol. For Andrew Cole, though, it was mammoth step towards placating his critics.

The following year (after Eric Cantona had surprisingly retired), Cole emerged as the club's alpha male in and around the penalty area; 25 goals, including 15 in the league marked a crucial contribution to the club's fortunes. A raft of spectacular goals had the United fans purring by now. His sumptuous chip, in a game against Everton, won their vote as United's goal of the season. Interestingly, Cole's development continued with Teddy Sheringham (the man he 'sent to Coventry') and the goals continued to come. When asked to identify the reason for his rediscovered form, his reply was a little deeper than what you might have received from some of his peers; he attributed his renewed appetite for goals to the joyous birth of his son, family life and becoming a Born-again Christian.

The following season saw Alex Ferguson bolster his squad with a cornucopia of striking talent. Given that his manager had previously made an unsuccessful bid to sign Alan Shearer in 1996, Cole may have been forgiven for fearing that his place was in great peril. The 98-99 season saw Cole, new arrivals Dwight Yorke, Ole Gunnar Solskjaer and Sheringham all vying for starting places. Whilst all four strikers made telling contributions, it was the electrifying union of Cole and Yorke which had the most dramatic impact. Yielding 53 goals between them, they played a huge part in propelling the team to stardom with the unique treble of the Premier League title, The FA Cup and the holy grail of the Champions League title – craved for so long by the fans and their manager. Their one-touch passing, mutual assists and ruthless finishing was simply spellbinding; seemingly telepathic. And they looked like they really enjoyed playing together – which is important; indeed there was a togetherness about the whole team and it was this spirit that carried them forward. Surely, in his dotage, Cole can reflect on being part of a team which eclipsed the heroics of even the 'Busby Babes' of 1968? Also, history repeated itself, as Cole enjoyed the kudos of scoring the decisive title-winning goal against Spurs on the final day of the season to pip Arsenal by a single point – a feat he'd achieved on the final day in 1997.

The following two and a half seasons saw Cole score 38 times in 91 games – though injury did restrict his appearances. His days at Old Trafford, however, were numbered. Whilst previous additions to United's strike-force had inspired Cole, the signing of Ruud van Nistelrooy was very different; Cole ultimately proved to be the Dutch forward's quarry and he was sold to Blackburn Rovers for nine million pounds.

Cole's stint at Ewood Park was far from a failure: 37 goals in 98 games and the winning goal in a League Cup Final demonstrated that he wasn't yet spent. Rovers' fans will remember with affection him chesting down a loose ball in a game at Liverpool's Anfield and lashing a right-foot howitzer into the roof of the net from all of 35 yards. He was also briefly reunited with Dwight Yorke – but the pairing were both now entering the autumn of their respective careers and were unable to perform at the level they had done so explosively in Manchester. Cole left Rovers in the summer of 2004 amid acrimony, culminating in him reporting manager Graeme Souness to the FA for alleged unfair treatment.

He then played for no fewer than seven clubs in just over four years. Fulham, Manchester City, Portsmouth, Birmingham City, Sunderland, Burnley and Nottingham Forest all hired Andrew Cole. The now peripatetic hitman added a further 33 goals in 117 matches, before retiring at the end of 2008.

Since retiring, Cole has coached at MK Dons, Huddersfield Town and returned to Manchester United to complete his coaching badges. It's also worthy of mention that Cole released his debut single, 'Outstanding', in 1999 – a cover of The Gap Band's 1982 hit. This venture into the music business did nothing to dent the widely-held belief that any record producer who coaxes a footballer into a recording studio should be summarily shackled and flogged through the high street of their local town – along with their deluded would-be pop star of course.

Elvis, James Brown or Will Smith he may not have been – but he was certainly 'outstanding' on the football field. The statistics speak for themselves and need no further lyrical embellishment – except to say 'thanks' for helping to illuminate our much envied league.

DAVID BATTY

"Being from Yorkshire is as much a state of mind as a geographical fact"

(Unknown)

David Batty was Leeds born and bred. He joined his hometown club on the old Youth Training Scheme or YTS. He broke into the first team as a raw 18-year-old in November 1987. He very soon earned a reputation as a tough, uncompromising midfielder, in the same mould as former Leeds player and Scots firebrand Billy Bremner, then Leeds manager. He was considered a bit lightweight at the time by Bremner – the Scot reputedly forced the lad to drink a glass of sherry mixed with raw egg each morning, in the hope it would bulk him up a bit. Imagine what the modern-day sport science guys would make of that nutritional plan!

Leeds had gained promotion to the old Division One in 1990 and their first season saw them finish a creditable fourth on their return to the top flight, with Batty being named the Leeds player of the year. Batty soon became a key influence in a talented Leeds outfit, which included the likes of Gary McAllister, Gary Speed and Gordon Strachan. As a mainly defensive midfielder, his ability to win the ball and distribute it to his more creative colleagues marked him out as a genuine talent. Known throughout his career as a ball-winner by most observers, it is easy to forget how capable he was at finding an accurate pass to initiate a counter-attack in tight situations. In 1991-92 he was an integral part of the team that were crowned League champions in the final season before the Premier League was created. It was a veritable dream-come-true for the Leeds boy to win the league with his hometown club.

After seven years of successful service with Leeds, it came as a big shock when manager Howard Wilkinson decided to sell Batty to Blackburn Rovers in November 1993 for a fee of £2.75m. It appears that Wilkinson was keen to rebuild his team, and with him and Batty not being, shall we say, bosom pals, had decided to offload the player to raise some funds.

Having been pipped to the signing of Roy Keane by Manchester United, Rovers manager Kenny Dalglish, armed with owner Jack Walker's treasure chest, was anxious to find a suitable replacement. He wasted no time in snapping up Batty to enhance his own team, which was fast becoming a force in the newly-formed Premier League. Wilkinson used the proceeds from the sale to buy Carlton Palmer from Sheffield Wednesday eight months later. Palmer was a sort of poor man's Patrick Viera, ostensibly a more attacking option than Batty with more of a goal threat. Answers on a postcard as to which manager got the best deal, but Batty's 42 senior appearances for England compared to Palmer's 18 may influence your decision.

In his first interview on his new club's radio station, Batty declared that it was Rovers' style of play that had most influenced his decision to join the club. This may have appeared a thinly-veiled dig at his former manager, whose own style of play wasn't deemed particularly attractive, more functional than pleasing on the eye. His parents, who followed his career with great pride, were away on holiday when the transfer was completed. They expressed disappointment that he had "crossed the great divide" into Red Rose territory but were seemingly heartened by his positive view of the Rovers under Dalglish.

Now sporting a shaved head, no doubt to enhance his hardman reputation, Batty's first outing in a Rovers shirt was a home match against Spurs. A 1-0 victory and several crunching tackles into the bargain soon had the Ewood faithful warming to a new hero, as the team went on to finish the season in second place behind the all-conquering Manchester United. The following season became a triumph for Rovers as they clinched The Premier League title on the last day of the season. Now a star-studded outfit with the likes of Shearer, Sutton, Le Saux etc, Rovers' big spending had finally paid off. Batty, however, had managed only five appearances in the season due to a foot injury. Ten appearances is normally the requirement for a winners' medal but the club offered to award one to 'Batts' – however, he couldn't bring himself to accept it in the light of his minimal contribution to the campaign.

Following their triumph in the league, Rovers embarked on their maiden outing on the European front in the Champions League. Having beaten some of football's giants to win the Premier League, Rovers were hoping to take on the greats of Spain and Italy, but a disappointing draw saw them grouped with less glamorous teams from Norway, Poland and Russia. Now back to full fitness, Batty was available to help Rovers' campaign, but regrettably they were unable to progress to the lucrative knock-out stages. Batty's one memorable contribution was an embarrassing punch-up with team-mate Graham Le Saux just four minutes into a tie against Spartak Moscow, which was broadcast on live TV. It's not clear what sparked the coming-together, but posh southerner versus gritty northener might have had a bearing on the matter. We can only speculate.

Following the departure of Dalglish in 1995, a certain amount of dressing room unrest became apparent under new boss Ray Harford. After a mere 54 game spell at Ewood, Batty thought it was time to move on and put in a transfer request in 1996. He was duly sold to Newcastle United, then managed by Kevin Keegan, for a fee of £3.75 million. He wasted no time in scoring his first goal for the Toon against who else but his former club Blackburn Rovers at Ewood Park. Newcastle went on to finish second that season and also the following one, with Manchester United pipping them on both occasions. Batty's midfield presence was a major factor in Newcastle being able to compete at the highest level. In praise of his new signing, Keegan commented that it was not until he worked with Batty on the training ground that he realised what a good player he was.

In only his first full season with the Toon, Batty saw the departure of Keegan, with Kenny Dalglish taking over. The 1997-98 season was a disappointing one, with the club finishing in only 13th place. They did, however, reach the FA Cup Final in which Batty played but failed to lift the trophy against Arsenal who triumphed in a 2-0 victory. In August 1998 Ruud Gullit took over the reins and started to re-shape the squad, and four months later Batty moved back to his spiritual home of Elland Road in a £4.4 million deal.

Leeds United were managed by former Gunner David O'Leary and were enjoying a degree of success at the time. Batty's experience and midfield bite were seen by O'Leary as an essential addition to his young squad. Unfortunately, he picked up a rib injury in his first outing and was sidelined for a lengthy period. The 1998-89 season saw him regain full fitness and he was able to cement a regular place in the team. However, during the following season, he sustained an Achilles injury from which he was slow to recover due to the side effects of the drugs he had been taking for heart problems caused by the earlier rib injury. This problem also prevented his taking part in England's Euro 2000 Championships campaign.

Batty's contribution was significant in enabling Leeds to qualify for the UEFA Champions League and in their cup runs in the UEFA Cup and Champions League. After the sacking of O'Leary in 2002, Batty became out of favour with subsequent managers and retired from football in the summer of 2004.

Batty's performances for Leeds resulted in him being called up for England duty under Graham Taylor. His first cap had come in a 3-0 victory against the USSR in May 1991 at the age of 22. He was a regular in Glen Hoddle's squad which competed in the 1998 World Cup, but regrettably he will be remembered for missing in a penalty shoot-out against Argentina (along with Paul Ince), which prevented England progressing to the quarter finals. His 42-cap international career is testimony to his much-admired ability as a combative midfielder. He bowed out from international football in a match against Poland in which he was dismissed in the 84th minute.

Little information about Batty's post-football life is on record. Apart from the occasional charity match and appearances in Leeds' promotional videos, he has largely kept himself hidden from public view. Clearly an individual who values his private life and who can blame him. As a player, his tough, no-nonsense demeanour may not have endeared him to every football watcher, but ask any of the guys who played alongside him and they will all tell you that every successful team needs a 'David Batty'.

On a lighter note, there will be many observers who viewed him as a rather stern and serious character, yet under the surface a dry sense of humour was definitely lurking. In his autobiography he recalls an occasion during his schooldays when his teacher asked the pupils to bring any unusual item of interest to class on the final day of term. Some years earlier Batty had lost the tips off two of his fingers in an accident with an iron gate and had kept the detached bits at home in a match box as a bizarre souvenir. He decided to take the aforementioned into school, now blackened after lying in his wardrobe for four years, as his 'unusual item'. Items such as stamps, coins, football programmes etc were produced by other pupils and when it came to Batty's turn, he revealed the gruesome contents to the class and asked if anyone could guess what they were. Not surprisingly no-one could guess the identity of the strange looking items. Finally, the form mistress held the mystery objects aloft and said "Okay, David, you've got us all baffled. What are they?" When he revealed the identity of the items, the teacher let out an ear-piercing scream and hurled them to the floor as though they were red-hot coals.

Nice one, David!

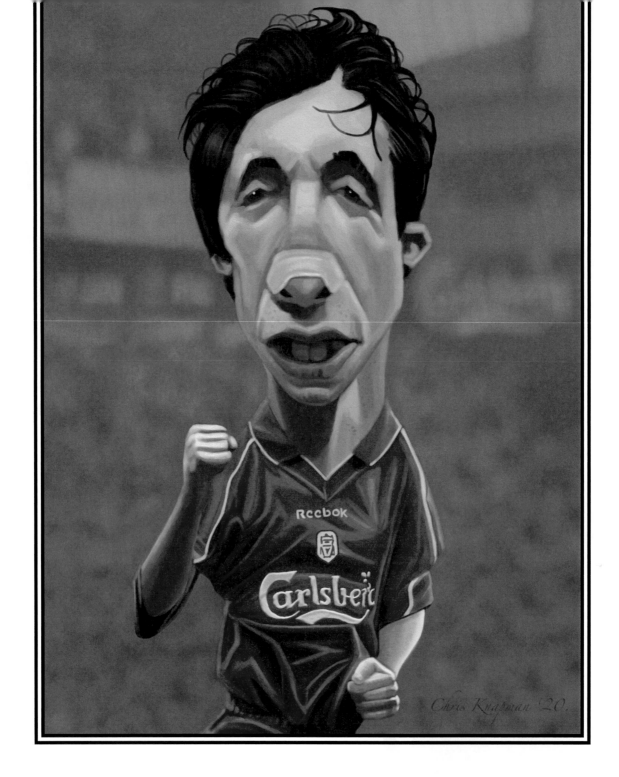

ROBBIE FOWLER

*"He was a god, such as men might
be, if men were gods."*

(Maxwell Anderson)

When fourteenth century poet William Langland penned the immortal maxim 'patience is a virtue' he did not know that 'patience' would become something we readily associate with the fans of Liverpool Football Club. In fact, he need not have said it at all where Robbie Fowler was concerned, in view of the alacrity with which the Toxteth-born forward set about first-team football.

Scoring on his debut in the first leg of a League Cup tie at Fulham's Craven Cottage in September 1993, he then proceeded to trouble the scorers on no fewer than five occasions in the return leg. He quickly translated his explosive cup entrance into league form and scored 13 goals in his first 12 games, including his first Premier League hat-trick against Southampton in what was only his fifth league game. So, the Anfield faithful's deep reserves of the admirable virtue 'patience' were never drawn upon, as the 'Toxteth Terror' caused utter havoc in his maiden season as a senior pro. Whilst he was never going to maintain the giddy goalscoring flourish of his first dozen games, he still finished the season having bagged a mightily impressive 18 goals in 34 games – and he was still a mere stripling at 19 years of age.

Born in the city, Fowler is often seen by outsiders as the embodiment and essence of Liverpool football club – a huge irony when one considers his roots. From a family of staunch Evertonians, Fowler was a boyhood Toffees fan before switching allegiances at the age of 11, when Liverpool scout Jim Aspinall persuaded the youngster to join Liverpool's Centre of Excellence. He had previously played regularly for schoolboy team Thorvald, for whom he once scored 16 goals in a 26-0 rout. This continued as, throughout his Anfield upbringing, the prolific local boy rewrote junior goalscoring records time after time.

Despite a lack of pace and height (5ft 9in), it quickly became apparent that the Reds had unearthed the most naturally-gifted goalscorer since the days of legendary Welshman Ian Rush. He clearly had a nose for poaching goals – whether it be a simple tap-in amidst the hurly-burly of a goalmouth scramble, or a superlative drive from 25 yards.

In his first four seasons at Liverpool, Fowler struck 83 times in 140 Premier League games and was paid the ultimate compliment when adoring Anfield regulars nicknamed him 'God'. If you then narrow the statistical focus to his first three full seasons, he is the only player in England to have scored 30-plus goals in all competitions within that timeframe.

The 1994-95 season saw him breach the 30-goal mark and he was unsurprisingly named PFA Player of the Year – a title he retained the following year with 28 Premier League goals in 38 appearances and 36 in total, as he forged a devastating partnership with Stan Collymore.

The 28th August 1994 is not a day Fowler, nor any Liverpool fan, will forget in a hurry. A sensational hat-trick against Arsenal added another entry to the Premier League record books. All three goals came in just 4 minutes and 33 seconds – a feat which stood for 20 years until eclipsed by another Liverpool player, Sadio Mane, in 2015. This performance is all the more impressive when you consider that he dismantled the normally watertight bastion of Dixon, Adams, Bould and Winterburn; the vastly experienced and most respected rearguard in the country wracked to distraction by a player still in his teens.

The same season saw Fowler notch some of his finest goals. One which readily springs to mind sealed a 2-0 victory over Manchester City. Steve McManaman rolled the ball to Fowler on the right flank about 25 yards from goal. Chaperoned by two City defenders, a hopeful ball into the box looked to be Fowler's only option. Instead, he flicked the ball to his left with the right instep, leaving his markers utterly statuesque, before dashing parallel to the 18 yard line and placing a firm left-footer into the far left-hand corner. A goal which exemplifies the fact that Fowler was more than a close-range predator; moreover, a footballer blessed with creative genius too.

Another goal, described by the man himself as one of his personal favourites, came in a 3-2 victory over Aston Villa. Right full-back Rob Jones sortied deep into the Villa half, only to see his shot cannon back off a Villa defender. Instinctively well-positioned, Fowler was on to the loose ball in an instant. Without an ounce of hesitation, he whacked a vicious left-foot drive high into the top left-hand corner. Technically perfect, Anfield can have witnessed few better executed finishes.

In December 1996, a four-goal salvo against Middlesbrough at Anfield put Fowler into the 'hundred club' – reaching a century in even quicker time than his striking mentor Ian Rush.

In nine fruitful seasons with the club, he was on the scoresheet 120 times in 226 Premier League appearances and 183 times in 369 games across all competitions, including those notched during a brief return in 2005. Playing at the highest level in arguably the most demanding league on the planet, Robbie Fowler consistently averaged a goal every two games: the unwritten – but universally accepted – hallmark of a 'quality' striker.

Statistically, Fowler's disciplinary record was generally unremarkable; however, in 1999 he was involved in two moments of unseemly and ill-judged theatre. His now notorious goal celebration against Everton led to him being charged with bringing the game into disrepute by his own club. Upon scoring against their Merseyside rivals, Fowler used the white line of the penalty area to simulate cocaine use. Liverpool manager Gérard Houllier hilariously defended his player, claiming that it was a Cameroonian grass-eating celebration, learnt from his team-mate Rigobert Song. The Anfield hierarchy were distinctly unimpressed by the Frenchman's risible explanation and presented Fowler with a £60,000 fine. Defending his actions, he later explained that he was mocking the Toffees' fans' baseless accusations of drug abuse. Fowler was banned for four matches at the subsequent FA hearing. Whilst attending the 'Sniffergate' hearing, the FA imposed a further two-match ban for taunting Chelsea's Graeme Le Saux by gyrating his backside at him. This homophobic jibe – also without foundation – was witnessed by Le Saux's wife and children, watching from the stands.

Conversely, there were occasions when he did show a strong sense of justice. In 1996, he won the UEFA Fair Play award for strenuously imploring the referee not to award a penalty after colliding with Arsenal keeper David Seaman. His pleas were ignored and the spot-kick was taken by Fowler. His weakly struck shot was blocked by Seaman, only for Jason McAteer to convert the rebound. Some observers felt that Fowler under-hit the ball deliberately because he felt the penalty was undeserved – something which he refuted. Also, in a UEFA Cup match against Brann Bergen, he celebrated scoring by lifting his shirt to reveal a slogan in support of recently sacked Liverpool dockers. A fine by UEFA swiftly followed.

His most successful season at the club in terms of honours was, paradoxically, far from his most prolific in front of goal. In 2001-02, Liverpool completed a unique treble sweep of the cup competitions, winning the UEFA Cup, the FA Cup and the League Cup, with Fowler contributing nine goals away from his Premier League duties.

The following season began in controversial fashion with a training ground bust-up with assistant manager Phil Thompson. He was dropped for the next game, sparking rumours that a host of clubs across Europe were vying for his services. Differences with manager Gérard Houllier persisted and the Frenchman edged towards Emile Heskey and Michael Owen as his favoured strike partnership. The club were also mindful of the potential financial loss, should Fowler reach the end of his contract and leave on a free transfer. (Steve McManaman had done just that, moving to Real Madrid that same year.) So, with the media peddling stories about his many suitors, Liverpool accepted an offer from Leeds United for £12 million. Interestingly, Fowler maintained that Houllier had driven him out; and that he'd manipulated the *Liverpool Echo* into propagating negative messages about him, thus turning a significant proportion of the Liverpool public against him.

Fowler continued to score with reasonable regularity in the white of the Yorkshire club; however, in 2002-03, the aggravation of a pre-existing hip injury stymied the England man's progress. When the season ended, Leeds were mired in a deepening financial crisis and Fowler was one of several stars to be sold off. A £3 million move to Manchester City was to follow and he was to remain there for four seasons. It was during this period that Fowler's star began to wane. Twenty goals in 79 appearances marked a slightly disappointing return by his previous standards; largely attributable to recurrent injury problems and a failure to recover a fitness level becoming of a Premier League footballer. His first employers, however, gambled on an Indian summer, and Fowler was to don the famous red shirt of Liverpool once again in 2006.

On returning to Anfield, he was greeted by a plethora of banners paying him lofty tributes such as "God – number eleven, welcome back to heaven". Fowler, himself, likened his return to "a kid waking up on Christmas morning every day". Although his 39 appearances during his second spell at the club yielded a respectable 12 goals (many a striker would be contented with such a return), he had lost a great deal of sharpness following a succession of injury setbacks and was clearly no longer the deadly marksman of the mid-90s. So, the return of Liverpool's not-so-prodigal son lasted just 15 months and Toxteth's finest export departed the club once more – and this time for good.

After a brief stint with Cardiff City (interrupted by keyhole surgery to his troublesome hip and a knee injury), Fowler brought the curtain down on his Premier League career with Blackburn Rovers. Next he was off to play in Australia for North Queensland Fury and Perth Glory, before joining Thai side Muanthong United, where he was player-coach. Since returning home he has coached both MK Dons and Bury. He has also spent time in the pundit's role for Sky Sports and other sport channels.

For some footballers, retirement is as traumatic a transition as release from Wormwood Scrubs after 25 years. Many harmlessly drift into anonymity, whilst others are gripped by indolence and vice. Mr Fowler, however, has not let the grass grow under his feet. In tandem with Steve McManaman, he's invested in a number of racehorses under the catchy trading moniker of *The Macca and Growler Partnership*. *Robbie Fowler Sports Promotions* is believed to have net assets of £1.58M, and in 2005 the *Sunday Times Rich List* placed Fowler in the top 1000 wealthiest Britons. Furthermore, he's also developed a property portfolio of at least 80. This startling fact prompted affectionate Manchester City fans to sing 'we all live in a Robbie Fowler house' to the tune of *The Beatles' Yellow Submarine*! The revered Liverpool quartet (along with their rock 'n' roll peers) might have been the pop stars of the 1960s, but Fowler's personal fortune, together with the attention footballers generally now receive, made them the pop stars of late twentieth century and beyond.

Looking back, Robbie Fowler was, in his prime, one of the most naturally-gifted goal-getters in Europe. Overlooked too often by his country (26 caps and 7 goals), this compact, explosive centre-forward never really made an impact on the world stage. Missing the 1998 World Cup through injury, and rarely used four years later, he never became the superstar his early years had promised. But, at club level at least, this shooting star burnt through the footballing firmament, enrapturing his fans and probably us all.

PAUL SCHOLES

"Finesse to most Americans means light, ... But it doesn't mean that in France. It means harmony, balance, completeness."

(Kermit Lynch)

Paul Scholes was good enough to play in midfield for a Manchester United team who almost completely dominated Premier League football from the mid 1990s to the early 2000s, claiming six titles in eight seasons. Good enough on 464 occasions no less. Those wondering whether this is the mark of a good player in a great team or, more specifically, a great player in his own right, might want to consider the lofty status of some of his admirers.

Zinedine Zidane rues not having played with him, citing it as the "biggest regret" of his career, adding "he is undoubtedly the greatest player of his generation". Spanish World Cup winner Xavi offers equally rich commendation: "For me, and I really mean this, he's the best central midfield player I've seen in the last 15, 20 years. He's spectacular, he has it all, the last pass, goals, he's strong, he doesn't lose the ball, vision. If he'd been Spanish he might have been rated more highly. Players love him."

Playing mainly in central midfield (though occasionally employed just behind a main striker), Paul Scholes has overcome athletic deficiency to become, quite remarkably, one of the most complete midfielders the Premier League has ever seen; perhaps even the greatest...

Five feet and seven inches tall, asthmatic, devoid of pace or stamina, Scholes thrived by developing other aspects of his game. He did more than simply eke out a career; he revelled in his role and became the team's most consistent and dependable player. A 'lack of technique' is the perennial reproof of English footballers – but Scholes was uniquely moulded in this sense. He had the ability to bring the ball to rest with one exquisite touch, thus affording him an extra split-second to use the ball wisely; whether that be a cunning, dangerous through-ball, or a simple lay-off in the interests of retaining possession. His ability to find a team-mate almost every time, due to effortless control and poise in possession, is his most salient attribute and perhaps the real hallmark of his greatness – *a la Xavi*. Statistical platitudes about ball retention – paradoxically impressive though they are – don't do his passing ability justice. He also had the vision to pick out the proverbial 'killer ball' on many occasions too.

Another arrow in the Scholes quiver is his eye for a goal; owing mainly to acute spatial awareness and the flawless technique. An enduring Manchester United image is the distinctively red-headed midfielder arriving late on the edge of the box and despatching the cleanest of volleys hard into a top corner. Having notched 104 Premier League goals, Scholes is one of just 19 'centurions' – forwards included.

Paul Scholes was quite simply a menace in and around the edge of the penalty area. His knack of being able to whack crisp, exocet drives from this territory, both from the ground and on the volley, have seen him garner a now opulent collection of long-range screamers. One such strike came at Villa Park in 06-07. Lurking about 25 yards from goal, he takes Grant McCann's headed clearance from a right-wing corner first time and, before the goalkeeper can blink, his flashing right-foot volley has thundered into the top left-hand corner – taking the paint on the underside of the crossbar with it. A masterclass in how to volley a ball which is coming across the body. Perfectly executed. Another example of Scholes's dazzling technique came when he scored a similar goal against Bradford at Valley Parade in 2000. As David Beckham's pin-point left-wing corner picks out the diminutive midfielder on the edge of the area, he still has it all to do. Rather than tee himself up to shoot, Scholes cracks a venomous right-foot volley through a crowded penalty area low into the bottom right-hand corner, igniting utter pandemonium amongst the United fans massed behind the goal. Risking an endorphinal overload, a trawl through the archives reminds one that Scholes scored a startling number of goals of this type. One outstanding strike, however, was more Giggs-like in its hue. It came against Blackburn in 2007. Picking up a loose ball on the edge of the area, the 'Ginger Prince' nips to the left of one stretching Blackburn defender, before balletically skipping to the right of two more. With his composure still intact, he drills a right-foot shot low into the left-hand corner.

Twice a Champions League winner (not to mention a host of other domestic trophies), there's just one disagreeable blot on the England international's otherwise stunning landscape: 121 bookings and 10 red cards in all competitions bear irrefutable evidence to the fact that Paul Scholes could not tackle. Lunging at opponents with all the timing of a mandrill on marijuana, his late and inglorious tackling brought notoriety. Countless rebukes and suspensions did not see Scholes improve this element of his game a jot. But when you do so many other things so well, does it really matter that much? Maradona was hardly noted for his aerial proficiency, was he.

Having said his farewell to Premier League football in 2011, Scholes made a surprise return to the United fold at the start of the 2012-13 season. He had been training with the United players, which rekindled his appetite for the game. This re-birth of his playing career lasted just the one season, but he helped United to claim yet another league title, making 33 appearances and chipping in with five goals. The season also proved to be Fergie's swansong, as he fittingly went out on a winning note.

In recent years he has embraced management with Oldham Athletic and Salford City, as well as becoming co-owner of the latter in conjunction with some of his former United team-mates. He also appears as a regular pundit on BT Sport, demonstrating quite forthright views on occasions.

Known as a quiet – almost diffident – family man off the field, the contrast with his on-field persona could not be greater. Tenacious, industrious and downright explosive in the last third of the field, the little man from Oldham will always be remembered as a giant of the Premier League. As some of his contemporaries incur the wrath of the authorities, as they lurch from gauche chatroom banter to fractious nightclub vagaries, Scholes (who rarely gives interviews) has led a life of equilibrium and dignity. Maybe it's this self-effacing and temperate approach that has enabled him to focus, flourish and give the game so much.

The 'Ginja Ninja' – thank you.

DENNIS BERGKAMP

"Intelligence is nothing without delight."

(Paul Claudel)

Universally regarded as one of the finest players to have performed in the Premier League, whether British or foreign. The breathtaking skill and ingenuity of Dennis Bergkamp will never be forgotten, and he remains the only Dutchman to be inducted into the English Football Hall of Fame, be named PFA Players' Player of the Year (1998) and Football Writers' Player of the Year in the same year.

Having starred and scored freely for his hometown club Ajax, it came as a surprise when he foundered in Serie A for Inter Milan – where a slow-tempo and emphasis on technique ought to have suited a player of his elegance and technical ability. Conversely, it was in the hurried and often brutal environment of the Premier League that Bergkamp began to flourish. Playing most effectively in the 'hole' just behind the main striker, Bergkamp displayed moments of unadulterated footballing brilliance. A first-class honours degree in mechanical engineering from the University of Bath points to a lively mind – something reflected by his acumen on the football field. Eighty-seven goals in 316 league appearances is respectable in itself for a secondary striker, but the sterling support he gave to successive strike partners (first Ian Wright and later Thierry Henry) is something for which he's just as well-regarded. Both these centre-forwards profited time and again from his close control, lightning brain and the ability to spot the minutest of openings in opposing defences. A deft flick or pass from the keen-eyed Dutchman saw Wright and Henry race clear to score on innumerable occasions.

Of the goals Bergkamp fashioned for himself, there are several which rank among the greatest the English top division has ever seen – even including those pre-dating the Premier League's inception. No other player has ever come first, second and third in Match of the Day's Goal of the Month competition. In 1998 Bergkamp scored a goal which won the Premier League Goal of the Season accolade. Just minutes into a game against Newcastle, Robert Pires issued a low ball from the left wing to Bergkamp, who was standing on the edge of the penalty area. With an outrageous flick of the left instep, he dumbfounded Niko Dabizas who was shoulder-to-shoulder, pirouetted the other way leaving the defender trailing, before calmly stroking the ball past the advancing Shay Given. A goal of sublime quality and possibly unique in terms of technique.

Surely his greatest goal in the Gunners' red and white came at the long-gone Filbert Street in 1997. Pegged back to 2-2 by a dogged Leicester City, Bergkamp lit up the dark Leicestershire evening to complete arguably the best hat-trick the Premier League has ever seen. A raking aerial pass from David Platt in midfield found Bergkamp, who was being marshalled by City defender Matt Elliot, on the left-hand corner of the six-yard box. The way he killed the ball dead with the outside of his right foot was a joy in itself. Then, with the ball yet to bounce, a gentle flick of the left boot took the ball to the right of Elliot. With the Leicester defender completely wrong-footed, he controlled the ball on the half volley with his left before sweeping the ball home with his right. A goal of rarefied class.

Another supreme goal, although scored away from the Premier League, saw Bergkamp put Argentina out of the 1998 World Cup in the last minute of the quarter-final and is deemed by many to be one of the greatest of all time. Leaping into the air to reach a lofted 60-yard ball from Frank de Boer, Bergkamp took the heat off the pass with the most delicate of controlling touches. He then brought the ball down with a flick through defender Robert Ayala's legs, before hammering a blistering volley with the outside of his right foot from a tight angle to the right of the goal. The awe inspired by this goal is as palpable now as it was back then.

Fabulous in its own right, a master-class in ball control, it is surely symbolic of what was happening back in England, with regard to the Premier League's burgeoning status. To see the goal of the tournament come from an English-based player was previously unheard of. Furthermore, it was indicative of the fact that the Premier League was starting to attract the best players in the world and soon to surpass Serie A and La Liga, and become the best league in the world. Scored on the world stage, yet a defining moment in the history of Premier League football.

As Arsenal prepared to leave Highbury for the Emirates Stadium in 2006, a series of themed match days were organised to celebrate the final season at the hallowed stadium. One particular day, themed as 'Supporters Day', was renamed 'Dennis Bergkamp Day' by the Arsenal fans. Standing second in a poll of Arsenal fans' all-time favourite players behind Thierry Henry, this was a glowing tribute and marked the final beatification of Dennis Bergkamp. Instrumental in three title-winning seasons, he was simply indispensable. One curious and well-documented aside to his career landed him the mildly reproachful nickname 'the non-flying Dutchman'. Whilst on board a flight with the Dutch national squad, a journalist jokingly claimed to be carrying a bomb. Following this incident, Bergkamp developed a fear of flying and has never boarded a plane since. So when Arsenal struggled in tough European away ties, with perhaps their most influential player in absentia, one might have forgiven their fans for feeling a degree of frustration and annoyance at the intractable Dutch forward. However, despite his most inconvenient of phobias, incalculable moments of astonishing brilliance in the Premier League – oh the goals – mean that the mercurial Amsterdammer has already gone down in Arsenal folklore.

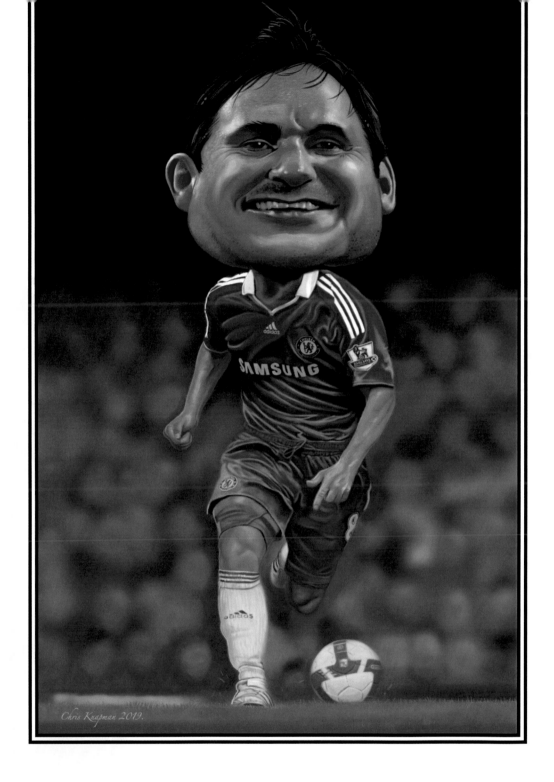

FRANK LAMPARD

"Ability is important in our quest for success, but dependability is critical"

(Zig Ziglar)

Frank Lampard was regarded by many pundits as one of the greatest midfielders of his generation. His undoubted footballing ability was allied to a level of consistency and dependability matched by few of his peers in the game. He was the ultimate 'box-to-box' midfielder with an engine that could conceivably have had Rolls-Royce stamped on it. His ability in terms of passing, tackling, goals and assists, plus his high work-rate marked him out as one of the great all-round players in Premier League history. Truly 'a man for all seasons' in every sense of the words.

Frank entered this world with football in his DNA. His father, Frank Lampard senior was a West Ham United player and assistant coach. His uncle Harry Redknapp also wore the famous claret and blue strip, whilst his cousin Jamie made the best part of 300 premier league appearances, mainly for Liverpool. Frank junior was destined to follow in the family footsteps and duly signed for the Hammers' youth team in 1994. He made his first team debut in January 1996 from the bench at the tender age of 17. He made one further substitute appearance that season.

The 1996-97 season saw Frank make his first start for West Ham on August 17th in a 2-0 away defeat to Arsenal. He was to make a further 15 appearances that season before sustaining a broken leg in a 0-0 draw against Aston Villa. He claims to have been booed by some West Ham fans as he was being stretchered from the pitch, hardly a fitting gesture to a young player who was one of their own!

The following season Frank was back to full fitness, and he quickly cemented his place as a first team regular. The opening fixture of that season was an away game against Barnsley, a club making the first appearance of its 110-year history in top-flight football. Lampard came on as a 76th minute substitute and, with barely a minute elapsing, he latched on to a Michael Hughes pass and with a neat flick scored what turned out to be the winner in a 2-1 victory. His eye for goal was further demonstrated later that season when he netted his first hat-trick in a League cup game against Walsall. He went on to make a total of 31 league appearances that season, scoring five goals in the process.

Frank went on to play three more seasons in West Ham colours. In 1999-2000, by now a regular in the side, he helped them to their highest ever Premier League position when they finished 5th and qualified for the then UEFA Intertoto Cup. The Hammers subsequently made it all the way to the final against French club Metz, but despite losing the home leg 1-0, they triumphed 3-1 in the away leg with goals from Trevor Sinclair, Paulo Wanchope and – who else? – Frank Lampard.

Later in the season, during a game against Bradford City, Lampard was involved in a bizarre incident with the notorious Paulo Di Canio. Having been awarded a penalty for a foul on Kitson, Lampard was about to take the spot kick when Di Canio wrestled the ball from his grasp and insisted on taking it himself. After a bit of toing and froing, Lampard conceded the initiative to the senior player, who coolly slotted home from the spot, much to everyone's relief – not least his own. Pure theatre! West Ham went on to win the game in a 5-4 goalfest. Lampard scored 14 goals in the season, a commendable return for a midfield player.

The following season saw a dip in West Ham's form and they slipped to a lowly 15th position from the heady heights of the previous year. Harry Redknapp left the club by mutual consent after seven years in charge, and Lampard's father also decided to wave goodbye to the club he had served for so many years. Not surprisingly perhaps, Frank junior eventually decided to part company with the Hammers and was scooped up by London rivals Chelsea for a transfer fee of £11m; and embarked on what transpired to be the most productive phase of his illustrious career.

In all, Lampard played in the Chelsea colours for 13 seasons. His goals-to-games ratio for the club (147 in 429 Premier League appearances) would have satisfied many a striker and in May 2013 in a match against Aston Villa he scored two goals, taking him past Bobby Tambling as Chelsea's all-time leading goalscorer with a staggering total of 211 goals in all competitions. He was an ever-present in the Chelsea team, which was further highlighted by him making 164 consecutive Premier League appearances, eclipsing the previous record holder, namely goalkeeper Brad Friedel. Furthermore, Frank is rightly lauded for his calm nerve and has scored a staggering 43 goals from the penalty spot during his Premier League career, which puts him in the top ten players' listing.

After reluctantly leaving Chelsea, Lampard was given a two-year contract by New York City FC, a club entering Major League Soccer for the 2015 season. However, NYC's parent club Manchester City had also offered him a contract to play for them on a six-month deal ending in January 2015. To cut a long story short, Lampard's stay at Man City was extended beyond the start of the MLS season, which angered their fans greatly. He eventually played 19 games for NYC, contributing a healthy 12 goals and hopefully placating the fans.

Frank collected many other accolades during his club and international career, too numerous to mention all of them here, but here are just a few to savour:

- 3 Premier League titles
- 4 FA Cup winners' medals
- 2 League Cup winners' medals
- UEFA Champions League winner
- UEFA Europa League winner
- FWA Footballer of the year 1995
- Premier League player of the season 2004-05
- UEFA Midfielder of the year 2008
- Premier League player of the decade 2001-10
- England Player of the Year Award 2004, 2005

Frank Lampard's impressive goals-to-games record for a midfield player is testament to his uncanny knack of arriving late into the opponents' penalty area. This made it difficult for defenders to pick him up and before anyone knew it, the ball was nestling in the back of their net after a fierce drive, often from the edge or just outside of their box. The surprised look on their faces said it all!

One of the finest testimonials of Frank's prowess came from no less a fellow professional than Lionel Messi. The Barcelona superstar, believed by many to be the greatest player of his generation, had this warning to his team-mates prior to their 2012 Champions League semi-final against Chelsea – "We know they have a great squad that contains some of the best players in Europe, but I particularly admire Frank Lampard. To have a midfield player who consistently scores so many goals at the top level is a rare thing. It is something we need to look out for in the two matches. For sure Frank is a big threat."

Frank's England international career was no less impressive than his club career. His 106 England caps puts him 8th in the all-time list of appearances. His goals tally of 29 in an England shirt compares favourably with his club form. Ironically, his England haul should read 30 goals but for a disallowed goal against Germany (who else!) in the last 16 of the 2010 World Cup in South Africa.

With the score at 2-1 in Germany's favour, Lampard latched on to a loose ball on the edge of the opponents' penalty area and thumped a powerful shot goalwards. The ball cannoned the underside of the German crossbar and bounced down clearly over the goal line and out again before being gathered by the keeper. To the dismay of Lampard and the rest of the England camp, the goal was disallowed, and Germany went on to win the game 4-1. Such a pity that goal line technology was not available at the time. It could have changed the outcome of the match, but we will never know.

Lampard has distinguished himself throughout his long career and this was recognised when he was awarded an OBE for services to football by the Duke of Cambridge in October 2015. He was an outstanding exponent of the beautiful game with a great deal of popular appeal. Consequently, he has appeared in TV series such as Play to the Whistle, as well as being employed as a TV pundit by BT Sport and the BBC. Unlike some footballers, he is also a man of great intelligence with an IQ over 150, which puts him in the top 0.1% of the population and above the likes of former Countdown mathematics expert Carol Vorderman. Albert Einstein's IQ at 160 was better than Frank's, but equally he was not noted for his football prowess.

Lampard has embraced the literary world by writing and publishing a series of children's novels. One of the books is called Frankie's New York adventure which involves Frankie and his footballing playmates being magically transported to the Big Apple. Remind you of someone?

And so, onward, upward, forward. The multi-talented Mr Lampard has now moved into the precarious world of football management. It's too early to pass judgement on him yet, but we eagerly await to see if the 'Man for all Seasons' can add yet more to his many and varied achievements.

JAMIE CARRAGHER

*"Nothing is more noble, nothing
more venerable, than loyalty."*

(Cicero)

Jamie Carragher is a rarity in the modern world of football, namely a one-club player. He loyally served Liverpool FC from joining the club's academy in 1988 until his retirement in 2013. Ironically, as a kid growing up in Bootle, he was an obsessive Everton fan like his father and attended matches both home and away. In recent years he has shared an early recollection of attending the 1985 FA Cup Final with his father and other family members, where an Everton win would have clinched a fantastic treble for the season. They had already won the First Division title and European Cup Winners' Cup, but succumbed to a 3–1 defeat at the hands of arch rivals Man United. Prior to the match Carragher senior was involved in a scuffle with a ticket tout and was promptly arrested by the police over the incident. He was later released having missed most of the match – let's hope he saw the funny side of it! Such was his father's obsession with Everton that Jamie was christened with the two middle names of Lee and Duncan, the former after the then Everton manager Gordon Lee and the latter in homage to former Blues idol Duncan McKenzie.

At the age of 11, Carragher, not surprisingly, attended the Everton School of Excellence, but a year later he switched his allegiance to the Liverpool youth set-up, which was regarded as superior, under the tutelage of former Reds favourite Steve Heighway. However, the blue blood continued to flow through his Everton veins as he reportedly turned up for training on numerous occasions wearing a Graham Sharpe Everton shirt!

His professional debut came in the 1996-97 season in a League Cup quarter final under Roy Evans, and by the following season he was a regular first team choice. The 1997-98 season saw them struggle to keep pace with Man United and Arsenal, despite having a quality line-up including Michael Owen, Robbie Fowler, Paul Ince and many more. Carragher's value to the club as a utility player was very much enhanced as he flitted from full back to centre back to defensive midfielder.

The 1998-99 season saw the arrival of Gérard Houllier as manager. The Frenchman soon took a liking to the versatile, hard-working Carragher and he was an ever-present in the side and was named as the club's Player of the Year ahead of his more famous team-mates.

After switching position to left back in the 2000-01 season, he won his first major honours as Liverpool won the FA Cup, League Cup, UEFA Cup, Community Shield and Super Cup in the space of a few months. Quite a haul! Henceforward he continued to play at full back with Houllier preferring to maintain the successful central pairing of Sami Hyypia and Stephane Henchoz. Over the next two seasons his progress was scuppered by a couple of serious injuries, but despite these setbacks, he was around to help Liverpool lift a second League Cup trophy in 2003 as well as being named as the club's vice-captain.

The 2004-05 season was undoubtedly a landmark in Carragher's career. New manager Rafa Benitez made the decision to switch him to centre back. This proved to be an astute move on the part of Benitez, with Carragher settling into his new role with ease alongside his new partner Sami Hyypia. He was to remain at centre back for the rest of his Liverpool career and he forged a reputation as a strong, uncompromising defender with great positional sense. His astute reading of the game has long been one of his key assets, making up for his slight lack of pace against the game's top players.

Liverpool's victory in the 2005 Champions League final was a stunning achievement. In Carlo Ancelloti's AC Milan they faced a team regarded as one of the best in the world. Following a dramatic penalty shoot-out, they triumphed against all the odds in Istanbul. Carragher featured prominently in the game, making two of his trademark last-ditch tackles during extra time, despite suffering from cramp through his whole-hearted efforts at the centre of Liverpool's rearguard. Such heroics saw him receive the Reds' Player of the Year Award that year, as well as a nomination for the prestigious Ballon d'Or.

Further success came the following year when Liverpool clinched an FA Cup Final win against West Ham after extra time and penalties yet again. Carragher blotted his copybook with an own goal in the first half, but this was soon forgotten when victory finally came and he picked up the second FA Cup Winners' medal of his career.

In 2007 Carragher surpassed Ian Callaghan's record of 89 club appearances in European competitions when he played in a Champions League semi-final against Chelsea. He was also voted the club's Player of the Year by the fans for the third time. Later in the season he called time on his international career, reportedly prompted by his lack of game time during Steve McClaren's tenure as England manager. He later returned to the England fold in 2010 when Fabio Capello's defensive options were limited by injury. He had generously responded to a request by the FA to make himself available for the FIFA World Cup. He featured in two group matches, picking up bookings in both, and received the compulsory one-match ban. He wasn't selected for the knock-out game against Germany which resulted in defeat for England. He subsequently announced his permanent retirement from the international stage.

In October 2010 Carragher scored his seventh own goal in the Premier League, three less than record holder Richard Dunne. A fascinating statistic, but whilst some of his critics may accuse him of being a serial own-goaler, those in the know will testify to his staunch defending efforts on so many occasions as the reason for this dubious honour.

In February 2013, Carragher called time on his distinguished football career. He clocked off and disappeared through the Anfield factory gates for the final time on May 19th that year, following a 1-0 win over QPR, having notched up a staggering 737 appearances in Liverpool colours, including a record 150 European matches for the club. He had many admirers in the game, none more so than Chelsea's Didier Drogba, who described him as the toughest opponent he had ever played against, but an aggressive and fair defender. Many in the game will no doubt echo that compliment.

Post retirement, Carragher has been working as a pundit for Sky Sports alongside old adversary Gary Neville, amongst others. (Who says Mancs and Scousers don't mix!) His immense football knowledge and analytical skills are without question, but the heavy Scouse accent has had many southern viewers reaching for the TV remote to hit the subtitles button.

The much-reported spitting incident, which led to a suspension of his job at Sky, should not be allowed to detract too much from his reputation as a person. His long-standing charity work for the 23 Foundation in Liverpool is testimony to his good nature. The political correctness demanded in public life these days means that everybody must be squeaky clean at all times. Any transgression is quickly posted on social media and soon the whole world knows you have scored another own goal!

On a lighter note, Carra's long career with Liverpool has seen him dutifully turn up at the Melwood training ground many hundreds of times. Hardly surprising that he was on autopilot one morning 18 months after his retirement when he arrived at the training ground once more. He was supposed to be going to the gym – old habits die hard, do they not!

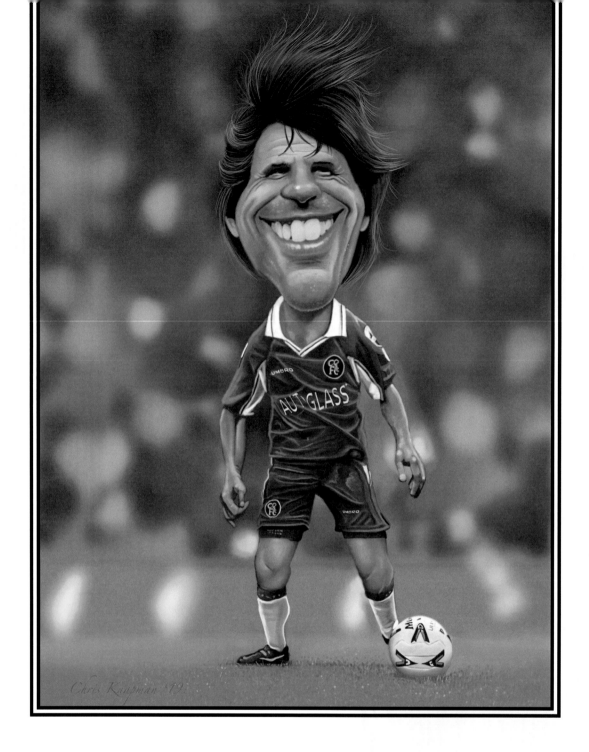

GIANFRANCO ZOLA

"I prefer to accept only one type of power: the power of art over trash, the triumph of magic over the brute."

(Vladimir Nabokov)

Whilst many leading lights of the Premier League are increasingly spotted at primary school and making their top-flight debuts barely out of secondary, Gianfranco Zola's emergence as a top-class footballer differed from this trend. Having spent his formative footballing years with hometown club Corrasi Oliena, in his native Sardinia, Zola signed his first professional contract when he was 18, when he joined fellow Sardinians Nuorese. Spent mostly in Serie D, Zola managed 10 goals in 31 appearances. This was enough to impress Torres, who took him up a division to Serie C2. After 21 goals in 88 games over three seasons with the Sassari-based club, Zola got his big chance at the highest level when Serie A Napoli came for him in 1989.

Zola played both alongside and understudy to the great Diego Maradona in Naples. He regards his time with the mercurial Argentinean as a period of huge growth as a player. The pair of them would stay on after training and spend hours practising free-kicks together. Zola has gone on record saying "I learned everything from Diego. I used to spy on him every time he trained and learned how to curl a free-kick just like him". The presence of a genuine legend of the game was a mixed blessing for Zola. As much as he learned from him, his role as Maradona's understudy slightly restricted his game time. He did, however, manage 105 games over four seasons, scoring a respectable 32 times. The undoubted high-point of his Napoli career was winning Serie A in his first season. Clinching their first title in years, Napoli were largely inspired by Maradona – but the little man from Sardinia played his part, making 18 appearances and scoring twice.

In 1993 Zola departed for Parma – a growing influence in Italy's top division. In just over three seasons, he contributed 49 league goals in 102 matches. It was during this time that Zola established himself as a top-drawer creative influence as well as a goalscorer. He was pivotal in Parma winning both the Italian Cup and the UEFA Cup in 1995. Also, although he'd debuted for Italy in 1991, his starring role at Parma won him more international recognition than at Napoli. Despite his obvious talent, manager Carlos Ancelotti sacrificed Zola because the blithe, impish, hard-to-pin-down forward didn't fit into his rigid formation. He was seen as the 'square peg'. He was frequently played out of position and the offer of a move to Premier League Chelsea suited both parties.

In November 1996 Zola was taken to Stamford Bridge by Ruud Gullit, as Chelsea – amongst others – sought to embroider teams built upon British grit and endeavour with a dash of continental panache. And, for £4.5 million, his acquisition proved to be excellent business. His debut season was marked by a number of stellar performances and some truly memorable goals. In short, Zola treated English football fans to a veritable cornucopia of wonderful goals. One such goal actually came in the FA Cup semi-final against Wimbledon during his debut season, rather than the Premier League, but it simply can't be overlooked due to its petulant brilliance. Darting right to left, skirting the edge of the area, Zola audaciously back-heels a through-ball with his right boot, before swivelling 180 degrees to dash right and retrieve his own back-heel (whilst the Dons defender was still running in the opposite and now wrong direction), before taking one touch and thumping a right-foot drive under the keeper from just inside the box. Another strike, again in his debut season, came against Manchester United – and it was as magnificently cheeky as his cup stunner. Latching onto Dan Petrescu's perfectly weighted through-ball where the right-hand corner of the area meets the byeline, Zola neatly tucks the ball to the left of Denis Irwin with his right instep. Having left the full-back trailing, with two more dabs of the right boot he dances along the edge of the six-yard box (ghosting past Phil Neville as if he wasn't there), before neatly sliding the ball home, to the right of a bemused Peter Schmeichel with his left. Even Alex Ferguson paid him a thinly-veiled compliment, calling the Sardinian wizard a "clever little so and so"; high praise indeed! For some, his finest goal came against Norwich City in the 2002 FA Cup – and it was as unorthodox as it was brilliant. Moving away from his marker on the edge of the penalty area, to find space on the right-hand corner of the six-yard box, Zola meets Graeme Le Saux's right-hand corner by leaping into the air and sublimely finishing with a back-heeled right-foot volley – a feat never before seen in the Premier League.

He then ran, arms aloft, to the advertising hoardings to celebrate before the jubilant Chelsea masses. But he wasn't just mobbed by his team-mates. No. A balding Blues fan encroached onto the pitch and gave him an enormous bear-hug. Unruffled by this, a grinning Zola responded likewise before despatching the ecstatic slap-head with an affectionate double-pat on the top of his head. Tragically, nowadays, any such player-fan synergy of celebration usually results in the player in question receiving the meanest of cautions. Another edict from the governing bodies which kills the spirit of the game. His manager, Claudio Ranieri, described the goal as "fantasy, magic", adding that "Gianfranco tries everything because he is a wizard and the wizard must try". And his wizardry was in evidence across all cup competitions

Away from the domestic scene, the Italian international was a totemic figure in various cup competitions, as Chelsea landed the FA Cup, League Cup, Cup Winners' Cup and the Super Cup. Few Chelsea fans will forget his decisive cameo role in the 1998 Cup Winners' Cup final against Stuttgart in Stockholm. Denied a starting berth by injury, he came off the bench to dramatically grab the winner after barely 30 seconds on the field. Running onto Dennis Wise's through-ball, Zola hammered the ball into the roof of the Germans' net with only his second touch. He also starred in Chelsea's run to the Champions League quarter-finals in 2000. He scored three goals en route, with a marvellous curling free-kick against Barcelona being his 'stand-out' moment.

Despite his influence in the cups, Zola's role in the Premier League was marginally limited during his last few seasons. Many of his appearances were from the substitutes' bench. In 1999, manager Gianluca Vialli adopted a squad rotation policy, often leaving Zola out. His successor, Claudio Ranieri, sought to decrease the average age of the squad, and ageing stars, such as Dennis Wise and Frank Leobeuf, were moved on. Zola himself saw his opportunities restricted. He did, however, finish his Chelsea career with a flourish. His final season, 2002-2003, saw him score 16 goals in 46 games across all competitions in what proved to be something of a renaissance. Despite not always starting or finishing, he played in every Premier League game. His last game was as substitute against Liverpool – and he shimmered for 20 final minutes. It is remembered for a mazy run, in which he left four Liverpool players in his wake, gaining a standing ovation from both sets of fans – a moment of class which epitomized his Chelsea career. It was to be his last act in Chelsea blue. He made 312 league and cup appearances, scoring 80 goals. At the end of the season, Zola was offered an improved contract, but opted to leave the Bridge and head home. Nobody has worn his hallowed number 25 shirt since his departure, fuelling speculation that it's been retired in his honour – though Chelsea have never made any announcement to that effect. One accolade that isn't in dispute is his OBE, awarded in 2004 at a special ceremony in Rome. His most notable personal honour came in 1997, when he was voted Football Writers' Association Player of the Year – the only player ever to receive the award without playing a full Premier League season and the first Chelsea player to win it.

Zola played two more seasons, returning to his roots to play for Cagliari in Sardinia. Helping steer them to promotion to Serie A in his first season, he played one season in the top-flight before retiring aged 38. Fittingly, he scored twice in his final professional game against Juventus. His number 10 Cagliari shirt was withdrawn for one season as a tribute to a truly wonderful footballer.

Since retiring, Zola has entered into the managerial fray. In 2006, he became assistant manager to Pierluigi Casiraghi with the Italian Under-21s - the pinnacle of which was progression to the quarter-finals of the Beijing Olympics in 2008. He also had two seasons at West Ham, where he blooded several promising youngsters and was commended for nurturing an attractive style of play. In his second season, the Hammers limped to a 17th-place finish. Amid speculation about his future, Zola revealed that he wasn't consulted over a bid for West Brom's Graham Dorrans, or with regard to chairman David Sullivan's mercantile announcement that the entire squad was for sale, with the exception of Scott Parker. Zola's contract was terminated in May 2010.

Next came Championship Watford – who'd been taken over by Italian club Udinese. This Anglo-Italian partnership enabled him to bring in some useful loan signings from the Serie A outfit, and the club secured a play-off spot at the end of his first season, only to lose 1-0 to Crystal Palace in the final. The following season saw the Hornets stutter somewhat. In December 2013, with the club lying 13th, Zola resigned on the back of five successive home defeats.

By the mid-nineties, players were rapidly pouring into the Premier League – and this metamorphosis received very mixed reviews. Caveat emptor? – many clubs were wowed by the so-called bargains they could procure from the continent against the backdrop of spiralling wage demands and rapidly inflating transfer fees at home. Some got their money's worth, but many a deal led to disillusionment and disappointment. Some imports, however, have played with such skill, technique and creativity that they've inducted themselves into the Premier League's 'hall of fame' – and in this number one must include Gianfranco Zola. He showed the British players ball-control, subtlety, perspicacity and invention few would recognise in themselves. Truly a pioneer when it came to helping the British remember how the game should be played. I don't support Chelsea, but I don't get bored of magic. I could take pleasure in watching Zola's goal against Wimbledon all day-long and beyond – which says it all really.

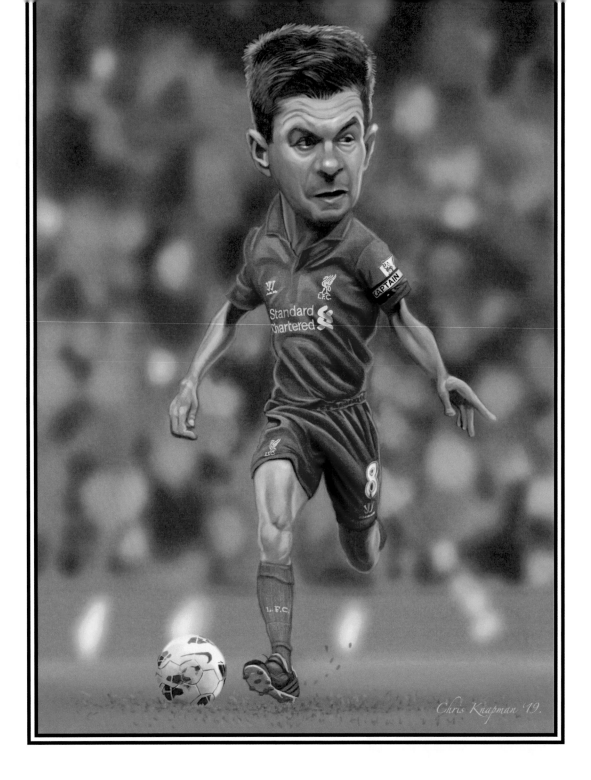

STEVEN GERRARD

"To do great things is difficult; but to command great things is more difficult."

(Friedrich Nietzsche)

For a long time, Premier League clubs have routinely scoured the globe, seeking to procure the services of the cream of available talent. In the case of Steven Gerrard, they needed to look no further than the Merseyside district of Whiston. Initially, Gerrard's football baptism wasn't really a happy one. He didn't meet with immediate success and travel seamlessly towards stardom. Although this young Liverpool supporter only really wanted to play for one club, it was clearly in his interests to maximise his chances by trialling at other clubs. Hard to envisage in view of what was to transpire, but Gerrard actually was rejected elsewhere, before penning a YTS contract with his beloved Liverpool. Even then, success still eluded him, and he failed to win a place in the England Schoolboys' side.

Football, like any other sphere of society, is supposed to operate along meritocratic lines; and in this case it delivered Gerrard the opportunity to showcase his talent. Making his debut as a last-minute substitute against Blackburn Rovers, he'd barely time to affect the game. Worse still, he was deployed on the right-wing and paralysed by nervousness. In a *Guardian* newspaper interview some years later, Gerrard recalled: "I was out of position and out of my depth." Ironically, as the years rolled by, he proved to be the most versatile of players, functioning effectively in a range of positions: holding midfielder, attacking midfielder, right-back, right winger and even second striker. However, ask any Liverpool fan or media pundit, and they will tell you with some conviction that Gerrard was at his best as a hard-working box-to-box central midfielder. Football's meritocratic values were very much intact as, in his central midfield niche, he grew from timid fledgling to become the Anfield club's talisman and one of the best players in the world. He was the go-to guy when the going got tough.

Gerrard began the new millennium in a midfield partnership with Jamie Redknapp. They bonded well as a duo. Disappointingly though, this proved to be a rather ephemeral arrangement, as the southerner's career was blighted by a succession of injuries. Gerrard, unshaken and absolutely driven, demonstrated that his career was going places; his rise was inexorable – despite suffering periodic injuries of his own – such was his quality.

Gerrard was becoming steadily more influential and showing that he'd the class to stamp his authority on matches. 2000-01 was to prove one of the most fertile seasons of his career. He made 50 league and cup appearances, and contributed 10 goals. By the spring of 2001, he'd won an impressive treble of the FA Cup, League Cup and the UEFA Cup. A superb haul for just one year and he was still only 20 years-old.

The next couple of years saw Gerrard continue to thrive in central midfield. Despite picking up the odd injury, he was still a regular starter and an integral part of the Liverpool machinery. In March 2003, Liverpool beat Manchester United 2-0, to clinch the League Cup at Cardiff's Millennium Stadium. From the perspective of fans on both sides of the M6, Liverpool's relationship with United has never been one of friendly rivalry – more like searing hostility. With that in mind, one suspects that Gerrard, a lifelong Liverpool fan himself, savoured that moment in particular.

The Champions League is a step-up in class from – and therefore a natural extension of – the English Premier League. Like every other European equivalent, the Premier League provides the springboard to play in the continent's senior-most competition. And aside from actually trying to win the darn thing, English competitors are indirectly advertising the Premier League and helping lure overseas players to the English game. (If they weren't already tempted by the filthy lucre!)

It was here that we saw Steven Gerrard, arguably, surely, play his finest football.

In 2005, Liverpool's progression in the Champions League was almost halted by Greece's Olympiacos. With five minutes remaining at Anfield, they led their Hellenic rivals 2-1, meaning that Olympiacos would claim second spot (having scored one away goal, compared to Liverpool's none in Greece) and qualify for the knockout stage, at the home side's expense. With just four minutes left on the clock, the home crowd were baying for someone to step up and be the hero; and a midfielder known affectionately as 'Stevie G' was ready to assume that mantle. Neil Mellor, who'd notched goal number two, showed great composure to adroitly cushion a header into the path of the arriving Gerrard. As the ball bounced up from the floodlit turf, he blasted a withering right-foot drive low to the goalkeeper's left, from about 22 yards. Anfield erupted in ecstasy – in a moment upon which peerless reputations are forged. This incredible escape was to prove more than telling, in view of Liverpool and Gerrard's absorbing journey thereafter.

Having side-stepped a Greek juggernaut, Liverpool went from strength-to-strength. And this was a competition which Gerrard seemed to enjoy, with his Champions League form making some of the game's observers start to take notice.

Bayer Leverkusen, then more notably Juventus and Chelsea, were all overcome en route to the final in Istanbul. The finale, however, against Italian royalty AC Milan, presented the greatest challenge. The Milanese line-up was one of formidable class: Maldini, Pirlo, Kaka, Crespo and Shevchenko. Steven Gerrard clearly wasn't bothered by this at all – even if his colleagues were quaking.

Things started disastrously for the Reds, with Milan taking a very early lead. Encouraged by Paulo Maldini's first minute opener, the Serie A side took control. This was followed by a brace from Hernan Crespo – and Liverpool's night looked to be over already. It's true to say that Milan's first-half offensive play was precise and utterly ruthless; however, it's also true to say that Liverpool defended like a miserable ragtag bunch of amateurs who'd just met for the very first time, in a pub about 20 minutes before kick-off. Every Milan surge into the depths of the Liverpool half was much like one of Oliver Cromwell's

Roundheads, armed with lance and rapier, setting about a block of Lurpak that's been left out of the fridge all night. When the beleaguered Reds trudged back to the dressing room at the break, not even the most optimistic of Liverpool supporters could've been hoping for what was to follow.

Still undismayed, Gerrard emerged from the dressing-room, took the game by the scruff of the neck and became the catalyst for a most unlikely revival. His valour and determination, as he fought his way into Italian territory, was starting to rattle their opponents. Inspired by the Whiston wonder, Liverpool subjected Milan to a truly devastating six-minute blitz. Here Gerrard showed real leadership. The once timid teenager was now the unshrinking alpha male and undaunted by what many thought to be a lost cause. Often from his own half, he began to make driving runs deep into the core of the Italian's defence. Foray after foray, raid after raid – an early second-half breakthrough was imperative and it was coming. Sure enough, Gerrard provided exactly that on 54 minutes. Latching onto John Arne Riise's left-wing cross, his lofted 12-yard header sailed past Dida into the right-hand corner. Steven Gerrard, already a folk-hero in one half of Merseyside, gained a totemic – almost mystical – status that night in Istanbul. His unflinching belief was now starting to radiate through the rest of the team; and just two minutes after Gerrard's reply, Vladimir Smicer smashed the ball home from distance. 3-2 and *I Rossoneri* were rocking. Liverpool and Gerrard could now smell blood. More Liverpool incursions followed and they equalised on the hour. Again, Liverpool's intrepid captain was instrumental. As he darted into the penalty area of their now trembling opponents, in anticipation of a through pass, Gennaro Gattuso then unceremoniously hacked him down and a penalty inevitably followed. Xabi Alonso saw his spot-kick saved by Dida, but knocked home the rebound. Extra-time saw missed opportunities for both teams and Liverpool held firm to eventually win on penalties. This improbable outcome was – and still is – the most stirring comeback in Champions League history; and it was largely down to Gerrard's fearless second-half performance and ability to inspire those around him. The 'man-of-the-match' award was only headed for one mantelpiece. Enshrined in Liverpool folklore, this game is known colloquially as *The Miracle of Istanbul*. His contribution, not just in the Turkish capital, but throughout the whole competition, wasn't lost on UEFA. Come the end of the season, he was named UEFA Club Footballer of the Year.

Gerrard carried his spellbinding European form into the following campaign, netting 23 goals in 53 league and cup games. At the end of the season, he was deservedly voted PFA Player of the Year by his peers. In doing so, he was the first Liverpool player to receive this endorsement since John Barnes – back in 1988.

Fittingly, he ended the season with a goal that will be forever etched into the collective Liverpool memory. Creating a moment of FA Cup iconography, in surely the best FA Cup Final since the turn of the millennium, Gerrard was on target twice against West Ham United; and this included a thunderous 35-yard pile driver – forcing extra-time with seconds remaining. He also slotted home from 12 yards, as Liverpool beat the broken Hammers in a climactic penalty shoot-out. These goals gave him the proud distinction of being the only player to have struck in the finals of the FA Cup, League Cup, Champions League and UEFA Cup; and his role as saviour and man-of-the-match was fast becoming the most salient feature of Liverpool's modus operandi.

The 2006-07 season saw AC Milan avenge their stirring defeat of 2005. Disappointing for club and player, of course, but Gerrard was quickly on the march once more. The following season started well for the midfield man, as he marked his 400th Liverpool appearance with a Premier League goal against Arsenal. Then in November, he scored in every domestic and cup game, bar one. The following month, Gerrard equalled a club record. He became the first Liverpool player since John Aldridge in 1989 to score in seven consecutive matches, in all competitions. As a midfielder, his finally tally of 21 goals was a laudable return.

His reputation stretched well beyond the Premier League – proven by his inclusion in the FIFA World XI of 2007. Indeed Ronaldinho, FIFA World Player of the Year that very season, was magnanimous in his assessment of the Liverpool captain:

"Gerrard is for me, in the position he plays, one of the best in the world. He has huge impact. For the job he performs, for me, he is one of the greatest."

Praise indeed.

As he continued to be Liverpool's lynchpin and leader, the 2008-09 season was a particularly good one for Gerrard. Though the club itself weren't amongst the honours this time around, he prospered on the pitch and the plaudits came thick and fast. Finishing the season with his career best goal haul (24 in all competitions), Gerrard received multiple awards. These included PFA Fans' Player of the Year and, even more prestigiously, the Football Writers' Association Footballer of the Year crown.

Having already been exalted by Ronaldinho, Gerrard was to receive even higher praise from the greatest player of the 21st century thus far – Zinadine Zidane:

"Is he the best in the world? He might not get the attention of Messi and Ronaldo, but yes, I think he might just be. He has great passing, can tackle and score goals, but most importantly, he gives the players around him confidence and belief. You can't just learn that – players like him are just born with that presence."

The Frenchman's remarks about Gerrard's rousing influence on others strongly evoke his influence in numerous Premier League games and, of course, the 2005 Champions League Final. It's also interesting that Zidane saw him as an excellent passer of the ball. At the outset of his career, he considered himself to be no more than a defensive ball-winner. Others weren't so sure and were concerned by his tendency to commit careless fouls. Zidane's viewpoint accorded with that of one of his later managers, Rafa Benitez. The Spaniard chose to employ him as a deep-lying playmaker, still in central midfield, and at that point he came into his own as a creative force.

In the spring of 2008, he marked his 300th Premier League appearance by opening the scoring in a 3-1 victory over Blackburn Rovers. A year later, March 2009 saw him make his 100th Liverpool appearance in European club competition. He celebrated this landmark by scoring twice in a 4-0 victory against Real Madrid. Against a club esteemed and feared in equal measure, this was a scoreline which reverberated across the continent. Statistical milestones appear to be something which Gerrard relishes. In 2012, he marked his 400th Liverpool game with an unforgettable hat-trick against city arch-rivals Everton. As a diehard Red this must've felt like sheer utopia – a footballing Shangri-La which cannot be surpassed!

Gerrard continued to be a one-man advertisement for the English Premier League in Europe. Debate has always raged as to which league is the best in Europe; is it the Premier League, La Liga or the Bundesliga? The Anfield man was certainly doing plenty to bolster the case for the Premier League; this included coming off the bench to blast a second-half hat-trick, in the Europa League, in a 3-1 victory over Napoli in 2010.

As we know, sponsorship, Sky Sports and latterly BT sport – indeed global television coverage – have all generated untold wealth. Furthermore, this affluence is augmented by foreign investment. It is, therefore, no surprise that the world's finest players are seduced by the sexiest and probably most entertaining league on the planet – not to mention significantly increasing their earning capacity. The downside of all of this for clubs is that players like Gerrard – basking in the Premier League limelight – will be perpetually coveted by other clubs. Football's heavyweights in England and abroad have relentlessly pursued Liverpool's very best player. He did, however, remain steadfast in his desire to stay on Merseyside – even when other clubs offered to match or better his wages. So, when Chelsea, Bayern Munich and numerous others were circling overhead, why did he remain a dyed-in-the-wool Red? Why did he stick with Liverpool during his heyday and beyond? He explains as follows:

"a traditional club like Liverpool still has value, that's the reason why I have stuck around for so long... ...it is more important to win a couple of trophies and achieve something. That is a lot more difficult than to go down the easy road and move to a club where it becomes easier."

It is clear from this that Gerrard thrived on the pressure and challenge of playing for a club whose fans demand, nay expect, a constant stream of silverware. And the rapture of playing for the club he loves was bound to guarantee his continued ebullience.

Liverpool's mesmeric recovery against AC Milan, to claim the European title, saw him almost single-handedly overcome seemingly insuperable odds. Ultimately though, not even the might of Stevie Gerrard could give Liverpool a long-awaited first Premier League title; nor the England national team an equally long-awaited World Cup triumph. And nobody can suggest that he didn't persevere on both fronts. A mammoth 700 league and cup appearances for the Anfield club, and an equally stupendous 114 caps for his country, both bear testament to his sheer tenacity and unflagging loyalty – both qualities which seem less and less apparent nowadays.

For all Gerrard's loyalty and ceaseless endeavour, the man himself ended the 2013-14 season with the most costly of blunders. When Liverpool faced fellow title contenders Chelsea, in their third-last game of the season, a gaffe from the Liverpool captain changed the whole complexion of the title race. His slip allowed Demba Ba to race clear and put the Londoners ahead – a game they went on to win 2-0. Whilst this certainly enhanced Chelsea's prospects, it put eventual champions Manchester City in the box seat. It has been argued that this pivotal mistake cost the Anfield side the Premier league title. In the context of what he did for Liverpool, this was a tragic irony of colossal proportions. *Faber est suae quisque fortunae*; well, if man is the artisan of his own fortunes, then, on this occasion, he was definitely the architect of his own misfortune. Sadly, this remains the one blot on Gerrard's Liverpool career.

When Gerrard finally bowed out at Liverpool, his career wasn't quite over. He could've hung up his boots there and then, slipped into smart-casual and then ensconced himself in the *Sky Sports* match studio. Instead, he chose to sample 'the beautiful game' in the United States, playing Major League Soccer for Los Angeles Galaxy. Westering stateside, on a sojourn which lasted just under two years, he was moderately successful. He'll be best remembered for his debut, in a 5-2 win over San Jose Earthquakes. He scored himself and provided an assist for former Liverpool team-mate Robbie Keane, who went on to complete a hat-trick.

Ultimately, however, the practicalities of playing in such a vast country as the USA proved too much of a burden. Upon leaving, he cited the journeys of gargantuan length to away games, the diversity of altitude and the capricious climate as being the reasons for his departure.

Only now, at 36, did Gerrard call time on his illustrious career.

Post-retirement, he's been back at Anfield to coach Liverpool's academy players, but later went on to become the manager at Glasgow Rangers and later Aston Villa. A more quirky off-pitch activity was his dalliance with the acting profession. With a nod to past triumph, Gerrard appeared in the 2015 film *Will* – about an orphaned Liverpool fan who hitch-hikes to the 2005 Champions League Final. He hasn't stood in front of a clapperboard since, and whether that disappoints anyone is open to conjecture... One thing we can safely assume, however, is that Eddie Redmayne and Leonardo DiCaprio needn't trouble their physicians for Valium just yet!

Stevie Gerrard is unquestionably amongst the best players to grace the Premier League; and at his peak, the pre-eminent midfield force in the division. He was blessed with tactical intelligence and a natural ability to read play – which enabled him to stymie the opposition's moves. Most of all, perhaps, he'll be remembered for his powerful running, sallying into areas of danger, and his signature drives from the edge of the box. Even without a Premier League title, he still boasts a most stately portfolio: two FA Cups, three League Cups, an FA Community Shield, a UEFA Super Cup, the UEFA Cup and the UEFA Champions League. And that's in addition to his many personal accolades. Good enough to captain both club and country, and good enough to pull on the England jersey more than a hundred times. But it's in the red jersey of Liverpool that he'll be remembered with the most affection.

For in the hearts and minds of the Liverpool faithful, when Stevie G pulled on that red shirt, it gleamed and dazzled vermillion. A player the great Bill Shankly would have been more than happy to have in his ranks.

JOHN TERRY

"Fortune Favours The Brave"

(Translation of Latin Proverb)

Love him or hate him, no-one can deny that John Terry stands out as one of the Premier League's most colourful characters. Sometimes the hero, often the villain, a veritable sports writer's dream, he was never out of the football headlines for very long. Despite his many transgressions, of which more later, he was one of the top defenders of his generation. A tough, uncompromising centre back, he was powerful in the air, very brave in the tackle and an excellent reader of the game.

Born in Barking, Essex, his football journey began when he played for a local Sunday league team called Senrab, named after Senrab Street in Stepney which was close to where the players trained. He was in good company at the East End set-up, where he rubbed shoulders with future star players such as Sol Campbell, Jermain Defoe and Ledley King. After initially joining the West Ham youth system, he later moved on to Chelsea as a 14-year-old. Although he started as a mid-field player, a shortage of centre backs prompted the coaching staff to deploy him at the back. He settled into his new position with ease and the ensuing years have shown this to be a fortuitous move.

After leaving school, Terry joined Chelsea on a YTS at the age of 16, signing professionally a year later. He debuted from the bench in October '98 in a League Cup tie against Aston Villa; his full debut came later that season in a 2-0 FA Cup win against Oldham. The 2000-01 season, in which he made 23 starts, saw him firmly cement his place in the Chelsea back four. The fans began to warm to his style of play and it was no surprise when was voted the club's Player of the Year. His good form continued through the 2001-02 season as he formed a strong partnership with fellow centre-back Marcel Desailly, the club captain. Terry himself captained the side for the first time during the season in a league match against Charlton Athletic.

Although his football career was progressing well at Chelsea, the unsavoury side to Terry's personality started to emerge. In 2002, following an altercation with a London nightclub bouncer, the Chelsea starlet was charged with assault and affray. Although acquitted of the charges by the court, the FA saw fit to give him a temporary ban from playing for the national team. It wasn't until June 2003 that he pulled on an England jersey for the first time.

In a prior incident in September 2001, Terry had been fined two weeks' wages by Chelsea for being drunk in public and harassing some grieving American tourists in the aftermath of the 9/11 terrorist attacks.

Meanwhile, Chelsea's 2003-04 season was going well as they finished a creditable sixth in the Premier League and made it to the final of the FA Cup, only to lose 2-0 to fellow London rivals Arsenal. Having scored the winner against Fulham to help secure Chelsea's passage to the final, Terry was suffering with a virus and was only able to make a token appearance from the bench. Terry continued to perform well and was consistently handed the captain's armband when Desailly was unavailable. He became a fixture in Chelsea's back four and formed a strong partnership with another Frenchman, William Gallas.

Following the departure of Claudio Ranieri in June 2004, José Mourinho was appointed Chelsea manager and decided on John Terry as his club captain after Desailly had retired from Premier League football. The new coach and captain pairing inspired a successful 2004-05 season for Chelsea as they romped home to the Premiership title with the best ever defensive record in Football League history. Terry was voted the Player of the Year by his fellow professionals and also voted best defender in the Champions League. To cap his outstanding season, he was selected in the World XI at the FIFPro awards, a team nominated by players from 40 different countries.

Things just got better and better for Terry and Chelsea. They successfully defended their Premier League title the following season with a 91-points haul and also had the satisfaction of beating rivals Man United 3-0 to secure the trophy. In the 2006-07 Premiership campaign, however, Terry experienced the first dismissal of his career, after receiving two yellow cards in an away match against Spurs. He further blotted his copybook after the match by questioning the integrity of match referee Graham Poll. He was fined £10,000 by the FA for this misconduct.

The 2006-07 season continued to disappoint for the Chelsea captain, with a recurring back problem hampering his progress. He missed several matches and was eventually forced to have a back operation to remove a disc in the lumbar region. The surgery proved successful and Terry was back playing in February 2007 after a three-month absence. His presence at the heart of the Chelsea back four was sorely missed, as Chelsea later surrendered their Premier League crown to Man United. Meanwhile, in a Champions League match away to Porto, he picked up an ankle injury, which looked like it would cause him to miss the 2007 League Cup final against Arsenal. He did manage to recover from the injury and was able to play in the final; but just when you thought it was safe to go into the water...! In attempting to score from an attacking corner, he flung himself at the ball in a diving header but his head came into firm contact with the boot of Arsenal's Diaby, as the hapless defender attempted to clear his lines. Terry was rendered unconscious for several minutes by the collision and was carted off to hospital for a precautionary check-up. Remarkably, he managed to discharge himself in time to return to the Millennium Stadium to help celebrate Chelsea's 2-1 victory.

Terry led his team to the Champions League semi-finals for the third time in four years, and he was again at the helm as Chelsea triumphed 1-0 against Man United in the first FA Cup Final at the new Wembley Stadium, thanks to an injury-time goal from Didier Drogba.

Prior to the start of the 2007-08 season, Terry signed a new five-year contract which made him the highest paid defender in the Premier League at the time. His season was again plagued by injuries including a broken foot and a dislocated elbow. However, he managed to stay injury-free to play in the 2008

Champions League Final against Man United. The match went to the dreaded penalty shoot-out, in which Terry missed a crucial penalty, which would have won Chelsea the match. He appeared to slip as he struck the ball and his effort finished on the wrong side of the post – disaster! United went on to triumph 6-5, and the unfortunate Chelsea captain was reduced to tears. Later on in the season the player received some consolation when he was awarded the Defender of the Year from UEFA, alongside Frank Lampard and Petr Cech for their respective positions.

Despite strong interest from Man City prior to the start of the 2009-10 season, Terry remained at Chelsea, now under the stewardship of Carlo Ancelotti. In another successful season, Chelsea won their fourth Premier League title, culminating in a thumping 8-0 victory against Wigan Athletic. They also lifted the FA Cup after defeating Portsmouth 1-0 in the final. By December 2011 Terry had completed 400 games as Chelsea Captain, a club record.

During Chelsea's 2011-12 Champions League semi-final against Barcelona, Terry was red-carded after an off-the-ball incident in which he appeared to knee Alexis Sanchez. Despite the sending-off, Chelsea were able to qualify for the final on a 3-2 aggregate, although Terry would be suspended for the final, which was to be played in Munich. Nevertheless, Chelsea triumphed in a 4-3 penalty shoot-out over Bayern Munich, with, yet again, that man Didier Drogba holding his nerve to slot home the winning penalty. This was Chelsea's first Champions League title, and a feather in the cap of caretaker manager Roberto Di Matteo.

After the much-publicised incident in which Terry was found guilty of racially abusing Anton Ferdinand, he received a four-match ban. On his return to action against Liverpool in November 2012, he recorded his 50th Chelsea goal. Chelsea, now managed by Rafa Benitez, had made it to FIFA Club World Cup, but a knee ligament injury precluded Terry from taking part. Chelsea were only capable of claiming the runners-up spot behind Corinthians.

October 2014 saw Terry captain the Blues for the 500th time. In a later match against Schalke, he scored the fastest ever Champions League goal with a header after 90 seconds. The following season, when Chelsea progressed to the League Cup final against Tottenham, he scored the opening goal in the team's 2-0 victory and was also named Man of the Match for his contribution. In May of the same season he notched up his 39th league goal and eclipsed the record held by David Unsworth, as the Premiership's highest scoring defender.

In February 2016, Terry announced that he would be leaving the club at the end of the season. However, he was persuaded to sign a contract extension taking him to the end of the 2016-17 season. Yet another new manager, in the shape of Antonio Conte, arrived at the club and confirmed that Terry would continue as club captain. In a largely uneventful season for Terry himself, the club did manage to claim the Premier League title once more. Following this triumph, he played his 717th and final match for Chelsea on May 21st in a 5-1 victory over Sunderland, receiving a guard of honour from his team-mates as he left the pitch.

In July 2017, Terry left Chelsea on a free transfer, having signed a one-year contract with Championship club Aston Villa. He scored his only goal for Villa in a 2-1 victory over Fulham in October 2017. On May 30th Terry ceased to be an Aston Villa player after the club failed to gain promotion to the Premier League, having lost 1-0 to Fulham in the play-off final. He did, however, return to the club a few months later as assistant manager under Dean Smith.

Terry's England career spanned nine years and included 78 appearances for his country. He scored six goals. He debuted in June 2003 against Serbia and Montenegro from the subs bench and made his first start in August of the same year against Croatia. He was partnered at the back by Rio Ferdinand, the duo forming a strong unit under manager Sven-Goran Eriksson. He was part of the England squad for Euro 2004, and the following season in a World Cup qualifier against Poland, he was handed the captain's armband after Michael

Owen had been substituted. He was selected in the squad for the 2006 FIFA World Cup and was fast becoming a fixture at the back for England. His first England goal came in a friendly against Hungary in May 2006.

August 2006 saw Terry named as England captain by new manager Steve McClaren, who commented: "I'm convinced he will prove to be one of the best captains England has ever had." No doubt buoyed by his new status, Terry scored on his debut as England captain in a friendly against Greece. The following year he had the distinction of becoming the first senior England player to score an international goal at the new Wembley Stadium, when he headed in a David Beckham cross. Terry resumed as England captain for the 2010 World Cup qualifying campaign, as England progressed to the finals. He had scored his first competitive England goal in a qualifier against Ukraine.

In February 2010, amid allegations about his private life, Terry was stripped of the England captaincy by manager Fabio Capello, the armband being passed to Rio Ferdinand instead. Later, in a media interview during the 2010 FIFA World Cup campaign, Terry openly criticised the England manager and was reprimanded for his comments. Despite this setback in their relationship, in March 2011 Terry was re-instated as captain when Ferdinand was absent with a long-term injury. However, in February 2012, when Terry was due to stand trial for allegedly racially abusing Anton Ferdinand, he was again relieved of the captaincy and, subsequently, Capello resigned as England manager.

Terry was again re-instated as captain, this time by new England boss Roy Hodgson for the Euro 2012 campaign and featured in all four of England's matches. During the tournament, a bizarre incident involving John Terry occurred in the final group match against Ukraine. A cross from the left found Marco Devic on the edge of the England penalty area. His firmly struck shot was parried by Joe Hart, but the ball looped over him and was heading into the unguarded net. With split-second timing Terry managed to scramble back and spectacularly hook the ball clear to prevent England from conceding an equaliser to Wayne Rooney's earlier goal. Video replays showed that the ball had in fact crossed the line fractionally and should have been given. Amazingly, the assistant referee, standing level with the goal-line and no more than five yards away, failed to give the goal. Once again, the incident prompted the debate about introducing goal-line technology. Ironically, justice was served as the replay also showed a Ukraine player clearly offside during the build-up to the goal attempt.

In a Premier League career punctuated by such controversy, it would be remiss not to recognise the many footballing achievements of John Terry. He is Chelsea's most successful captain, having led the club to five Premier League titles, four FA Cups, three League Cups, one Europa League and one Champions League title. An inspirational captain, a courageous defender and great leader, he has certainly left his mark on the Premier League as a player and will no doubt continue to make the headlines as his coaching career develops.

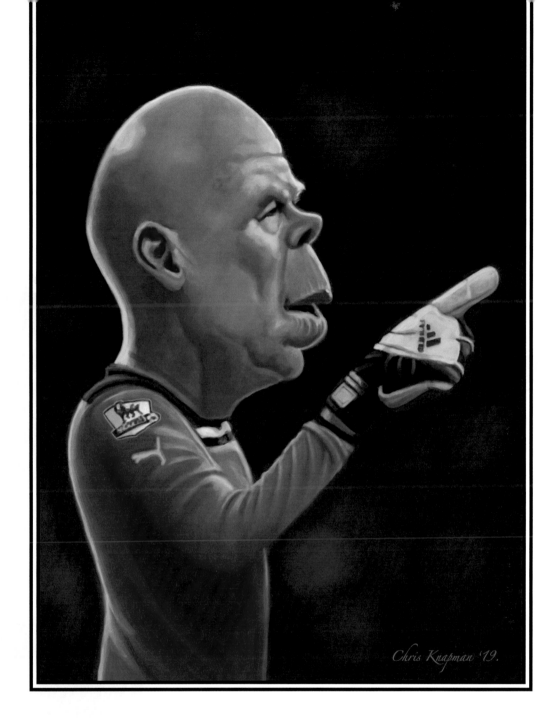

BRAD FRIEDEL

"If you wish to succeed in life, make perseverance your bosom friend, experience your wise counsellor, caution your elder brother, and hope your guardian genius."

(Joseph Addison)

Established denizen and elder statesman of the Premier League, it now seems an absurdity that Bradley Howard Friedel endured such a gargantuan struggle in earning the right to play here at all. But Nottingham Forest, Newcastle United and Sunderland all tried – and failed – to bring the rugged American to English shores. Having failed to gain a work permit to play for Brian Clough's Forest (he had no top-class experience to speak of), his problem was aggravated when he signed a contract with the United States Soccer Federation, to play exclusively for the United States national team in preparation for their hosting of the 1994 World Cup. So when Newcastle and Sunderland expressed interest after the tournament, he still did not meet the criteria at club level. It was only when Graeme Souness took him to Champions League regulars Galatasaray that Friedel managed to get some experience at a credible level of European club football. With 30 games under his belt for the Turkish side, Friedel pitched up at Liverpool in 1997 (after a brief stint in the MLS with Columbus Crew). Even at the fourth time of asking, he was only granted a work permit upon appeal – quite a saga for man who was still playing in the Premier League 468 appearance later at the age of 42.

Friedel's time at Anfield proved difficult. He was distinctly third-choice behind David James and Sander Westerveld, and accrued just 25 Premier League games in three years.

The year 2000 proved to be a pivotal one in Friedel's career – when he was reunited with his Galatasaray boss Graeme Souness at Blackburn Rovers. Unlike at Liverpool, where he was often 'waiting in the wings', the man from Lakewood, Ohio was straight into the cut 'n' thrust of a Championship promotion battle, as Souness sought to mastermind a return to the top division. Unbowed by the challenge, a series of assured performances from Friedel aided an ultimately successful promotion push.

In the following few seasons, Friedel was consistency personified; in fact, his errors were so infrequent that their rarity made them perversely memorable.

Equally rare was a Rovers' victory at Highbury, over an Arsenal team en route to the title in 2002. This notable scalp owed much to a catalogue of brilliant Friedel saves. Away from the Premier League, Friedel's 'Man of the Match'-winning performance inspired Rovers to League Cup Final glory as they beat Tottenham 2-1. After another stirring performance, away to Southampton, Saints' manager Gordon Strachan drew comparisons with Superman: "I wouldn't be surprised if, when he takes his shirt off, there's a blue jersey with an 'S' on underneath it."

At the end of the 2002-03 season his 15 clean sheets were rewarded when he won the club's Player of the Year award and was prestigiously named in the 'Premiership Starting XI'. Having also performed heroically at the World Cup the previous summer, was there a better goalkeeper on the planet at that time?

Friedel also holds the distinction of belonging to a select band of goalkeepers who've scored a Premier League goal. In February 2004, with his team trailing Charlton 2-1 at the Valley, he ran up-field to swell the ranks at a corner-kick. His last-minute strike from open play appeared to have pinched the Lancastrians a point – until Claus Jensen scored Charlton's winner practically from the re-start. A cruel twist; there seems to be something rather unholy and unacceptable about a goal-scoring goalkeeper finishing on the losing side!

Another of Friedel's finest games was against Sheffield United in 2006. Not content with making smart save after save, as the Blades peppered the Rovers' goal, he also saved two penalties – rendering the 'Man of the Match' award a formality.

The burly stopper from Ohio extended his contract with the club in April 2006 and again in February 2008. Upon penning this contractual extension, he expressed his affection for Blackburn Rovers, saying: "I am delighted to have extended this agreement. It was not a difficult decision to make. Blackburn Rovers is home to me. This is my club and I have a special affinity with it."

So when the club hero – and hitherto loyal servant – signed for Aston Villa just a few months later as the season ended, this 'declaration of love' for the Rovers must've sounded hollow and shocking in equal measure to the club's faithful. On balance, Friedel had, however, missed just four league games for the club from a possible 266 over seven seasons – a staggering feat unlikely to be outdone.

Record-breaking was also the most salient feature of his time at Villa Park. In February 2011, he became the Midlands club's oldest ever player at the tender age of 39 and 259 days. Also, in November 2008, he surpassed the record for continuous Premier League matches when game number 167 finished 0-0 against Fulham.

When Friedel's contract ended at the end of the 2010-11 season, a new club beckoned (Tottenham Hotspur) and the records continued to be broken. During the 2011-12 campaign, he became the oldest ever player to grace Premier League turf. Not even newly arrived French international goalkeeping captain Hugo Lloris found it easy to dislodge the American, who had achieved a staggering 310 consecutive Premier League games by October 2012.

Perhaps the most sobering thought with regard to this enduring North American is that football could quite easily have lost him to basketball or tennis – as he excelled at both. In his youth he was invited to represent the University of California basketball team. By comparison to football, basketball is a comparatively insular and almost exclusively North American sport; in electing to play football, more sporting fans worldwide have been privileged to enjoy seeing this quiet and modest man display his immense goalkeeping talents.

A stranger to scandal (sporting journalists would die of terminal boredom if they were to set-up camp outside his home), Brad Friedel just gets on with his job – and boy does he do it well. Amongst the most reliable goalkeepers British football has ever seen and an Ewood Park legend.

THIERRY HENRY

"Be not afraid of greatness: Some men are born great, some achieve greatness and some have greatness thrust upon them"

(William Shakespeare)

Thierry Henry was undoubtedly one of the greatest strikers in the history of the Premier League. He was the epitome of French flair and style combined with a speed and power which made him a formidable opponent for even the best of defenders. This French footballing icon had everything in his repertoire: exquisite technique, phenomenal pace, surprising strength, awareness of others and a lethal touch in front of goal. Like all top goalscorers, Henry possessed great composure and rarely squandered a scoring opportunity. On his day, he was simply unplayable.

Henry was born to parents of Antillean heritage in Les Ulis, a tough commune in the south-west of Paris, an area which also spawned other notable Premier League players such as Patrice Evra and Anthony Martial. He was signed by Monaco as a 13-year old after club coach Arnold Catalano saw him score all six goals in a match for his local side. He was so impressed with Henry that the club welcomed him into their ranks without even the customary trial.

He went on to make his professional debut for the club in 1994 and was initially deployed as a left winger by manager Arsène Wenger, who believed his blistering pace would be more effective against full backs than centre backs. He played a total of 105 games for the club over a five-year period, scoring a total of 20 goals. His good form led to an international call-up in 1998 and a year later he moved to Italian giants Juventus. However, his playing time at Juve was severely limited, as he struggled against the highly defensive teams that characterised Italy's Serie A league and he made an early decision to re-join his former Monaco manager Wenger who had been in charge at Arsenal since 1996. He signed for Arsenal in 1999 for an estimated fee of £11m.

It was at Arsenal that Henry made his name as a world-class player, where he became a prolific striker and Arsenal's all-time leading goal scorer with 228 goals in all competitions, eclipsing previous record holder Ian Wright. Wenger made the astute decision to play Henry as an out-and-out striker, a move which would pay dividends in the longer term. He played in tandem with Dennis

Bergkamp many times and having that sort of creative player alongside you can only increase your scoring opportunities.

Henry was also called upon to play as a lone striker in a 4-5-1 formation adopted by Wenger. He adapted well to this new role and the goals continued to flow. Wenger was inspired to heap praise on his protege with comments such as "Thierry Henry could take the ball in the middle of the park and score a goal that no one else could score". I'll second that! Henry had a multiple of ways to find the net: thumping drives, delicate chips, jinking runs, audacious backheels, the occasional header. You name it – Henry had it!

Words alone cannot do justice to the high class goals scored by Henry during his illustrious career – they have to be seen to be believed. One such classic was his goal against Man United in October 2000, where he received the ball with his back to goal on the edge of the box with a defender tight behind him. In one continuous movement, he flicked the ball a couple of feet off the ground, turned and volleyed it into the opposition net in the blink of an eye. Breathtaking!

His time at Arsenal was littered with many notable achievements. He won the Premier League Golden Boot four times and collected two FA Cup and two Premier League winners' medals. He was part of the so-called 'Invincibles' side of 2003-04, who went the entire season undefeated. He was runner-up for the FIFA Player of the Year award in the same year. He was voted the PFA Player of the Year twice and the FWA Footballer of the Year on three occasions.

He captained the Gunners during his last two seasons at the club and led them to the UEFA Champions League final in 2006, where they succumbed to a 2-1 defeat at the hands of an emerging Barcelona team. The Arsenal keeper Jens Lehmann had been sent off early in the match, which clearly reduced their chances of victory. Ironically, the following year Henry ended his eight-year association with Arsenal, when he signed for Barcelona for a fee of €24 million.

On his departure from Arsenal he made this emotional farewell statement –
"Arsenal will be in my blood as well as my heart. I will always, always, always
remember you guys (the fans). I said I was going to be a gunner for life and I
did not lie because when you are a Gunner you will always be a Gunner. The
club is in my heart and will remain in my heart forever." As a lasting tribute
to their former superstar, the club unveiled a bronze statue of Henry at the
Emirates Stadium as part of their 125th anniversary celebrations. The statue
showed him in classic knee-sliding pose after scoring against arch-rivals Spurs
in 2002.

In 2009 he was an integral part of the Barca's historic treble when they won La
Liga, the Copa del Rey and the UEFA Champions League. The club went on
to clinch an incredible sextuple when they also added Supercopa de Espana,
the UEFA Super Cup and the FIFA World Cup to add to their burgeoning list
of achievements.

Henry enjoyed further success in his international career, winning the 1998
FIFA World Cup, UEFA Euro 2000 and 2003 FIFA Confederations Cup. In
October 2007, he surpassed Michel Platini's record to become France's all-time
leading goalscorer. He was capped by his country a staggering 123 times and
scored a total of 51 goals. He retired from international duty after the 2010
FIFA World Cup.

In 2010 Henry ended his spell at Barcelona, when he signed for New York Red
Bulls.

During his four-season spell with them, he helped the club to the first major
honour of their 17-year history, when they were awarded the Supporters Shield.
This trophy is awarded to the Major League Soccer team with the best regular
season record, as determined by the M.L.S. points system. At one point he was
reported to be the highest paid player in the M.L.S. on a salary of around $5
million, even surpassing that of David Beckham.

In January 2012 Henry briefly returned for a cameo appearance at his spiritual home Arsenal. During the MLS off-season, he had been training with the Gunners and signed a two-month loan deal to provide cover for Gervinho and Chamakh, who were on Africa Cup of Nations duty with their national teams. He played in seven league and cup matches, scoring two goals to show that his predatory instinct was still intact.

In December 2014, it was announced that Henry was leaving Red Bulls after a successful four-and-a-half years at the club. Shortly after this, he announced his retirement as a player and stated he had signed a contract with Sky Sports as a pundit. After more than three years at Sky, he parted company with them to focus on his career in coaching.

His first coaching role was as assistant to Belgian National team manager Roberto Martinez, whom he joined in August 2016. His coaching skills and the value of his playing experience were significant in helping Belgium reach the semi-finals of the 2018 FIFA World Cup. They lost to his home country of France but won the Bronze medal when they defeated England 2-0 in the third place play-off final. In October 2018 he accepted the role of head coach at former club Monaco but he was unable to turn round the club's fortunes and was dismissed the following January after only 20 games in charge. He is currently back as an assistant with the Belgian national team.

Off the field, Thierry Henry was viewed as a highly marketable footballer and endorsed the brands of many global companies. He is probably best remembered for his work with a leading French car maker, a relationship which enabled him to meet his future wife, Claire Merry. He has also espoused several worthwhile social causes, including working with Unicef to promote football as a game to be played on behalf of children, as well as being an active spokesperson against racism in football.

RIO FERDINAND

"The superior man is modest in his speech, but exceeds in his actions"

(Confucius)

Rio Gavin Ferdinand was rightly regarded by many as one of the best defenders of his generation. You could argue that he was ahead of his time in that he was supremely capable in his defensive duties, but also had the technical skills to play out from the back, exactly in the way that modern football coaches have come to demand. Always comfortable on the ball, having thwarted an opposition attack, he instinctively strode forward to instigate a counter-attack and invariably found one of his team-mates with an accurate pass. He was able to replicate this style of play in a long and distinguished international career.

Ferdinand was a stylish defender, who had pace as well as tackling ability. He was powerful in the air and had an intuitive ability to read the game. His good positional sense enabled him to snuff out opposition strikers with ease and he was good at marshalling his fellow defenders in the heat of battle. He possessed excellent leadership skills and went on to captain at both club and international level with great aplomb.

The son of an Irish mother and a Saint Lucian father, he grew up in the South London suburb of Peckham. His brother Anton Ferdinand and cousin Les were also destined to become professional footballers. It all started for Rio Ferdinand back in 1992, when he joined the youth system at West Ham United at the age of 16, alongside the likes of Frank Lampard. Around this time, he was also selected to play for the England youth-team, representing his country at the UEFA European Championship.

His professional debut in the Premier League came four years later in 1996 and he quickly became a firm favourite with the fans, winning the Hammer of the Year award the following season. During the summer of 1997, Manchester United had been watching the talented youngster, but the West Ham management resisted their approaches and Ferdinand stayed put. After a short loan spell at Bournemouth, he returned to the West Ham ranks in January 1997.

His time at Upton Park came to an end in November 2000, when he was transferred to Premier League rivals Leeds United for a British record fee of £18 million. This hefty price-tag also made him the world's most expensive defender at the time, quite a burden for the 22-year-old to carry. Seemingly undaunted by the pressure of his new status, Ferdinand settled quickly at Elland Road and became an integral member of the side that reached the semi-final stage of the Champions League that year, having contributed a headed goal in the quarter final against Deportivo La Coruna to help get them there.

The following season saw Ferdinand handed the captain's armband and his good form continued as the ambitious Leeds outfit, under the stewardship of chairman Peter Ridsdale and manager Terry Venables, strove to emulate the previous season's success in qualifying for the Champions League a second time. Regrettably, it was not to be, as Leeds failed to break into the top three and what followed was a period of instability at the club. Having invested heavily in their quest for success, Leeds ran into financial difficulties and were eventually forced to sell their prime asset to Manchester United for a fee in the region of £33 million in June 2002.

This new chapter in the Ferdinand career was destined to be his most successful. Although he again carried the millstone of being the most expensive player in British football, he went on to win the Premier League with Manchester United in only his first season. His start to the 2003-04 season, however, was marred by controversy when he failed to turn up for a scheduled drugs test at United's Carrington training ground, having allegedly forgotten about the appointment. Although the club appealed against the charge, the FIFA judgement was that the charge should stand and the FA Discipline Committee meted out a severe punishment in the shape of an eight-month playing ban at both club and international level, plus a £50,000 fine. The reality of this meant he would miss the rest of that season and part of the next one, as well as being unable to participate for England in Euro 2004. During his absence, United lifted the FA Cup with a win against Millwall at the Millennium Stadium, a goal from Ronaldo and two from van Nistelrooy sealing the victory for the Reds.

On his return to action, he soon re-established himself in the United team and his performances continued to reflect his outstanding ability and determination. His next winners' medal came in the 2006 League Cup after a 3-1 victory against Wigan Athletic. His consistent good form throughout the season earned his inclusion in the 2006-07 PFA Premiership Team of the Season, along with no fewer than seven of his United team-mates. In the following season, during an FA Cup quarter final match against Portsmouth, Ferdinand turned from defender into goalkeeper when Edwin van der Sar left the field injured and the substitute keeper Tomasz Kuszczak was subsequently sent off after conceding a penalty. Ferdinand managed to dive the right way but was unable save the penalty, and United were eliminated from the competition. Portsmouth went on to lift the trophy that season, beating Cardiff City 1-0 in the final.

In May 2008, Ferdinand captained United in their Champions League Final victory over Chelsea. Both he and Ryan Giggs accepted the trophy jointly, since the latter had worn the armband for most of that season's matches. The 2009-10 season, however, was something of a disaster for him with a series of back and knee injuries hampering his progress for several months. On his return to action in January 2010, he received a four-match ban for violent conduct during a match against Hull City. His woes continued when he suffered a further knee injury in the summer of that year, which prevented him from taking part in England's World Cup campaign. He also missed United's pre-season phase, the Community Shield and the first four fixtures of the 2010-11 campaign.

In December 2012 during the Manchester derby, Ferdinand had the misfortune to be struck by a coin thrown by a City fan as he was celebrating Robin van Persie's winning goal. He picked up the offending object, a 2p piece, and handed it to the referee. He later tweeted his effrontery that it was only a 2p coin and not at least a pound coin!

Ferdinand's career with United had produced a staggering six Premier League titles and 14 trophies. He scored a mere eight goals in his 455-match career but none was perhaps more poignant than his winner on May 12th 2013 against Swansea. Standing at the far post for a United corner, he volleyed home from close range to register the final goal of the Alex Ferguson Old Trafford era.

After one further season with United, Ferdinand chose to sign for the newly promoted QPR in July 2014. His solitary season with the Loftus Road club produced only 12 appearances, and on May 30th he finally brought the curtain down on his distinguished football career.

As mentioned earlier, he had an exceptional international career with England, making 81 appearances and scoring three goals for his country. On his debut in 1997, at the age of 19 years and eight days, he was the youngest ever defender to play for his country. He was a fixture in the England squad for well over a decade, featuring in four World Cup squads but missing out on two potential Euro Championship campaigns, firstly in 2008 when England failed to qualify, and secondly in 2010 due to his drug test related ban. In March 2008 Ferdinand was handed the captain's armband by then manager Fabio Capello. However, under Capello's policy of rotating the captaincy in the run-up to the World Cup qualifiers before actually naming the official captain, he lost out to John Terry but was named vice-captain instead. Ferdinand regained the captaincy in February 2010. Although selected as captain for the 2010 World Cup, injury ruled him out of the tournament, with the armband returning to John Terry once more.

Ferdinand failed to gain inclusion in Roy Hodgson's Euro 2012 squad, fuelling speculation that John Terry's inclusion had influenced the decision. Terry had earlier been accused of racially abusing Rio's brother Anton and, with a trial pending, many thought the decision to exclude Rio was politically motivated. He was subsequently recalled to the England squad on March 2013 for the 2014 World Cup qualifiers but had to withdraw through fitness problems. The following May came the announcement that he was retiring from the international scene.

During his football career Ferdinand has, to say the least, courted controversy on many occasions. The earlier mentioned missed drug test of September 2003 was but one of a number of incidents to whet the appetites of the tabloid press. In 2000, along with fellow professionals Frank Lampard and Kieron Dyer, he was reported to have taken part in a sexually explicit video filmed in a Cyprus holiday resort.

Another drink-fuelled incident in a Leeds nightclub resulted in Ferdinand being accused of threatening a woman. However, after a police interview, the CPS announced he and fellow accused Michael Duberry would not face any charges.

A somewhat embarrassing radio interview on the Chris Moyles Show involved Ferdinand calling the host a faggot, after he jokingly suggested he was homosexual. He promptly apologised for this transgression, after complaints from listeners and also gay rights campaigner Peter Tatchell.

Like many a modern footballer, Ferdinand's comments on Twitter have sometimes got him into hot water, resulting in fines from the FA for using offensive language. Notably, his comments about Ashley Cole, who supported John Terry in the trial in which he was accused of racially abusing Ferdinand's brother, resulted in him receiving a £45,000 fine for bringing the game into disrepute.

On the plus side, Ferdinand has made several documentaries dealing with sensitive subjects such as bereavement, following the untimely death of his first wife Rebecca, and more recently, one dealing with the problems of step families focussing on his second wife Kate and his three children. He has also filmed a documentary about Peckham, which aimed to persuade the youngsters of his home borough away from a life of crime. He has also set up the Rio Ferdinand Live the Dream Foundation to nurture and develop children from deprived communities seeking careers in sport and entertainment. He has also been an outspoken campaigner against racism in football.

As a pundit with BT Sport, he will continue to be a high profile figure in the game. One thing is for certain, he will never shy away from debating sensitive issues, either on or off the field.

PETER CROUCH

"I can believe anything, provided that it is quite incredible"

(Oscar Wilde)

Anyone casting an eye on the physique of Peter Crouch would probably doubt that this was the body of a professional footballer. High jumper or basketball player maybe, but not, surely not, a footballer! Never judge a book by its cover, for Peter James Crouch was a successful Premier League footballer and a man of many talents. He was a prolific goal scorer and became a Premier League legend. Everybody has a soft spot for 'Crouchy'. He is famous for his height of 6'7", earning him the nickname of '2 metres of Peter'. His most powerful weapon was his head, witnessed by his record of scoring the most headed goals in Premier League history. In his illustrious career, in which he played for ten different clubs, he scored an impressive 108 times in his 500 Premier League appearances

Crouch started his career as a trainee at Tottenham Hotspur. He failed to make an impact there at this time and was loaned out to Dulwich Hamlet and Swedish Club IFK Hässleholm, before joining Gerry Francis's QPR where he really started to prove himself, scoring 10 times in 42 appearances, showing the footballing world his talents.

After QPR's relegation at the end of the 2000-01 season, Portsmouth paid £1.5 million to acquire the young striker's services. He wasn't just there to make up the numbers as the goals flowed at Fratton Park, scoring a creditable 19 times during the season. Big clubs like his old club, Spurs, and Liverpool started looking in closely on the striker's progress. This was a huge season for Crouch: he scored 19 times for Pompey, but after one season Portsmouth sold him for a whopping £5 million to Aston Villa. Crouch got off to the perfect start, scoring the equaliser against Newcastle on his debut. Unfortunately, his spell at Villa wasn't as successful as he would have wanted. In the following 2002-03 season, Crouch failed to hold down a regular place in the team, as he went 18 games without a goal and he was eventually loaned out to Norwich. This wasn't seen as a setback to him, it was seen as an opportunity to show the world the talents he had. At the end of the three-month loan deal, Crouch was sold to Southampton for £2.5 million. Crouchy had been a magnificent player for his new club's bitter rivals Portsmouth, but this was seen as a new and more challenging chapter for the lofty striker. He added to their numerous attacking options, with James Beattie and Kevin Phillips already in their ranks. However, it was Crouch who became the main attacking threat at St Mary's, as he went on to score 12 goals in 37 games. Again, after only one season at Southampton, he joined the mighty Liverpool for a £7 million fee.

Things started badly at Anfield; Crouch became the focus of abuse from the Liverpool faithful after failing to score in his first 19 games. He finally scored his first goal against Wigan Athletic where he bagged a brace. This was to be the catalyst for the tall, dangerous striker as he scored vital goals along the way to winning the Community Shield and the FA Cup with his new club. He later participated in the 2007 UEFA Champions League Final, coming on as a substitute for Javier Mascherano. The game ended in bitter disappointment as Liverpool were unable to repeat their heroics of Istanbul two years earlier, as Milan avenged themselves with a 2-1 victory. He ended the 2006–07 season as Liverpool's top goal scorer in all competitions, with 18 goals.

His form at Liverpool led to an England call up to the squad for the 2006 World Cup. He was partnered up front for the Three Lions by former Liverpool favourite Michael Owen. Crouch scored his first goal in an England jersey against Trinidad and Tobago, causing some debate. The goal should not have counted, as he was seen grabbing an opponent's hair in creating the scoring chance. England were knocked out in the quarter-final against Portugal, yet again on the dreaded spot kicks! On a personal level, Crouch played a big part in a great tournament for England. He had a very good international career, scoring 22 goals in 42 appearances. He was a real fan favourite. Not just for his goal scoring but for the 'robot' – this was his classic goal celebration that everybody seemed to embrace.

By the end of his three-year spell on Merseyside, he had scored 22 goals in 85 games. In July 2008 he re-joined Portsmouth for £11m. Yet again, as seemed to be customary, Crouch only lasted one season at the club, where he scored 16 goals in 46 games before joining North London outfit Tottenham. Portsmouth had lost £1m on the Crouch transfer, as he was sold for £10m. Crouch was brilliant this time around for Tottenham as he scored vital goals in the Premier League. Most importantly he scored in a match that was labelled a £15m game against Manchester City, where a coolly taken cushioned header was enough to earn a 0-1 away victory and guided Tottenham back into the lucrative Champions League. Spurs fans were absolutely delighted and fell in love with their new striker.

In his next campaign in the Champions League, Crouch scored a memorable hat-trick against Young Boys, which was followed up against Inter Milan away from home at the famous San Siro, when poking home an Aaron Lennon cross to get Spurs a vital away goal and victory.

After so many good memories for the North London outfit, Crouch moved up north to Stoke City for a club record fee for the Potters at the time of £10m. Crouch would serve Stoke for more than seven years, much longer than any of the other clubs he played for. In that time, he scored some quality strikes including a sweet volley against fellow England colleague Joe Hart. Crouch scored 46 times in the Premier League for Stoke in 225 Premiership games.

Towards the end of his career he joined Burnley on a six-month contract. This was to be Crouch's last club. He was used as an impact player for the last 10-15 minutes to try and rescue a goal. Crouch announced on his hilariously funny podcast 'THAT PETER CROUCH PODCAST' that he had spoken to Sean Dyche, saying that he didn't want to be remembered as a bit-part player who team-mates just lumped the ball up to in desperation. Dyche did want to keep Crouchy on for another season; however, Crouch decided to call time on his long career, retiring at the ripe old age of 38.

His departure was definitely the end of an era, but sadly all good things must come to an end.

Peter Crouch was well known for being a bit of a joker. He was once asked, "What would you be if you weren't a footballer?" Crouch replied, "A virgin!" – illustrating his great sense of humour and all-round likeability. The modern footballer is often castigated for being, well not very bright, a little dull, lacking in wit or wisdom. This cannot be levelled at Peter Crouch. He was a great talent on the pitch and is very warm, witty and engaging off it. Fans will remember his famous robot celebration, some brilliant goals, an impressive set of teeth and of course his very long physique, but mostly I think they will remember him as a warm-hearted, funny individual who acquitted himself well at every club he played for. Since retiring he has been doing punditry on BT Sport and BBC Match of the Day, as well as his own podcasts that are so insightful into a footballer's life. There is still a lot of Crouch to come.

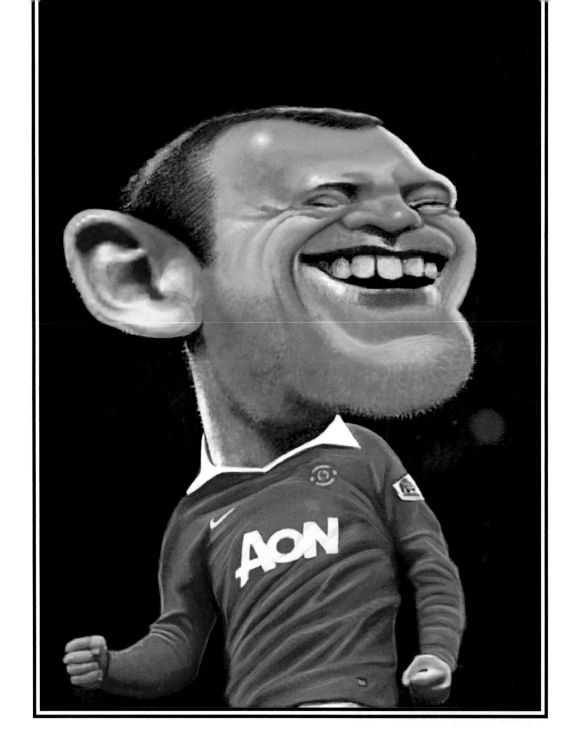

WAYNE ROONEY

"When the goal is in sight, all your physical pain disappears, and your mental determination shall carry you the rest of the way."

(Trey Patty)

We've all heard the jokes: 'Rooney wants to go to Juventus – he'll never turn down an approach from an old lady'; 'Rooney's planning a move to Real after hearing that Madrid was "full of senior Ritas"; 'Odds on Wayne Rooney's next club have been shortened. It's now 8/11 Stringfellows, 3/1 Spearmint Rhino'; and, finally, 'Rooney's press statement was delayed – as he broke three crayons writing it'. Whether you perceive such jibes and jokes as 'fair game' for a high-profile and scandalously well-remunerated sportsman, or demur at what may be seen as a cheap brand of humour – one thing is clear: personalities who attract 'witty' public broadsides usually have something the authors of mockery patently don't. And, as we queue up to deliver our castigation (the media in particular), we might be well-served by the succinct words of writer Max Beerbohm: 'the dullard's envy of brilliant men is always assuaged by the suspicion that they will come to a bad end'.

Born in Croxteth, Liverpool and raised as an Everton fan, Rooney was on the books at Goodison Park at just nine years-old and went on to make his debut whilst still 16. Before breaking into the Everton first team, he outshone his peers in youth football. Representing Liverpool schoolboys, this young Everton fan once managed an improbable 72 goals in just one season. Rooney also sparkled for Copplehouse Boys' Club in the Walton and Kirkdale Junior League – his staggering final season haul of 99 goals alerting Everton scout Bob Pendleton. No less startling was his form for Everton under-10s and under-11s, for whom he racked up 114 goals in 29 games. And he even found time to be Everton mascot in the Merseyside derby!

Every great player does something special to herald their arrival on the footballing stage and this young Liverpudlian was no exception. Having debuted a couple of months short of his 17th birthday (making him Everton's second youngest player in their history behind Joe Royle), Rooney faced formidable champions Arsenal, who were unbeaten in 30 matches. Unfazed by the class of the opposition, he revelled in the limelight and hammered a last-minute winner to send Goodison Park into unbridled pandemonium. With the game seemingly petering out to a 1-1 draw, a hopeful punt up-field fell into the path of the youngster. Exquisitely controlling the ball in the air as it came over his shoulder with the outside of his right foot, he spun 180 degrees to escape the attentions of an Arsenal defender. He then swivelled to complete the full 'three-sixty' and face the goal once more. Still appearing as though he still had it all to do, he unleashed a vicious right-foot drive which thundered into the top left-hand corner, leaving England's David Seaman vainly clutching at air. This goal made him the youngest ever Premier League scorer – though this record has since been surpassed. A new star had appeared in the Premier League firmament. Even Arsenal's manager, Arsène Wenger, not exactly known for his magnanimity towards opponents in post-match interviews, saw fit to laud the teenage starlet: "Rooney is the biggest England talent I've seen since I arrived in England. There has certainly not been a player under 20 as good as him since I became manager here." High praise indeed from one of the game's most exacting scrutineers. Having set the division ablaze, Rooney capped a memorable year by landing the BBC's Young Sports Personality of the Year award.

As a Toffee, Rooney netted 15 times in 67 appearances – but there was clearly much more in the offing and this was not lost on Manchester United supremo Alex Ferguson, who was prepared to pay a gargantuan £25.6 million for a boy of just 18. In the mercantile arena of the Premier League, Everton fans might argue that pursuit of boundless wealth outweighed an alleged quest for silverware, when Rooney made the perfidious choice to leave his lifelong footballing home.

When Wayne Rooney arrived at Old Trafford in 2004, Manchester United had already enjoyed the success of 'Fergie's Fledglings' in the late 1990s, but were keen to savour a new idol. And in this young Evertonian, their manager felt he'd found the man to provide such a tonic.

In nine seasons at Old Trafford, Rooney managed 141 goals in 277 Premier League games. He would obviously never come close to the prodigious return he garnered in youth football – but a goal every other game in arguably the world's most unforgiving league does, nevertheless, command the utmost respect. And he is, in fact, a double-centurion with 214 goals if you take into consideration his exploits in domestic and European cup competitions. Not to mention his free-scoring exploits for his country.

It would be wholly unjust to use Rooney's goal-to-games ratio as the sole measure of his worth; there is substantially more to his game than simply being a marksman. And the United faithful didn't have to wait too long to marvel at the full panoply of his talents. Whilst some new recruits at big clubs languish in the reserves for a time, or cut their teeth on loan to lower league outfits, Ferguson felt he could unleash his protégé straight into the hurly-burly of Premier League football. Not quite as bold a move as one might think at first glance, given his considerable skills. Rooney is tenacious, robust, boasts frightening acceleration and can shoot powerfully from distance or finish deftly from close-range. He's also a useful dribbler and passes the ball with the finesse of an accomplished midfielder. Add to that a propensity for a mean free-kick and you have an awesome footballer. Also, what he lacks in height, he compensates for with his physical strength, enabling him to stoutly hold the ball up with his back to goal and bring other attackers into play. He also has the ability to drop very deep when exerting his creative influence. His astute footballing brain and awareness of other players make him the consummate team player. His purring United manager, Alex Ferguson, has welcomed comparisons with South American strikers – Pele in particular – saying "there are similarities that way in strength, speed and determination". He goes on to say: "Look at Pele. He was a very aggressive attacker as well, who could look after himself. So can Rooney." The Latin-American theme was continued by Benfica coach Jorge Jesus who, speaking ahead of his club's Champions League tie with United, remarked that "Rooney is the best British player so far. But he plays like an Argentinian or a Brazilian. He can decide a match in the last third of the field".

Rooney has also won the *Match of the Day* 'Goal of the Season' award on three occasions, with his spectacularly improbable bicycle kick against arch-rivals Manchester City surely being the pick of the bunch and perhaps the most salient reminder of his penchant for the 'Latin'. A benign influence on the game for the first 78 minutes, Rooney showed us that he can illuminate proceedings in a flash. Hovering around the City penalty spot, he appeared to pose no immediate threat as Nani's right-wing cross sailed in slightly behind him. But cleverly swivelling into a better position, the predatory striker, with his back to goal, leapt acrobatically to hook a ferocious right-footed bicycle-kick into the top right-hand corner. England goalkeeper Joe Hart was as bemused as he was stationary. A master-class in footballing athleticism, worthily securing all three points. It perfectly exemplified Rooney's flawless technical ability – the absence of which in English players is frequently bemoaned.

With United, success came thick and fast: four Premier League titles, the UEFA Champions League and two League Cups while still only in his twenties. Personally, he's been decorated by peers and even the fickle, pernicious press alike. Voted PFA Players' Player of the Year in 2010; also scooping the FWA Footballer of the Year award in the same year. 2011 also saw him voted an impressive fifth in the prestigious Ballon D'Or and earn a place in the FIFPro World XI. Furthermore, Rooney offers rich pickings for those of us who are of a statistical bent, having also been PFA Young Footballer of the Year in 2005. He was the youngest player to reach 200 league appearances and is only the fourth ever player to net hat-tricks in successive Premier League games; in fact, only three other Manchester United players have bagged more top-flight hat-tricks than Rooney. He's currently tied on seven with Bobby Charlton. Also, along with Ryan Giggs and Paul Scholes, he's only one of three United players to score 100 Premier League goals.

He's courted much controversy off the pitch. We've all seen the photos of him relieving himself behind a skip, or read the tales of sordid extra-marital shenanigans, but, ultimately, Wayne Rooney has the armoury to do battle with the best players in the world and will hopefully be remembered solely as a gifted footballer, as opposed for the lewd, tawdry baggage so many modern players seem to carry. He doesn't take kindly to defeat and his qualities ensure that he rarely has to. Always pugnacious and usually victorious through attrition. In the words of Napoleon Bonaparte, "the truest wisdom is a resolute determination" and Wayne Rooney is the embodiment of exactly that.

DIDIER DROGBA

*"Nurture your mind with great thoughts;
to believe in the heroic makes heroes."*

(Benjamin Disraeli)

To say that Didier Drogba is regarded as a hero by the Chelsea fans is an understatement of mega proportions. During his nine seasons at Chelsea, Drogba helped his club win four Premier League titles, four FA Cups, four Football League cups and, the jewel in the crown, The Champions League. He was named as Chelsea's greatest ever player in a poll of 20,000 fans conducted by Chelsea Magazine in November 2012. When one considers the plethora of Chelsea greats who have graced this football hotbed – Osgood, Tambling, Dixon, Hudson, Zola, Lampard, Vialli, Cole, Hollins, Wilkins, Cooke, Gullit, Terry etc, etc, this iconic footballer has undoubtedly earned a special place in the hearts of the Chelsea faithful.

His Premier League goal tally of 164 in 382 games, is highly commendable from a man who played numerous times as a lone striker. His physical strength, coupled with his ability to hold up play and allow his team-mates to get forward was exceptional. His manager José Mourinho harnessed this feature of Drogba's skills with great success during his time at The Bridge. The Ivorian created numerous assists as well as goals, and terrorised many a centre back with his robust, no-nonsense style of play. He won the Golden Boot in 2006-07 and 2009-10.

José Mourinho, his manager at Chelsea during two separate spells at the club, formed a strong and successful partnership with him. Not one for lavishing high praise very often on players under his management, Mourinho said this of him: "I have always refused to say which is my favourite player or the best person, because so many have given soul and blood to play and to fight with me. But if I have to choose one who represents all the good things you want in a player and a man, I think in this moment I would choose Didier." A fitting tribute indeed!

Drogba's route to the top was by no means the stereotype of the modern professional footballer. He never attended a football academy and he was 21 by the time he signed his first professional contract. His early career began at

French Ligue 2 side Le Mans, where he struggled with injuries as a result of the arduous training and match schedule demanded of a football pro. During the 2001-02 season he was sold to Ligue 1 side Guingamp.

His first season with his new club was decidedly modest, yielding only three goals in 11 appearances, as his team just managed to stave off relegation. His next season was more productive with 17 goals in 34 starts, helping Guingamp achieve their best-ever league position of seventh. This goal return prompted interest from larger clubs and he moved up to Ligue 1 Side Marseille at the end of the season for a fee of £3.3 million. His one and only season at Marseille produced 19 goals, as well as a further five UEFA Champions League goals and six in the UEFA Cup. It also resulted in this burgeoning talent being snapped up by Chelsea for a club record fee of £24 million. Thus began the phase of his career which brought him to the notice of the wider football world.

His first season at Chelsea was relatively quiet, yielding 16 goals in 41 games, although the club did win the Premier League title. Their only previous top-flight success had been 50 years earlier in the old English First Division. They also won the League Cup that season with Drogba scoring an injury-time winner to deny Liverpool at the Millennium Stadium. The following season saw Chelsea retain the League Title with Drogba contributing 12 goals to the cause.

The 2006-07 season saw Drogba's star in the ascendancy. He switched to the departed Damian Duff's number 11 shirt from 15, and proceeded to amass 33 goals in all competitions, picking up the Golden Boot award in the process for his 20 league goals. Not since Kerry Dixon in 1984-85 had a Chelsea player reached the 30-goal mark in a season. He began to build a reputation as a big-game player with a knack of scoring vital goals at key moments in the heat of battle. An injury time equaliser against Barcelona at the Camp Nou, was one such moment. Having scored the only goal in the first leg at The Bridge, Drogba was again on target. A long ball into the Barca penalty area was headed back across goal by John Terry, Drogba chested it down, strode forward and stabbed the ball past an on-rushing Victor Valdez from close range. This gave Chelsea a 3-2 aggregate win against the favourites and, such was the emotion of the occasion, that the normally phlegmatic José Mourinho famously slid across the turf on his knees in a typical goal scorer celebration despite his expensive suit getting covered in mud. I'm sure he didn't mind the dry cleaning bill!

A pair of hat-tricks followed later, one in the league against Watford plus one against Levski Sofia in the Champions League. In the final game of the season Drogba scored the winner against Man United in the first FA Cup Final at the new Wembley Stadium and joined a select few who have netted in both domestic finals – Norman Whiteside and Mark Hughes being the others. Drogba, however, was the only one of the trio who was on the winning side in both finals.

2007-08 season saw the departure of Mourinho, which upset the equilibrium at Chelsea in Drogba's eyes. His initial reaction was to suggest he might leave the club, but he later regretted his words and vowed to throw himself wholeheartedly into the Chelsea cause. His football career was never without controversy of some form or another. He was accused by many of his detractors of being a 'serial diver', eliciting such comments as 'for a big man, he doesn't half fall over a lot'! The biggest critic of this feature of his play was then Liverpool Manager Rafa Benitez, who claimed to have compiled a dossier of Drogba's 'dives' over a four-year period.

Further transgressions, including an elbowing incident with United's Nemanja Vidic, which resulted in the Serbian needing stitches to a cut lip after losing a tooth, did nothing to enhance his reputation. Drogba was also sent off in the Champions League final for slapping the same player, only the second ever player to be sent off in a European Cup Final, Jens Lehmann being the other culprit. It was Chelsea's first Champions League final and the incident marred Drogba's achievement of becoming the club's highest goalscorer in European competition after scoring two goals in the earlier semi-final victory over Liverpool, eclipsing the record set previously by Peter Osgood. Chelsea lost the game 6-5 to Man U on penalties after a one-all final score. It is regrettable that this great footballer's reputation was tarnished by these incidents. He was never awarded the Premier League Player of the Month during his career and some people have gone so far as to cite his on-field antics as the reason he was overlooked.

After an indifferent 2008-09 season, the arrival of interim manager Guus Hiddink heralded an improvement in his form, witnessed by his scoring four goals in the first five games under the Dutchman. He scored a further four times in the Champions League to help Chelsea reach that year's semi-final. They eventually suffered defeat to Barcelona, and Drogba, feeling that too many decisions had gone against Chelsea, confronted and swore at the referee after the match. He received a yellow card for his outburst and was subsequently handed a six-match European ban, later reduced to five on appeal. On a brighter note, he was on target along with Frank Lampard in Chelsea's 2-1 triumph over Everton in the 2009 FA Cup Final.

The 2009-10 season saw Drogba score his 100th goal in Chelsea colours. His fine scoring form continued throughout the rest of the season, interrupted only by a four-week stint in the African Cup of Nations for The Ivory Coast. On his return to Chelsea duty in February, he scored against Hull City and the following month reached the prized 30-goal milestone against Portsmouth. In May, Chelsea secured the Premier League title with Drogba scoring a hat-trick along the way in an 8-0 drubbing of Wigan. This gave him his third League winner's medal and he secured the Golden Boot when he scored his 29th league goal from the penalty spot. Regular penalty taker Frank Lampard had generously allowed him to take the spot-kick, knowing its significance.

His fine form continued the following season with a hat-trick against West Brom. In the Autumn, Drogba revealed he had suffered a bout of malaria, not the usual footballer's ailment by any stretch. Prompt treatment enabled him to make a full and speedy recovery. December 2011 saw him reach another career landmark when he scored his 150th Chelsea goal in all competitions, putting him level with past greats Peter Osgood and Roy Bentley. In March 2012, yet another landmark was passed when he scored his 100th Premier League goal, the first African player to do so.

The Champions League Final of 2012 was undoubtedly Drogba's finest hour. Just as the game seemed to be slipping from their grasp, Chelsea were awarded a right wing corner in the 88th minute. Juan Mata's away swinger, hit firmly towards the near post, saw Drogba stride manfully through a ruck of defenders and produce a powerful glancing header which rocketed into the roof of the Bayern net, sending the match into extra time and the crowd ecstatic. No further goals ensued and the dreaded penalties loomed. At 3-3 in the penalty shoot-out, Drogba stepped up to take what would be the match winner. He calmly sent the keeper the wrong way and the net bulged to the delight of the crowd. The big match specialist had delivered again!

Having left Chelsea in May 2012, Drogba was lured to the Chinese Super League club Shanghai Shenhua, but left in the following January amid claims of breach of contract, unpaid wages and legal wrangles. He then signed for Turkish giants Galatasary and enjoyed a short but productive stay in Istanbul, scoring 20 goals in 53 appearances for the club over two seasons. In July 2014 he returned to his spiritual home when Chelsea signed him on a free transfer. José Mourinho was in his second spell at the club and Drogba couldn't resist the chance to work with him again. The highlights of his second spell at The Bridge were reaching his 350th appearance for the club and scoring his 50th European goal against Schalke.

Following his departure from Chelsea he had two spells in America at MLS side Montreal Impact and USL side Phoenix Rising. In November 2018 he brought the curtain down on his illustrious playing career at the age of 40.

Drogba proudly represented his home country Ivory Coast over a 12-year period from 2002 to 2014, scoring 65 goals in 105 appearances. He helped them to qualify for their first FIFA World Cup in 2006, but since their qualifying group contained Netherlands, Argentina, Serbia and Montenegro, the so-called 'Group of Death', a tough route to the knock-out stages looked on the cards. Alas, so it proved and although he scored his first World Cup goal in the opening match against Argentina, they were sadly eliminated from the competition after a further defeat by Holland. They managed to win their final two games against Serbia and Montenegro, but it was not enough to progress.

Drogba was included in the Ivory Coast's squad for the 2014 World Cup and collected his 100th cap in a friendly during the run-up to the finals. He retired from international football in August 2014.

He was immensely proud of his country, and he was famously credited with influencing a ceasefire between the rival factions involved in the civil war that had raged for five years in the Ivory Coast. His efforts were subsequently recognised when he was later appointed by the UN as a Goodwill Ambassador. He has been involved in many charitable projects since retirement and has always been willing to use his high-profile status for the greater good. His hometown Abidjan benefited from the player's generosity in the shape of a £3m donation towards the cost of building a new hospital.

Didier Drogba will be fittingly remembered as one of the greatest African players of his generation.

CRISTIANO RONALDO

"If you have talent, use it in every which way possible. Don't hoard it. Don't dole it out like a miser. Spend it lavishly like a millionaire intent on going broke."

(Brendan Francis)

Cristiano Ronaldo dos Santos Aveiro, to give him his full title, not only had footballing talent in abundance, he also had film star good looks to go with it. He was destined for fame and fortune (current net worth in excess of $500m!!!) from the moment he left his home town of Funchal on the beautiful Portuguese island of Madeira. It will be difficult to encapsulate the staggering number of his achievements in the ensuing few paragraphs – but attempt it we must.

His father worked as a part-time kit man for a local team called Andorinha, for whom Ronaldo played as a schoolboy. At the age of 12 he joined the youth set-up of Sporting CP, who were based near Lisbon. His football career looked in doubt, however, before it had hardly got off the ground, when he had to give up playing, having been diagnosed with racing heart at the age of 15. The problem was later rectified following surgery with laser treatment and the young Ronaldo was soon back in training. In his younger days, Ronaldo frequently demonstrated a somewhat volatile personality. He was expelled from school for throwing a chair at his teacher, who he believed had disrespected him. This aspect of his make-up manifested itself on a number of occasions during his playing career, as we shall hear later.

During a busy summer of transfer activity, in which Manchester United parted company with David Beckham to Real Madrid, their bid to sign Ronaldinho as his replacement from P.S.G. failed to materialise. United duly turned their attention to a Portuguese teenage sensation, one Cristiano Ronaldo, with a view to transforming him into a world star. Their initial plan was to sign him from Sporting Lisbon, and then loan him back to the club for a season. However, a pre-season friendly against Sporting brought about a change in United manager Alex Ferguson's mind. In a famous half-time phone call to chief executive Peter Kenyon, the United manager pleaded with his boss – "Rather than leave him here, can we take him home please?" The United team left for home, as Fergie and Kenyon stayed behind to re-negotiate the deal with Sporting. The loan deal was subsequently scrapped, leaving Ronaldo free to join United with immediate effect.

So the 18-year-old Ronaldo became the first ever Portuguese player to sign for the club. A fee of £12.24m was the outlay for his services, making him the costliest-ever teenage player at the time. For flair players like Ronaldo, the cut and thrust of the English game presented a daunting challenge to say the least. Others of his ilk had followed the same path and failed to prosper in the intense environment of Premier League football. Ronaldo, however, soon transformed into the stand-out player in United's star-studded squad. He proudly wore the number 7 shirt previously donned by such sporting greats as Best, Cantona and Beckham; he undoubtedly saw it as a challenge to emulate the achievements of his illustrious predecessors. Emulate them he did – his six-year stint at the club yielded an FA Cup winners' medal, three consecutive Premier League titles, a Champions League title, two League Cup winners' medals and the FIFA Club World Cup. Furthermore, his contribution of 84 goals from 196 appearances ranks as an excellent return for a player who was predominantly deployed in a wide role.

His first match for United was against Bolton Wanderers, when he came on as a sub in the 60th minute. He managed to impress the fans and showcase his outstanding talent in this cameo appearance, with the watching George Best praising "an outstanding debut". He capped his first season at the club by scoring the opening goal in United's 3-0 victory over Millwall in the FA Cup final, picking up the first of his many honours. A red card against Aston Villa on the final day of the PL season was the only thing to mar his first campaign for United.

The 2004-05 season saw him establish himself in the side and earned him a two-year extension to his United contract. The following season will be remembered for some unsavoury moments, not least his one-fingered gesture to Benfica fans, which earned him a one-match ban from FIFA. He was also sent off in the Manchester derby for kicking former Reds favourite Andy Cole.

A further incident occurred during the 2006 World Cup quarter finals when Wayne Rooney was sent off for stamping on Portugal's Ricardo Carvalho. Ronaldo controversially ran over and remonstrated with the referee and appeared to influence the decision to dismiss the Englishman. Ronaldo's wink to the Portuguese bench following the dismissal seemed to justify the view that he got his United buddy sent off. There followed an unsavoury clash between the two players in the tunnel after the match. Ronaldo allegedly asked United for a transfer on the basis that the club refused to back him over the incident, but nothing came of the request and things returned to normal by the start of the 2006-07 season, save for the regular booing meted out to him by the United fans.

Despite these problems, Ronaldo had a successful season, notably picking up back-to-back Premier League Player of the Month awards in November and December, and also taking his goal tally above the 20-mark for the first time. He attributed his improved goalscoring to the work done with United coach at the time, Rene Meulensteen.

The 2007-08 season was an outstanding one for Ronaldo. He won the PFA Players' Player of the Year, Fans' Player of the Year and PFA Young Player of the Year awards. He also picked up the Football Writers' Association Footballer of the Year award, becoming the first ever player to collect all four honours in a single season. He was also runner up to Kaka for the Ballon d'Or and came third behind Kaka and Messi for the FIFA World Player of the Year award. His first and only hat-trick for United came during the campaign in a 6-0 win over Newcastle United. His 50th goal for the club came in the 1-0 win in that season's Manchester derby, as United went on to clinch the Premier League title after a four-year hiatus. More success came the way of the talented Portuguese in the shape of the PFA Players' Player of the Year and the FWA Footballer of the Year awards for the second year running. If that wasn't enough, his 31 league goals won him the Premier League Golden Boot award, and his overall goal tally of 42 surpassed the record for most goals in a season, previously held by

George Best. United also reached the final of the Champions League against Chelsea, with Ronaldo netting the opening goal, but failing with his spot kick in the ensuing penalty shoot-out. United, however, triumphed, giving Ronaldo yet another winners' medal. He also received the UEFA Club Footballer of the Year award, to add to his growing collection of honours. The one black mark in his otherwise perfect season had come early on, when he was dismissed for foolishly headbutting a Portsmouth player.

Ronaldo's final season at Old Trafford got off to a bad start when he missed the first ten weeks after picking up an ankle injury in pre-season. Nevertheless, his 26 goals from 53 appearances helped United win the FIFA World Club Cup, as he also went on to emulate George Best by winning the Ballon d'Or; also becoming the first Premier League player to be named FIFA World Player of the Year. His goal in a second leg Champions League match against Porto, a screamer from 40 yards, earned him the goal of the year award from FIFA. He later described this as his best ever goal. His final game in United colours was in the Manchester derby, in which he scored with a neat free kick to bring the curtain down on his Premier League career (or so we thought!).

Ronaldo scored many memorable goals for Manchester United – spectacular long-range strikes with either foot, devastating free kicks, as well as powerful headers; the list is too long to itemise here. One goal he scored against Southampton, however, typified his superb skill and awareness. Picking up the ball on the left side of the Saints' penalty area, Ronaldo spots Rooney making a run on the right-hand side of the box and skilfully curls the ball with the outside of his right foot away from the keeper's reach and into Rooney's path. Closed down by the Southampton defence, Rooney chips the ball back across goal where Ronaldo meets it with a thumping volley which whistles into the net, leaving the Southampton defenders open-mouthed.

Ronaldo's career went into overdrive following his move to Real Madrid and later Juventus, eclipsing even his outstanding Premier League achievements.

Suffice it to say, the high-flying Portuguese didn't disappoint his new fan base and at the age of 35 he was still performing in the top flight, a testimony to his outstanding fitness.

It would be remiss not to mention his brilliant international career. A staggering 164 matches had produced a goal tally of 99 until during a UEFA Nations League group match against Sweden, a stunning free kick that flew into the top corner saw him reach the landmark century. He was the first European in men's football to achieve this feat. A second goal in the same match put him only eight goals adrift of the then world record held by Iran's Ali Daei. Only a fool would have bet against him surpassing even this target. By the time Euro 2020 came round, albeit delayed to 2021 by the Covid pandemic, Ronaldo had the world record goals target within sight. His five goals not only saw him reach 111 goals in his 180 appearances, passing Daei's record in the process, but also netted him the tournament's Golden Boot award.

In 2021 Ronaldo made a triumphant return to the Premier League by re-joining Manchester United after 12 years away, in what was seen as a major coup for the Reds. His first two games yielded three goals, proving that even at the ripe old age of 36 he hadn't lost the golden touch. His outstanding fitness is by no means down to luck. It has been well documented that he follows a strict low-fat diet, doesn't drink alcohol and makes several trips a week to the gym, in addition to the normal club training programme. His outstanding hat-trick against Tottenham on March 12th 2022 will be long remembered as the highlight of his return season in Premier League football. With United having a fairly indifferent season by their own standards, speculation is beginning to mount that this cameo spell will be the Portuguese star's last in United colours. Although he has the option of a one-year extension to his contract, the rumour mongers are already predicting his departure. If that's the case, it was nice while it lasted.

Ronaldo is undoubtedly one of the greatest football players of all time. He can easily be mentioned in the same breath as Pele, Messi, Best et al, without fear of contradiction. His fitness is second to none; his goalscoring prowess, heading ability and awareness of others around him, make him the supreme footballer we see today. In his own words – "I see myself as the best footballer in the world. If you don't believe you are the best, you will never achieve all that you are capable of."

Sir Alex Ferguson once said "The reason I speak of Messi and Ronaldo is consistency first of all; the consistency, the balance, their excellence on the ball and the courage. They are never dented by a tackle. They get up and ask for the ball again. I think everyone will agree with me that these two guys are above everyone. There's no question about that. They are fantastic to watch and they never miss a game. They have given value to everyone in the world by playing all the time."

Finally, it's worth mentioning that Ronaldo is also one of the most well-known sports stars off the field, and numerous studies of athletes' popularity have shown him to be the most beloved athlete in the world during his playing peak. His extreme popularity made him one of the highest-paid endorsers in sports history, and in November 2016 he became only the third person (after basketball superstars Michael Jordan and LeBron James) to earn a 'lifetime' contract from the sportswear company Nike. For good measure, he has also had an airport named after him. Quite some achievement!

VINCENT KOMPANY

"Let me tell you the secret that has led me to my goal. My strength lies solely in my tenacity"

(Louis Pasteur)

The 'Muscles from Brussels' is a nickname which may well be applied to Vincent Company as well as his Belgian compatriot Jean-Claude Van Damme. His strength and tenacity at the heart of the Manchester City defence characterised his Premier League playing career for a decade or more since arriving on these shores. Film star he is not, but the star of this much-admired central defender will always sit high in the firmament of English football.

Vincent's senior playing career started at hometown club Anderlecht, where he joined as a hopeful 17-year-old in Millennium year. In 2004 he won the Belgian Golden Shoe, an annual award given to the best footballer in their First Division. He also won the Belgian Ebony Shoe in seasons 2004 and 2005, which is awarded to the best African or African origin player in the top flight.

Such accolades had brought him to the attention of several leading European clubs at that time, but he decided that he needed to further hone his skills before moving on. He stayed on at Anderlecht until June 2006, when it was announced SV Hamburg had acquired his services for a fee of €10m. His debut season at the German club was thwarted by an Achilles injury, which restricted him to a mere six starts. After a disappointing season, his inclusion in a 30-man provisional squad for the 2007 UEFA European Under-21 Football Championship provided some consolation.

The following year Kompany's career at Hamburg had been called into question due to him insisting on playing for Belgium in the Olympic Games against the club's wishes. In fact, he had proudly helped Belgium to reach the semi-finals of the competition in Beijing that year, but the club insisted he return from the games in time for the first Bundesliga game of the season. The strained relationship between Hamburg and Kompany proved to be a major factor in him eventually moving to Manchester City.

If his two-year spell in the Bundesliga proved largely uneventful, the next decade by contrast thrust him into the Premier League and international limelight, earning him so many admirers in the world of football. The former Liverpool defender Alan Hansen, no mean central defender himself, said this of him during the 2014 World Cup in Brazil: "If I was a Premier League manager with £100 million to spend on the best two central defenders in this World Cup, I would probably spend it all on Vincent Kompany." Praise indeed.

Kompany duly signed for Manchester City in August 2008 under the then manager Mark Hughes. He was signed on a four-year deal for an undisclosed fee, believed to be £10m and what a signing it proved to be! In October 2009 following a successful first season, Kompany signed a new five-year contract which would keep him at the club until 2014. "Vincent is a model professional who has proved his worth in a variety of positions," commented City boss Mark Hughes.

He started his City career as a holding midfield player, however, when Nedum Onuoha moved on loan to Sunderland, Kompany was handed the number 4 jersey, initially partnering Kolo Touré at the heart of the defence. During the 2010-11 season he was handed the captain's armband in the absence of Carlos Tevez. In the April of that season, Kompany captained City's victory over fierce rivals Man United in the FA Cup semi-final at Wembley. City triumphed 1-0 and he was later named in the PFA Team of the Year alongside team-mate Tevez.

City managed a 1-0 victory over Stoke City in the final, their first major trophy for 35 years. At the end of the 2010-11 season, in which City qualified for the UEFA Champions League for the first time, then manager Roberto Mancini praised Kompany's "incredible season" and claimed that "with his attitude and mentality, he can become one of the best defenders in Europe".

At the end of that campaign, he also won the Supporter's Player of the Year and Players' Player of the Year awards, as well as the Premier League Player of the Season; fitting tributes to his outstanding season. In the 2011-12 season he was firmly established as club captain, Carlos Tevez having expressed his desire to leave the club.

On April 30th, 2012 Kompany scored with a header from a David Silva corner in the Manchester derby, which proved to be the winning goal and put City at the top of the Premier League ahead of United on goal difference, with only two games remaining. On May 13th, the final day of the season, Kompany led the team against a struggling QPR side with the match ending in a dramatic 3-2 victory for City, clinching the league title for the club for the first time since 1968. The occasion was somewhat soured by the sending off of one Joey Barton after his elbow came firmly into contact with the face of Carlos Tevez, producing a straight red card. In the ensuing melee, Barton kicked Sergio Aguero on the back of his leg and attempted a head butt on Vincent Kompany to complete a rather unsavoury hat-trick.

In March 2014, Kompany captained the Manchester City team that won the League Cup Final with a 3-1 victory over Sunderland. On May 11th, he scored City's second goal in a 2-0 win over West Ham which secured the 2013-14 Premier Title for the club. 2014-15 proved a modest season for City and late in the season Kompany sustained a muscle injury, which heralded a prolonged chapter of injuries and strains for the unfortunate Belgian. After scoring in City's two opening fixtures of 2015-16, he was again sidelined with a calf strain and injury kept him out for most of the season. He did, however, manage to take part in that season's League Cup Final, scooping the man-of-the-match award in the victory over Liverpool. His international career was also hampered by injury problems, resulting in him pulling out of the Belgium squad for Euro 2016. His lengthy spell of injuries over the first eight seasons following his move to City was reported to have cost him more than two years of playing time. A huge amount of credit must go to the player for achieving so much in the English game against this background of injury problems.

The 2016-17 season passed by without City acquiring any silverware. Kompany himself managed just 15 appearances during the campaign. However, when fit he was immediately back in the starting line-up which highlighted his great importance to the team. The next season followed a similar pattern for him, plagued by various injuries. In February 2018 he made a rare appearance, scoring City's second goal in a 3-0 victory over Arsenal in the EFL Cup Final and was named man of the match. That season he lifted the Premier League Trophy as City won the title with a record 100 points.

In 2018-19 he made a limited number of appearances but towards the end of that season, as a two-horse title race with Liverpool unfolded, he popped up with a stunning goal in the penultimate match to give City a 1-0 victory over Leicester. Not known for his long-range shooting, he latched on to a pass from the right and unleashed a 25-yard screamer into the top right-hand corner of the net, leaving Casper Schmeichel clutching at thin air. His manager Pep Guardiola admitted after the match that he was willing Kompany not to shoot but was greatly relieved as the ball whistled into the net, his only ever goal scored from outside the box. This victory took them a point clear of Liverpool at the top of the table and meant that their title destiny was in their own hands. City subsequently lifted the title with a 4-1 victory over Brighton, and six days later, clinched an incredible domestic treble by thrashing Watford to win the FA Cup Final.

Twenty-four hours after lifting the FA Cup trophy, Vincent Kompany brought the curtain down on his outstanding Manchester City career when he announced his intention to leave the club to become the player-manager of Anderlecht, the club he had first joined as a six-year-old. In an emotional statement he said it was the "most passionate yet rational" decision he has ever made.

Khaldoon Al Mubarak, the City chairman, summed up Kompany's contribution by saying: "He defines the essence of the club. For a decade he has been the life blood, the soul, and the beating heart. A booming voice in the dressing room yet a quiet and measured ambassador off it, Vincent can be as proud of himself as we are of him."

On the international front, Kompany has represented Belgium on 84 occasions, scoring four goals. He was part of the team which took the FIFA World Cup third place spot in 2018. He captained the national side on 35 occasions from 2010 to 2017.

Kompany has shown great compassion and leadership both on and off the field. He is an official FIFA ambassador for SOS Children. In his father's native Congo, he has invested and engaged in projects which aim to provide an education and safe living accommodation for children living in poverty. In March 2013, Kompany bought the Belgian third division club FC Bleid as a "social commitment towards the youngsters of Brussels, with the intention of offering disadvantaged youngsters the opportunity to use sport as a vehicle for self-improvement". He has an active interest in politics and graduated with an MBA at Manchester Business School in 2018, fitting in several years of study alongside his football duties.

Early in 2019 Vincent Kompany made a truly magnanimous gesture when he announced that he would donate proceeds from his testimonial season to try and help the homeless in Manchester. In a joint initiative with the mayor of Manchester, Andy Burnham, he launched a campaign to tackle rough sleeping in the city.

The modest Belgian summed up his feelings in this statement. "I've received much from Manchester – a great career at the highest level, unconditional support from the fans through thick and thin, a lovely family and much more to be grateful for."

He added: "Over the past decade I've been lucky to have witnessed and played a part in Manchester City's rise as a club and a brand. This has also run parallel alongside the rise of a whole region." Inspiring words from an inspirational player who has graced English football with his ability and leadership, and has won the respect of all those who share his love of the beautiful game.

GARETH BALE

"The primary factor in a successful attack is speed"

(Lord Mountbatten)

A succinct statement from the former Admiral of the Fleet which pertains to the field of battle but is equally true in relation to the field of play in football. Talk to any player, coach, manager or football pundit, and they will all tell you that a player with genuine pace is worth his weight in gold to any team.

Gareth Bale not only possesses electric pace to carry him past most defenders, he has the unique ability to maintain that pace when running with the ball. In a recent study he was rated the fastest player in the world with the ball at his feet. He has been recorded at an incredible speed of 22.9mph or 36.9km/h. As a comparison, Olympic legend Usain Bolt recorded 28 mph in his world record setting 100 metres, but *he* didn't need to control a football at the same time!

This Welsh football prodigy was born in Cardiff and possessed great athletic ability from an early age. At the age of 14 he ran the 100 metres in a time of 11.4 seconds and excelled at all sports, including rugby, hockey, running and not least football. Such was his sporting prowess at primary school, pro club scouts soon started showing an interest in the young Welshman. He was invited to train at Southampton's satellite academy in Bath while still at junior school and eventually he was signed up on professional forms by the south coast outfit. In April 2006 he made his debut at the age of 16 years and 275 days, the second youngest player to do so after Theo Walcott, who was 132 days younger. And so, a highly promising career got under way at a club noted for nurturing young talent, and soon the world of football began to take notice.

His professional career at Southampton saw him deployed in the left back role, from where he made the occasional flurry forward with the blistering pace that has now become his hallmark. His magic wand of a left foot was soon paying dividends and his first goal for the club was a free kick against Derby, a 25-yard scorcher over the defensive wall which levelled the scores. In all he scored five goals in his 45 appearances for Southampton, three of which came from free kicks. At the end of 2006-07, his first full season at Saints, he was named the Football League Young Player of the Year.

His final game for the club was ironically against Derby in the first leg of the Championship play-off semi-final. The game ended in a 2-1 defeat for Saints and saw Bale pick up a second half injury that was to keep him out of the second leg in which Derby triumphed after extra time and penalties. Later the same month Bale was sold to Tottenham Hotspur in a £5m + deal.

His competitive debut for Spurs came against Man United at Old Trafford in September 2007. The following week he scored his first goal for the club in a 3-3 draw with Fulham. He also scored from a free kick against Arsenal in his first North London derby. Another goal against Middlesbrough in a League cup game made it three goals in his first four games for Spurs. Not a bad start for the 18-year-old Welshman, and undoubtedly a precursor of great things to come.

However, in December 2007 he was seriously injured following a heavy tackle from Birmingham's Fabrice Mamba. He was diagnosed with ligament damage to his right ankle following a scan, which meant a sustained period on the sidelines. His club were adamant that their young star should be allowed time to recover properly from his injury and were in no hurry to rush him back into action. His next competitive game was as a substitute in the League Cup final against Man United at the end of the 2008-09 season, when he came on in the 98th minute but was unable to make any impact on a match that ended 0-0. The subsequent penalty shoot-out ended in a 4-1 win for United.

His Tottenham career stalled again in June 2009, when he had to go under the surgeon's knife to repair a knee injury. Another two months on the sidelines beckoned for the hapless youngster. His next appearance came in late September 2009, when he appeared as a substitute in Spurs' 5-0 thrashing of Burnley. Undaunted by two serious injuries, Bale set about trying to establish himself as a first team regular, but his opportunities were limited by the excellent form of Spurs first choice left back Assou-Ekotto, who was a naturally gifted full back with good pace and tackling ability and also a firm favourite of Spurs manager Harry Redknapp.

However, it's an ill wind that blows no-one any good as they say, and an injury to Assou-Ekotto proved fortunate for Bale when Redknapp decided to give him a chance to prove his worth. The manager's confidence in Bale's potential was duly rewarded when he made impressive contributions in the next few games, culminating in him being named Man of the Match when he scored Spurs' winning goal in a 2-1 victory over high-fliers Chelsea. He also scooped the Premier League Player of the Month award for April 2010 and soon after was rewarded with a new four-year contract. The prospect of Champions League football was now on the horizon for Bale as Spurs finished in the Premiership top four to qualify for the competition.

In a memorable 2-1 away win against Stoke City in August 2010, Bale scored both goals including a magnificent left foot volley which was later voted goal of the month. A cross by Aaron Lennon from the right floated over the Stoke defenders and found Bale in space on the left corner of the box who connected with a head-high volley which thundered into the top right corner of the Stoke goal, the net billowing before the keeper could even react. Sublime!

Bale's good form continued and even though regular left back Assou-Ekotto had returned to the side, the manager decided to accommodate the Welshman in a left wing role. This proved to be a significant turning point in his career, giving him more freedom to push forward into the opposition half and making better use of his pace and crossing ability. Later that year he scored his first senior hat-trick against Inter Milan at the San Siro stadium in the Champions League. Spurs looked like they were dead and buried at 4-0 down, but Bale stepped forward with a magnificent second-half treble, all scored with sublime left foot strikes. Spurs eventually lost the match 4-3, a creditable result given the fact they played with ten men after their keeper Gomes was sent off in the eighth minute for a professional foul. The return match at White Hart Lane saw Spurs triumph in an outstanding 3-1 victory, with Bale setting up two of the goals in a man-of-the-match performance.

Further recognition of Bale's burgeoning talent came when he was voted PFA Players' Player of the Year by his fellow professionals in April 2010. The 2010-11 season got underway with the now established Bale scoring on a regular basis for his club. One particular goal against Bolton stands out in the memory. After scoring the first goal, Bale removed his left boot to reveal a poignant tribute to a Welsh legend, which simply said "RIP Gary Speed" and was applauded by the Bolton fans in recognition of one of their former players. In all he scored ten goals in the season and in January 2012 he was named Premier League Player of the Month for the second time after contributing three goals and two assists.

At the start of the 2012-13 season, Bale was handed the number 11 shirt in recognition of his transition from full back to left winger. In January of that season he netted his first Premier League hat-trick against Aston Villa. He scored many memorable goals in his career including a stunning effort against Norwich City when he picked the ball up just inside his own half, rode a firm tackle which would have decked lesser players, and accelerated into the opposing penalty area and past two defenders before unleashing a spectacular shot into the bottom corner of the Norwich net. A goal worth the admission money alone! A series of great performances and stunning goals over the remainder of the season saw him awarded PFA's Player of the Year and also Young Player of the Year. He later completed his hat-trick by picking up the FWA Footballer of the Year award from the Football Writers Association, only the second player to achieve this after Cristiano Ronaldo. His goal tally in league and cup for the season was a creditable 26 in 44 appearances.

After his appearances for Spurs in the Champions League, Bale attracted interest from top European clubs and in September 2013 he was transferred to Real Madrid for what later transpired to be a record fee of €100.8m (£85.1m). His first season at the Bernabeu was hampered somewhat by injury. His hefty price tag meant greater scrutiny from the Spanish press, and he flitted from hero to villain on several occasions when his form varied in the early part of the season. As the season progressed, the goals started to come and in late November he scored his first hat-trick in a 4-0 victory against Real Villadolid.

In April 2014 he scored the winning goal to defeat Barcelona in the final of the Copa del Rey. In arguably one of the best goals of his career, he received the ball in his own half and sped along the left touchline, running off the pitch at one point to enable him to round a retreating defender who was trying to block his path to the ball. He then drove into the penalty area and slid the ball under the advancing goalkeeper for a truly spectacular finish.

He again endeared himself to the fans by scoring the winner in the 2014 Champions League final against Atletico Madrid. After a shaky start he finished the season with 22 goals and 16 assists in all competitions. He scored in yet another final when Real Madrid lifted the FIFA Club World Cup in December 2014.

The 2015-16 season saw the Welshman score two hat-tricks, the latter in Zinedine Zidane's first match as head coach in January 2016. Later in the season he scored his 43rd La Liga goal surpassing Gary Lineker as the highest British goalscorer in the league's history. He continued to be an integral member of the team as they went on to win the Champions League that season.

In the 2017-18 season he featured regularly in the side as Los Blancos picked up three trophies, namely the UEFA Super Cup, the Supercopa de Espana and the FIFA World Club Championship. Bale contributed 16 goals in 26 La Liga appearances but they could only finish third in the competition behind Barcelona and Atletico Madrid.

In the season's Champions League final, however, Bale scored two goals in a 3-1 victory over Liverpool, including his now famous overhead kick from just inside the box. He was named Man of the Match as Real amassed their 13th European Cup triumph.

2018-19 saw the departure of Zidane and also Ronaldo. Bale continued to perform well under the new manager Julen Lopetegui and won Player of the Month in the August. He later won the Golden Ball award in the FIFA World Club Cup, having scored a hat-trick in the semi-final stage. By February 2019 Bale had notched up his 100th goal for Real against Madrid rivals Atletico.

September 2020 saw Bale return to Tottenham on a season-long loan deal, during which he made 20 appearances and contributed 11 Premier League goals, including a hat-trick in a 4-0 defeat of Sheffield United. His return season at Real has been fairly limited in terms of appearances and he is expected to leave the club in the near future.

The International career of the wing-heeled Welshman is no less impressive. Selected 50 days before his 17th birthday, he came on as sub in a friendly match to become, at the time, the youngest ever debutant for his country. He was also the youngest player to score an international goal at senior level when he netted in a Euro 2008 qualifier against Slovakia. His international goals tally of 38 in 102 appearances makes him Wales' all-time leading goalscorer.

He was a key figure in Wales reaching the semi-finals of UEFA Euro 2016, contributing three goals in the country's best ever performance in a major tournament. In May 2021 he was selected as Welsh captain for the delayed Euro 2020 tournament. In the World Cup of 2022, he scored two goals in the qualifying play-off semi-final against Austria. Bale is fiercely proud to represent his country and never misses a game if fit to play.

Bale has received many plaudits throughout his career from managers and fellow professionals alike. BBC pundit Mark Lawrenson said of him in 2011: "He is one of the quickest players I have ever seen, but he has another gear and the ability to find that extra pace within his next stride. He has the ability to perform and use his technique at great pace."

The pony-tailed Welsh Apollo with the heart-shaped goal celebration has undoubtedly become a superstar in Premier League and European football. May he long continue to entertain us with the spectacular goals which have become his trademark!

CHARLIE ADAM

"Battle against obscurity"

(Robert Henri)

Chris Knapman '19.

Blackpool Football Club had been in the doldrums for years. Fans able to recall, with vivid affection, the heady days of Matthews and Mortensen, were already thinning in number. It was time for someone to return the feelgood factor to Bloomfield Road. That 'someone' was from north of the border; enter knight errant, Charles Graham Adam.

Young Charlie was born in Dundee and is the son of a former professional player, Charlie Adam, who played for various Scottish clubs in the 1980s and 1990s. Tragically Charlie Snr died in 2015 – he was only 50 years old.

His son signed for Rangers aged 17, helping them to win the Scottish Youth Cup in 2001-02. He was unable to command a regular place in the first team and was loaned out for spells at Ross County in 2004-05 and then at the 1st Division side St Mirren in 2005-06. He returned to Rangers for the 2006-2007 campaign. Vital goals in the UEFA Cup and a glorious free kick in an Old Firm derby won the hearts of 'The Gers' fans, who voted him their Young Player of the Year.

In February 2009 Adam was loaned to the Fylde Coast outfit on a six-month loan deal from Rangers. Tony Parkes, the caretaker manager of Blackpool, was appointed to steady the ship after Simon Grayson switched to their fierce rivals Preston North End. Parkes could see the Scot was the real deal, possessing a great footballing brain, a delightful range of passing, and great confidence and authority on the ball. Parkes felt that he had a real gem on his hands. However, his spell at the club didn't start gloriously. He was sent off five days after he had joined the club, on his debut in the 3-2 defeat to Doncaster Rovers. After his three-game ban, he was starting to make a significant impression at the club. The Scottish ace turned out for the reserve team against local rivals Accrington Stanley. He scored a brace in the 4-2 victory, including a goal from just inside the halfway line, with an audacious long-range strike. Inevitably, this made a great impression on the caretaker boss.

In March 2009 Adam scored his first league goal for the club in a fine 2-0 win over Norwich. Two days later he received due recognition, when he was named in the Championship Team of the Week. If Blackpool fans weren't warming to him already, it got even better in April – as he scored the only goal in the 1-0 West Lancashire Derby win over Preston; made even sweeter victory for Blackpool fans, as this was only four months on from Simon Grayson defecting to old enemy Preston. Shortly after this, Adam's outstanding performances were very much noticed by the managerial team. It came as little surprise when the caretaker boss publicly admitted he was desperate to lure the 24-year-old to Bloomfield Road on a permanent basis.

At the end of the 2008-09 campaign Blackpool finished 16th with Adam playing a pivotal role in helping Blackpool to avoid the drop. During the 2009-10 campaign, Tony Parkes left the club and Ian Holloway was appointed as the new manager. 'Ollie', as he was to be affectionately known, signed Charlie for £500,000, a bargain in hindsight, but a massive outlay for the cash-strapped Seasiders. The deal was protracted, and it took till August 3rd before it was finally confirmed, and he signed a two-year contract with the offer of a 12-month extension. He made his competitive debut as a fully contracted Blackpool player in the 1-1 draw away with QPR at Loftus Road. Adam had a remarkable season taking Blackpool FC to 6th place in the Championship, a marked improvement of ten places above the previous season. He scored some vital goals in the season as well as earning the Player of the Month accolade in January 2010. The awards kept coming for the Scottish midfield dynamo as he capped his 50th appearance for Blackpool by scoring in a 2-0 victory over Plymouth Argyle.

Following his impressive 17 goals, Adam was named in the Championship Team of the Year.

He was chiefly deployed as Blackpool's attacking midfielder, while his partners in the three-man midfield were the more defensive David Vaughan and Keith Southern.

Blackpool won nine out the last 11 league games to sneak themselves into the play-offs on the final day. In the play-offs, Blackpool always had that belief factor that if they conceded they could still go and win the game. Blackpool were drawn to play Nottingham Forest and even though Forest started well with a sensational goal through Matt Cohen, Blackpool's response was swift. Keith Southern scored neatly to bring the Fylde Coast side level. In the second half Adam confidently struck home a penalty to give them a slender 2-1 advantage, going into the away leg.

At the City Ground, Blackpool were greeted by the most intimidating of atmospheres. However, having beaten Forest three times that season, they were hoping to make it four and secure a fantastic trip to Wembley. In a pulsating encounter, Blackpool eventually triumphed 4-3. The style of football Blackpool were playing was breathtaking. The 6-4 aggregate win secured their place in the Wembley final with Cardiff City. Blackpool had defied the odds yet again, showing how to play football with style.

Saturday, May 22nd, 2010. The capital was basking in glorious sunshine, it was the day when Wembley Way turned a vivid tangerine. History was about to be made when, with 85,000+ in attendance, a financially momentous showdown beckoned in tropical north London weather! Blackpool versus Cardiff City in the Championship Play-off final. Charlie Adam was Blackpool's inspiration throughout the season. A thrilling 3-2 victory ensured Blackpool's remarkable, nay improbable, promotion to the big time. The Scottish midfielder notched an impressive tally of 19 goals in all competitions, with 17 of them coming in the Championship campaign. Possibly the best and certainly one of seismic importance, was Adam's Play-off Final equaliser. With less than ten minutes gone, Michael Chopra had put the Bluebirds in front; however, Blackpool's riposte was swift. Presented with a free-kick, Charlie Adam was the man to step forward. I'm sure Cardiff had done their homework and were cognisant of the Dundonian's expertise in such matters. Despite this, they were powerless to stop his precision strike flying over the wall and into the top right of the goal.

Charlie Adam was a key part to Blackpool's Premier League campaign. In January 2011 he was targeted by Liverpool. Liverpool subsequently made an initial bid for the player of £4.5 million which was summarily rejected by Blackpool and was described as "an absolutely disgraceful offer" by Manager Ian Holloway. At the end of the season, Blackpool were relegated following a 4-2 defeat at the home of the champions Manchester United. Old Trafford was agape at Adam's world-class free kick (curled around the wall, from around 25 yards, nestling in the bottom right-hand corner). That gave Blackpool hope, but unfortunately it wasn't enough; sadly, Blackpool slipped out of the Premier League after just one season back in the top-flight. They had accumulated 38 points in the season, scoring the most goals a relegated team has ever scored. Their problem was seeing out games in which they were ahead. They lost a two-goal lead to the likes of Bolton away, Manchester United at home and Blackburn away. Blackpool won many plaudits for playing with great attacking flair. Adam was one of seven players nominated for the 2010-11 PFA Players' Player of the Year.

The following season Adam was sold to Liverpool for £6.75 million. Sadly, his spell on Merseyside wasn't nearly as impressive as his stint at Blackpool. He scored a mere two goals in his 28 appearances for the club; however, he did have the satisfaction of helping Liverpool beat their Merseyside rivals Everton. That season he also helped Liverpool reach the Football League Cup final where they took on Cardiff City. Liverpool won the tie on penalties; unfortunately Charlie missed his spot kick.

After one season at Anfield, Adam was sold to Stoke City. He joined the Potters for a rumoured £4 million. He hoped the move to Stoke would guarantee him more playing time, having been mainly a squad player at Liverpool. He wanted to enjoy his football again and the move proved successful as Charlie spent seven happy years at Stoke.

One moment Potters fans won't forget in a hurry came at Chelsea, in 2015. After a Chelsea attack was thwarted, the ball found its way to Adam, who was still comfortably inside his own half. The Blues keeper, Thibaut Courtois, had wandered from his goal towards the penalty spot. Adam, totally unperturbed by the distance, launched a speculative punt from in excess of 60 yards. Desperately scampering in retreat, there was nothing the Belgian international could do to prevent the ball sailing beyond him, giving Stoke parity. During this time, he made 156 league appearances scoring 19 goals. Charlie had played under five different managers during his time at the club, starting with Tony Pulis and ending with Nathan Jones. Towards the end of his time at Stoke, Adam found playing time increasingly hard to come by and his time with the club drew to a close.

On the international scene, Adam was capped 26 times at senior level by Scotland, making his debut in 2007 under manager Alex McLeish. He represented his country between 2007 and 2015. He didn't manage any goals during his Scotland career, but provided many assists for his playing colleagues.

Charlie Adam went on to ply his trade at Championship side Reading. Recently he has been acting as a pundit on various media channels and he has also started the process of taking his coaching badges. We await to see the next phase of the likeable Scot's career with great interest. Emerging from relative footballing wilderness, Blackpool's recent history tainted by lower league turmoil, the club needed someone to marshal the team; and the supporters, a new paladin, whom they could hero worship.

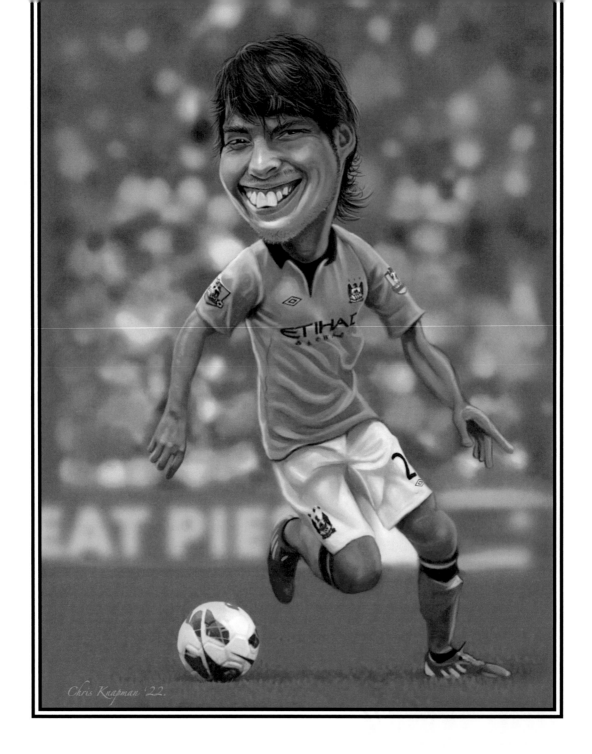

DAVID SILVA

'Making the simple complicated is commonplace; making the complicated simple, awesomely simple, that's creativity.'

(Charles Mingus)

David Silva wasn't born and raised in some football-crazed suburb of Madrid or Valencia. He couldn't hear the dull and distant cacophony of the Bernabeu, as he kicked a tin can against the rusting facade of the family shack, harbouring giddy dreams of being the next Raul – no, he actually hails from Arguineguin (which translates as 'quiet water'), a small fishing village in the south of Gran Canaria in the Canary Islands. And he was a keeper! He played as a goalkeeper in UD San Fernando's youth team – surely an ill-conceived idea, for a kid of his height and frame. It was in his teens that he decided to switch to outfield. The waif-like Silva soon found himself very much at home on the left-wing. When he was 14, Valencia spotted his potential and offered him youth terms. Remaining with their youth set-up until he was 17, this precocious talent made his senior bow on loan with Segunda Division Eibar, playing week-in, week-out. Again the following season, he found himself out on loan – but this time gaining invaluable top-flight experience with Celta Vigo where, again, he was a regular starter.

Silva returned to his parent club in the summer of 2006 and was pitched straight into Valencia's starting line-up and the blistering thermosphere of La Liga Primera Division. Assuming the mantle of creator-in-chief for one of Spain – if not Europe's – biggest clubs (twice Champions League finalists at the start of the decade) and still only 20, Silva let nobody down. Over the next four seasons he made 188 appearances, scoring 29 goals. Most importantly of all though, it was here that the template for a distinguished career was cast: Silva the playmaker – the man who selflessly makes it possible for others to score.

Some say that a move to the Premier League was inevitable and it was no surprise when Silva signed for Manchester City, who were the emerging force in English football. Interestingly, though, Silva has stated that he declined offers from both Barcelona and Real Madrid, in preference for Manchester City and the glitz of the Premier League. That in itself speaks volumes about the financial might and ever-growing popularity of England's Premier League. Comparisons, here, may be drawn with Italy's Serie A, 25 years earlier.

When Silva joined City in 2010, he continued in much the same fashion as he did at Valencia: his almost unparalleled skill and vision delighting fans and colleagues alike, as he again began racking up the 'assists'. Before long, he began to pick up 'player of the month' awards at both club and Premier League level. As those who worship all things OPTA drooled over his heavy contribution, City were moving up the Premier League pecking order at a pace. Whilst he enjoyed Champions League football at Valencia, he won just a solitary Copa del Rey (2008). Unlike during his time on the east coast of Spain, he, notwithstanding his own considerable influence, was now with a club capable of winning domestic honours. His impressive list of honours boasts four Premier League titles, two FA Cups, five League Cups and three FA Community Shields. He was also, unsurprisingly, named in the PFA Premier League Team of the Year on no less than three occasions during his decade at Man City. Now with Real Sociedad, at the ripe old age of 36 he is far from waning and is still adding to his already impressive haul, having won a second Copa del Rey in 2019-20.

Silva is a lustrous, shimmering talent and always a vibrant presence on the field. You can almost see the workings of his febrile footballing brain as the boy from Gran Canaria flits between bewildered opponents. Mainly left-footed, his agility and unpredictable movement makes him a nightmare to man-mark. With a god-given gossamer first touch, Silva brings the ball to bear with ease, then seamlessly accelerates away from defenders, with a mazy run into dangerous territory for the opposition. His ability to simply ghost past seasoned Premier League defenders as though they're not there must be rather alarming for opposing managers and supporters alike. In addition to intelligent forward play, Silva is also gifted with spotless technical ability – an attribute which enables him to retain possession in the tightest of spaces. Having created space for himself, in situations where most players would have run into a cul-de-sac, he shows telling composure on the ball, followed by the intelligence and vision to find the deadly accurate pass needed to carve open the opposition. An archetypal 'number 10' and wonderful reader of the game, his array of skills allow him to dictate the tempo of a game. In this position, he's one of the finest players in the world. Silva can, however, operate most effectively in more than one position. For Valencia, Manchester City and the Spanish national team he's undertaken the roles of 'attacking midfeld player', 'winger' and 'second striker' – the point being that his mercurial talent enables him to play pretty much anywhere. In addition to his creative bent, whilst far from prolific, he does carry a goal threat and occasionally pitches in with important goals.

Admired throughout the game, perhaps the greatest testament to his talents comes from within the club itself. The late Colin Bell, widely regarded as Manchester City's greatest ever player and dubbed 'King of the Kippax', said this of the Spanish playmaker:

"David Silva would walk into any City team. He is in my greatest all-time XI and is just fantastic to watch. When he's on the ball he makes the whole team tick and we don't look the same side without him. He has an incredible awareness and is the perfect player for the modern game."

He's also been rightly lauded in the media on numerous occasions – the remarks of Sky Sports analyst Jamie Redknapp typifying the consensus:

"He is the maestro; he knows where the passes are going to go. He runs the game. A joy to watch."

A further – almost tacit – endorsement of his abilities is his international records. Put in the simplest of terms: you don't win 125 caps for Spain if you're not a player who occupies the very highest echelon of the ability scale. Silva's talents have also yielded the greatest rewards at this level, winning three successive titles: UEFA Euro 2008, the 2010 FIFA World Cup and UEFA Euro 2012 – playing an integral role every time.

David Silva is living-proof that, in a league often stereotyped as being obsessed by brawn and physicality, the artist can flourish as well as the artisan; the sophisticate as well as the grafter – for this elfin, will-o'-the-wisp of a footballer from the Atlantic, is as good as anything the Premier League has ever seen.

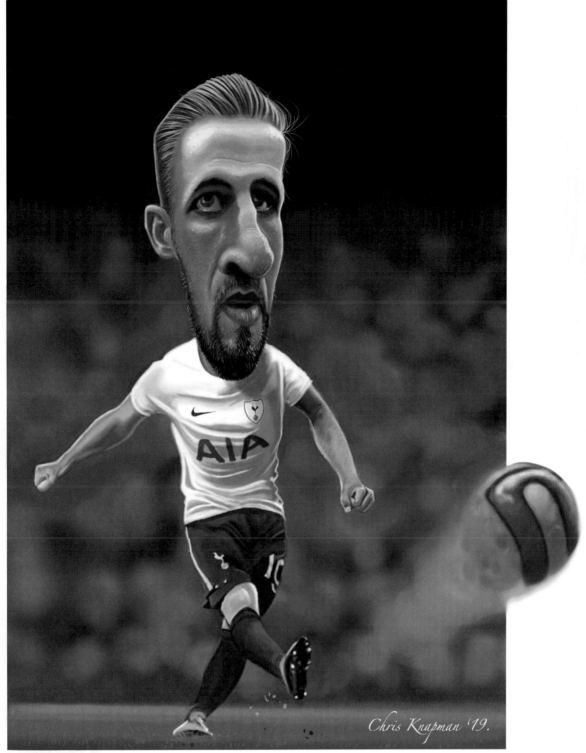

HARRY KANE

"Always bear in mind that your own resolution to succeed is more important than any one thing"

(Abraham Lincoln)

Harry Edward Kane MBE is arguably in the top three greatest English centre forwards of the Premier League era, alongside Alan Shearer and Wayne Rooney. Kane needed just 141 appearances to rack up 100 Premier League goals, a feat only surpassed by Alan Shearer, who netted his century in 124 appearances. Former Tottenham manager David Pleat described Kane as an "old-fashioned traditional centre-forward", but he is more than that. He tracks back and plays for the team and not just for himself. He is a very clinical finisher, and I am sure like all strikers, Kane has a selfish streak, but if another player is in a more advantageous position, more often than not Kane will make the right choice and play the man in. Harry is a strapping 6ft 2in tall and is an excellent header of the ball. He has great awareness in and around the opposition box and is quick to seize on any opportunity to strike on goal. He has an instinctive ability to fashion a shot at goal from any angle and invariably hits the target, as his goal tally testifies. He strikes the ball with great power using his favoured right foot, but he can also produce a little bit of magic with his left peg when needed.

It is ironic that the young Harry, a self-confessed life-long Spurs fan, initially joined rivals Arsenal's Youth academy. Liam Brady, the academy coach released him after only one season, saying he was "a little chubby and not very athletic"! This was something that Arsène Wenger and Arsenal would come to regret over time.

Tottenham themselves were not sure about Kane's potential; he was rejected by them at first. Given a short trial by Watford, Kane came to Spurs' attention again when playing against them at junior level. Harry was obviously a late developer; in his early career he wasn't tall or quick, that came later. He was loaned out to various clubs in the football league pyramid including Leyton Orient, Millwall, Norwich City and Leicester City. Four loan spells took a staggering four years out of the young Kane's career. He played 56 times in total across the various clubs, scoring 19 goals., However, this was just a stepping stone to coming back to North London and to work his way into Mauricio Pochettino's plans.

Kane's involvement started under Pochettino in 2014 and this was the year Harry Kane took the Premier League by storm. He scored 31 goals across all competitions in his first full season at Tottenham, finishing second top goal scorer in the Premier League with 21, behind the prolific Argentine Sergio Aguero with 26.

He collected the PFA Young Player of the Year award, and was also named in the 2014-2015 Team of the Season. Following this first amazing season some expected a young Harry Kane to flop and be a 'one season wonder'. However, he came back with a bang, scoring 25 goals and becoming the league's top goal scorer ahead of another prolific English striker, namely Jamie Vardy. Kane's goals helped secure the club's Champions League place for the following season, finishing in third spot behind the champions Leicester and one point behind arch-rivals Arsenal.

Kane proved the doubters wrong once again. The following season the Englishman's goal scoring record would improve drastically as he scored 41 goals in 48 games in all competitions. Kane's scoring prowess brought him to the attention of the football world. He holds the record of winning six English Premier League Player of the Month awards alongside Steven Gerrard and Sergio Aguero.

Harry Kane isn't just an exceptional goalscorer at club level, he has also done it on the international stage. He has played 69 games currently for his country, scoring 49 goals, an excellent goal-to-games ratio by any standard. Kane made his England debut under Roy Hodgson in March 2015 scoring just 90 seconds after coming on as a substitute and helping England see off Lithuania 4-0 in a UEFA Euro 2016 qualifier at Wembley. Eleven days later Harry started upfront with Wayne Rooney in a friendly against Italy at the Juventus stadium, where England came away with a positive 1-1 draw.

He is a natural leader and it was no surprise that in June 2017, Kane captained England for the first time in their 2018 FIFA World Cup qualifier against Scotland at Hampden Park, scoring an added-time equaliser to rescue a 2–2 draw. He was to follow this up by scoring a last gasp winner against Slovenia, which confirmed England's qualification for the 2018 FIFA World Cup finals.

In the finals in France, he helped the nation believe that Football could finally be coming home. England progressed all the way through to the semi-finals before succumbing to a very gifted Croatia. His tally of six goals in the finals was enough to earn him the prestigious Golden Boot award for the tournament.

Harry Kane's rise to the top is testament to his work ethic as well as his athleticism and skill. He is a very humble individual and is always looking to improve his game and is reportedly the last player to leave the training pitch at Spurs. Kane's work rate and dedication to his craft has been noted by his fellow professionals. In 2015 Match of the Day pundit Danny Murphy said that the England team should be built around Kane, stating, "I'm struggling to see a weakness in the lad's game". He has proven himself as a prolific Premier League goal scorer and is potentially on course to become the Premier League's top goal scorer. In addition to scoring more than 100 Premier League goals for Tottenham, Kane is also the club's top goal scorer in European competitions with 24 goals in 50 appearances.

His biggest hoodoo at Tottenham was that he had never scored a goal in August, having to wait till September before he found the net. However, his luck soon changed at the start of the 2018-19 season when Fulham came to face Spurs at Wembley, their temporary home whilst the building of their new stadium at White Hart Lane was in progress. Kane struck in a 2-1 victory with fellow Englishman Kieran Trippier scoring a delightful free kick to earn Spurs a vital three points. Shortly after, Kane also then netted against Manchester United, which meant he had scored against all of the so called 'Premier League Big 6' both home and away.

Kane isn't just an out-and-out goal scorer, he has so much more in his repertoire. ESPN reporter Michael Cox stated that "Kane was initially considered a pure goal scorer, he's actually a good all-round player, often playing as an attacking midfielder", pointing out that during the 2018 FIFA World Cup "Kane's contributions in deeper positions were outstanding, his back-to-goal work as impressive as ever". The way he can drop into midfield and create chances with that excellent passing ability is a great asset to his game. He can switch play in a blink of an eye. This is why he is considered to be one of the Premier League's elite strikers every single year. Kane has been the club's talisman; he was pivotal in maintaining Tottenham's Champions League qualification.

In 2018-19 Kane played a huge role in helping Spurs to secure their place in the final! He scored a very important double against PSV that just kept their slim chances of progressing alive. He also assisted Lucas Moura to equalise against Barcelona at the Nou Camp. This saw Spurs through to the last 16. Kane was involved again when Spurs comfortably beat Borussia Dortmund 3-0 at Wembley. He also scored away at Dortmund to clinch 0-1 victory to make it 4-0 to Spurs on aggregate.

Next up in the quarter finals were Premier League Champions Manchester City. This was to prove a titanic struggle, one which would lead to victory against all the odds. In the first leg Kane unfortunately injured himself in a tense 1-0 victory at their brand-new Tottenham Hotspur Stadium. He had to watch the away fixture and the subsequent round against Ajax from the stands. The quarter and semi-finals were to become two of the most dramatic nights of Champions League football ever. Tottenham lost a pulsating game against

City 4-3, but went through on the away goals rule with the dreaded VAR having a big say in the eventual outcome.

In the semi-final against Ajax, Tottenham Hotspur pulled off a miracle of a turnaround with Lucas Moura scoring a brilliant second half hat-trick. Kane couldn't contain his excitement – at the final whistle he sprinted onto the pitch to congratulate his victorious and heroic team-mates. This was surely a sign he was ready for the final against fellow Premier League giants Liverpool!

Unfortunately for Kane and for Tottenham there was to be no fairy tale ending this time. Kane started but didn't make much of an impact in the game. Tottenham lost the match 2-0 with Mo Salah slotting home a penalty conceded in the first minute, with Divock Origi sealing their fate late on in proceedings.

Kane's efforts during the season were noted, however, as he was chosen to be in the PFA Team of the Year, an honour that he has achieved an amazing four times. In the New Year's Honours List of 2019, Kane was awarded the MBE for his achievements in The Beautiful Game.

His 19-20 season was hampered by injury problems but he still made a creditable contribution to the Spurs cause with 24 goals in all competitions. He also notched up his 200th league appearance during the campaign.

In the 20-21 season Kane came roaring back. Notably he was on the score sheet in a 5-2 drubbing of Southampton, as well as providing all the assists for his 'partner in crime' Son Heung-min, who scored the other four goals. It was the first time in Premier League history that a player had contributed four assists to the same team-mate in a single match. Quite an amazing achievement!

On 23 May, he scored a goal in a 4–2 win over Leicester City, to reach his 23rd goal of the season and to win the third Golden Boot award of his career. He also won the Premier League Playmaker of the Season award for most assists in a season, becoming only the third player to have won both the Golden Boot and Playmaker awards in the same season since the introduction of the playmaker award in 2018.

At the start of the 21-22 season there was much speculation that Kane would leave Spurs and he reportedly claimed to have an agreement with the club's hierarchy to go on the transfer list, following interest from Manchester City. However, the move did not materialise and Kane registered his protest by failing to turn up for pre-season training. He later pledged his allegiance to the club and his desire seemed to be rekindled under new manager Antonio Conte, whose stewardship has guided Spurs into contention for a top-four finish.

Despite the disappointment of losing out in the Champions League final, Harry Kane has continued to work hard to achieve as much as possible in his career. He is very strong mentally and will keep working hard to break more records, such as scoring 200 Premier League Goals and breaking Wayne Rooney's England goals total. At the time of writing, he sits level with the great Bobby Charlton on 49 goals, with Rooney's haul of 53 well within his grasp. He will be 29 years old at the end of the 21-22 season and he can already claim to be a footballing great. The only thing missing from his impressive CV is silverware. He came so close with England and Tottenham in 2018 and 2019, but time is still on his side to win a major trophy at either club or national level. Let's hope he makes it – he surely deserves it.

SERGIO AGUERO

*"A single dream is more powerful
than a thousand realities"*

(J.R.R. Tolkien)

When, in July 2011, Sergio 'Kun' Aguero swapped the Spanish sunshine for the altogether capricious weather that passes for an English summer, hopes were high that Manchester City had found the man to do justice to the creative talents being introduced elsewhere in the team. With the likes of Yaya Touré and David Silva happily embedded in their line-up, City just needed someone to provide the coup de grâce to their stylish build-up play; and they had found it – 'Kun' Aguero was simply lethal in front of goal. Unlike the dismal summer – that followed a hugely promising spring that year – Aguero had been no faux-ami. Unlike the weather, flatter-to-deceive he certainly hasn't; moreover, it seems more a case of pathetic fallacy in reverse, as in view of Aguero's unpredictability around the penalty area, it's as though Mother Nature has imbued the little Argentinian with the vagaries of the Manchester weather! Belief and determination were crucial to Aguero prospering.

What Aguero lacked in height and heading ability, he generously compensated for in physical strength and unabated desire. Stylistically, he was not from the same mould of his nation's finest attacking predecessors, or current doyen – Lionel Messi. Messi, Maradona, Aimar and D'Alessandro all preferred to make winding runs from deep, using both feet in the process. Aguero was altogether different and atypically South American; instead, he's better compared to European forwards, such as Jimmy Greaves or the almost incomparable Gerd Muller. Both of the above were small in stature, strong and well-balanced, lightning quick over ten yards and deadly in front of goal – all qualities that Aguero possessed in spades. He also showed an appetite for curling – or sometimes simply smashing – the ball home from greater range. Striking the ball from distance is something you were more likely to see from Greaves than Muller; however, the attribute which unites all three is the movement – that mercurial burst in and around the penalty area – to leave defenders floundering haplessly in their wake. Many of his attributes have drawn comparison with past greats from well-respected figures in the game. Former City manager Roberto Mancini likened him to the Brazilian ace Romario – due to his pace, positional sense and goalscoring ability. The great

Lionel Messi has said that his international team-mate possessed "immense power, strength and an incredible work ethic". Aguero also possesses natural close control, superb vision, astoundingly quick feet and a range of passing normally the preserve of a midfield playmaker; and to that end Argentinian World Cup winner Ossie Ardiles described him as "sharp and clever". So there's no doubting his stature amongst the great and the good in the game.

Aguero grew up in Los Eucaliptos, a villa miseria or slum, in southern Buenos Aires. His childhood, in this shanty town, was impoverished to say the least. Meals often amounted to no more than mate, a herbal tea, served with stale bread. Without the income to sample the delights a capital city can offer its more affluent residents, the thoughts of young Sergio focused upon his favourite pastime; and in the absence of affordable alternatives to kicking a ball in the street, a desire to play football crystallised in this young Argentinian mind. So if you want to read about someone who embodies the 'rags to riches' archetype, then look no further.

A question people often ask of the diminutive, stocky Argentinian is why his shirt bears the name 'Kun'. Apparently this epithet was coined by his grandfather. Kum-Kum is a Japanese cartoon character. This was Aguero's favourite television programme as a boy. His grandfather likened him to Kum-Kum because young Sergio shared the cartoon character's penchant for making mischief. Many a Premier League defender can vouch for his proficiency in this area! His right arm also bears a tattooed inscription written in J.R.R. Tolkien's fictional language of 'Tengwar', which features in Lord of the Rings. It transliterates roughly to 'Kun Aguero'.

Having joined Argentinian giants Independiente at just nine, he debuted at 15 – setting a Primera Division record in doing so. As the goals started to flow, Aguero was soon turning a few European heads. Whilst still 17, he was snapped up by Spanish heavyweights Atletico Madrid. A brand new continent to contend with didn't appear to faze him – certainly not on the pitch. Whilst his 74 goals in 175 games for Los Colchoneros certainly brought kudos, his halcyon days (and counting) were to come a little further north.

The summer of 2011 left several crack European sides, including some in the Premier League, rather deflated, as Aguero signed for Manchester City. Culturally, Britain has less in common with Argentina and, after ten years on English soil, he had yet to master the native tongue. If he found life difficult off the field, it clearly wasn't affecting his performance on it – not even in the early stages. If a new player is supposed to respectfully endure a bedding-in period, nobody had told this dynamic Argentinian. Just nine minutes into his début, after coming off the bench almost on the hour, he was nonchalantly stroking Micah Richard's pass into the Swansea City net. He then turned creator, teeing-up David Silva to compound Welsh dismay; and, if that wasn't sufficient, he rounded off an effervescent and truly sparkling début by cracking home a 30-yard drive in the dying seconds. If Carlsberg did débuts...

Seemingly at home in his new environs, Aguero truly tormented Wigan Athletic in only his third City start. Sometimes referred to as 'pie-eaters', the Latics faithful were treated to a hat-trick by a man more accustomed to tapas. They had no answer to Aguero, as City breezed to a 3-0 victory. It wasn't long before onlookers sensed that he wasn't an ephemeral sensation, a flash in the pan – but here for the foreseeable, and hell-bent on helping City gain a long-awaited stranglehold on the Premier League. Yep, his fearsome reputation appeared justified and his presence to defenders was about as welcome as hemlock in a rose garden.

He ended his first season, 2011-12, with 30 goals in 48 outings, including 23 in the Premier League itself. He was also named Manchester City Player of the Year, in addition to being short-listed for the coveted FIFA Ballon d'Or in the November. The notion of 'second season syndrome' appears to be lost on Aguero; in almost ten years on English soil, he plundered no fewer than 184

Premier League goals – not to mention wreaking equal havoc across both domestic and European cup competitions.

Unsurprisingly, Aguero's prolific goalscoring has seen him break a number of records, bag various awards and ensure City's trophy cabinet does more than simply illustrate the club's impeccable taste in elegant period furniture. Five Premier League titles, six League Cups, one FA Cup and three Community Shields brought home to the Etihad and all achieved with Aguero, hungry and unfettered, providing the deadly endgame to his team's polished, flowing football. His success has extended into European competition – a European Super Cup winner (with Atletico Madrid) and part of the same Spanish side that won the 2010 Europa League. On a personal level, Aguero continued to break new ground. In November 2013, he scored twice in the 6-0 drubbing of Tottenham to overtake Thierry Henry, no less, to achieve the best goals per minute ratio in Premier League history. This reflects the fact that successive managers have often deployed him tellingly from the bench and, conversely, also subbed him on occasions when his race is run. Another landmark occasion came in May 2014, when his quadruple strike in the 4-1 dismantling of Spurs (yes, another!), took him to 61 Manchester City goals, surpassing Carlos Tevez as the club's all-time leading scorer in the Premier League. The following season, he struck 26 goals and was awarded the Premier League Golden Boot. Still the red-letter days came: in October 2015, Aguero helped himself to five goals in a 6-1 routing of Newcastle United, becoming only the fifth player to score as many in a single match. By November of the same year, he'd become the most prolific South American the Premier League has seen – again overtaking compatriot and former team-mate, Carlos Tevez. In the spring of 2016, he reached a century of Premier League goals. Achieved in 147 games, only the great Alan Shearer has done it quicker (124). The following season, he became the top-scoring non-European in the competition, moving ahead of Trinidadian Dwight Yorke. In the autumn of 2017, he netted goal number 177 in all competitions for City, equalling Eric Book's long-standing record (one which takes account of the days of the old First Division). January 2018 saw the arguably peerless Argentinian hammer a hat-trick, as Newcastle were brushed aside 3-1. The second of these was the 350th of an incredibly impressive career and duly earned him his fifth Premier Player of The Month award. The following month saw him hammer four goals in a 5-1 thrashing of Leicester, his third hat-trick of the campaign. City secured a 3-0 victory in the EFL Cup Final later in the month, with Aguero yet again on the score sheet with a deft chip over the Arsenal keeper for the opening goal.

More notable Aguero scoring feats punctuated the 2018-19 season – two goals in the FA Community Shield saw him pass the 200-goal mark for his club, also a ninth Premier League hat-trick against Huddersfield put him within reach of Alan Shearer's tally of 11. He also entered the top ten leading PL scorers and achieved second spot in the listing of foreign scorers in the Premier League, behind Thierry Henry. He was rewarded with a new contract extension which would keep him at the club until 2021. As the season progressed the records just kept on coming. September saw him score his 150th PL goal, in February, a hat-trick against Arsenal brought him level with Alan Shearer's record of 11 and took him past the club's record goalscoring tally of 158.

In January 2020 Aguero netted his 12th PL hat-trick, eclipsing Alan Shearer's record in the process and also taking him past Henry's record goals tally (175) for a foreign player in the Premier League. On May 23rd he made his final league appearance for City, scoring twice after coming off the bench in a 5-0 drubbing of Everton and helping his club to lift the Premier League title. City narrowly missed out on winning the Champions League title, a 1-0 defeat by Chelsea in what would have been the 'icing on the cake' for Aguero's fantastic PL career.

In May 2021 Aguero signed for Spanish giants Barcelona and showed his goalscoring instincts were still intact as he scored on his debut against Valencia, after coming off the bench. In October he made his first El Clasico appearance and scored a last-minute goal in the 2-1 home defeat to Real Madrid. A week later during a home match against Alaves, he came off the pitch complaining of chest pains and was later diagnosed with cardiac arrhythmia. Alas, this proved to be the Argentinian's last match and on December 15th he announced his retirement from football on medical advice.

Many Aguero fans will certainly remember him for the variety in the type of goals he scored. One strike which defied the norm came in a 2-2 draw with Liverpool in February 2013. The ever-eager Argentinian tore down the Merseysiders' right flank in pursuit of what some players might have deemed a lost cause. In a race to the ball with keeper Pepe Reina, Aguero won and proceeded to clip the ball back across goal from a near impossible angle, finding the bottom left-hand corner. This level of audacity is often hand in glove with genius. Another moment for the City faithful to savour came a couple of months later – at none other than Old Trafford, to dramatically settle the Manchester derby, 2-1 in City's favour. A rapid turn of pace saw Aguero nip in front of Danny Welbeck to receive a short Yaya Touré pass. Around 25 yards from goal, he was confronted by Ferdinand and Jones. With the two defenders bearing down on him, it looked as though he'd be thwarted; little 'Kun', however, had other ideas. Just when you thought he'd reached top gear, he suddenly – most unexpectedly – moved into what can only be termed as 'overdrive'; having found this 'non-existent' gear, he seemed to effortlessly glide past the two centre-halves and smash the ball into the roof of the United net from eight or nine yards. The sheer acceleration was, to some extent, disguised by the fact that he made it look so terribly easy. This gilded manoeuvre oozed class and made two England internationals look like they'd been brought in off the parks. Sheer class.

Whatever achievements Sergio Aguero's considerable talent produced in his illustrious career, one particular game, one particular moment, is highly unlikely to be eclipsed. Easter came and went as the Premier League approached its critical final weeks. Returning after being sidelined with a foot problem, Aguero was pivotal as City strung together five successive victories

– obliterating the eight-point lead of City rivals Manchester United. In the final game at home to QPR, City were required to match or better the result of the Red Devils. QPR appeared to be aiding City's cause when, with just over an hour on the clock, the bellicose Joey Barton was dismissed for violent conduct. Despite this, QPR went into a 2-1 lead, with Manchester United 1-0 ahead against Sunderland. Manager Roberto Mancini bolstered his attack by introducing Dzeko and Balotelli. With time running out, Dzeko equalised to give City faint hope. News soon filtered through that United had taken all three points in their game: City needed a third and they needed a man undaunted by gargantuan pressure and with real class and charisma; enter Argentina's finest centre-forward; that man was Sergio Aguero. Latching on to a short pass from Balotelli, Aguero drove into the penalty area, drifted away from one interested QPR defender, before drilling low and hard across the keeper from about nine yards. Nobody – and I don't just mean Manchester City fans – will forget Aguero wheeling away in celebration, shirt in hand and the arm rotating almost Channonesque. Mobbed by equally jubilant team-mates, he collapsed in a tearful heap before the frenzied sky blue hordes – as City, and Aguero, had finally brought the Premier League title to a different part of Manchester. Stirring, heart-stopping – this was surely a career-defining moment and a huge shot in the arm for those concerned with marketing, arguably, the most theatrical, breathtaking and wonderfully entertaining league in the world.

KEVIN DE BRUYNE

"The ability to focus attention on important things is a defining characteristic of intelligence"

(Robert J. Shiller)

Kevin De Bruyne, in a nutshell, is a class act. The midfield star is the stand-out player, along with Eden Hazard, from a rich crop of Belgian talent which has lit up the Premier League in recent years. His innate intelligence and ability to read the game are rivalled only by the very elite of the football world.

Described by many as the complete footballer, he possesses great passing, tackling and shooting ability, as well as an innate ability to read the game and make the right decisions. He has stated many times that he gains more satisfaction from making a telling pass than from actually scoring a goal. In his own words, "When you score, it is obviously a great feeling, but to give a great pass is also something special for me. I think it is also very underrated, what we do".

Born in the Flemish town of Ghent, his professional career began at Genk in the Belgian Pro League in 2005. He progressed to the first team squad three years later, making his league debut in a 3-0 defeat against Charleroi in May 2009. In February 2010, now a first team regular, he scored his maiden goal in a 1-0 victory against Standard Liège. His tally of five goals and 16 assists in the 2010-11 season helped Genk to become Belgian champions for only the third time in the club's history. His first hat-trick came in a 5-4 win over Club Brugge in October 2011. He finished the season with eight goals from 28 appearances, having been signed by Chelsea in the January 2012 transfer window for a reputed transfer fee of £7 million. He remained with Genk for the remainder of the season before his permanent move to Stamford Bridge.

Having had just a couple of appearances in friendly games for Chelsea, the new recruit was put out on a season-long loan deal to Werder Bremen in the German Bundesliga. A return of 10 goals from 33 games at Bremen showed him to be a competent player with bags of potential. His loan spell now completed, his imminent return to Chelsea was clouded in rumours that he was about to be sold on to Borussia Dortmund or Bayer Leverkusen. Incoming manager José

Mourinho, however, assured the lad that he was part of the club's future plans and De Bruyne officially returned to the Chelsea squad in July 2013.

He made a solitary appearance for the club on the opening day of the 2013-14 Premier League season, before being sold to Wolfsburg in the following January for a fee of £18 million. Little did 'The Special One' realise what a potential superstar he had let slip through his fingers. Eat your heart out, José!

So, it was goodbye Chelsea, hello Wolfsburg and this next phase of his career proved very successful for the baby-faced Belgian. He began to build a reputation as a goal creator as well as a goal scorer. In the 2014-15 season he scored 10 goals and chipped in with an amazing 21 assists, the latter being a new Bundesliga record. This contribution from De Bruyne was significant in enabling Wolfsburg to finish second in the league and thus qualify for the Champions League. His final tally of 16 goals and 27 assists in all competitions earned him the 2015 German Footballer of the Year award.

The start of the 2015-16 season saw De Bruyne collect a winners' medal in the DFL-Supercup win over Bayern Munich. This is a one-off match between the German league and cup winners, similar to our own Community Shield. In a one-all draw, De Bruyne had made the assist for Nicklas Bendtner to score the equalising goal in the 89th minute. He also netted in the ensuing penalty shoot-out as Wolfsburg finally triumphed.

In August 2015 speculation began to arise suggesting De Bruyne might be a target for Manchester City. The Light Blues were fast becoming a major force in the Premier League and sought to improve their squad with top quality players. Although he played down the speculation at first, he did not totally rule out a move to the Premier League saying, "I do not have to go to England. If I go there it's because for me and for my family it is a good choice." After two unsuccessful bids, City came in with a club record offer of £55 million which was too tempting for the Wolfsburg hierarchy to refuse. It was also reported that City had made an "astonishing" wage offer to De Bruyne and so the deal was sealed. City got their man and what a signing it proved to be!

At the time, De Bruyne was the second most expensive signing in British football history. Only Angel Di Maria's move to Man U had cost more. The Belgian star made his City debut on September 12th against Palace, coming on as a sub for the injured Aguero. His first goal came a week later against West Ham. More goals and assists followed, and in October his name appeared on a list of possibles for the Ballon d'Or award, alongside team-mates Yaya Touré and Sergio Aguero.

In January 2016 he scored a goal in a 3-1 League Cup semi-final victory over Everton, but picked up a knee injury in the process, which kept him sidelined for two months. On his return in April, he scored in a 4-1 victory against Bournemouth. He was again on the score sheet four days later in a Champions League quarter final 2-2 draw with PSG in Paris. In the return leg, despite a rare missed penalty by Aguero, City were triumphant and that man De Bruyne scored one of his trademark goals, curling a low shot around the PSG keeper from 20 yards out. A truly stunning goal, which took City through to the Champions League final for the first time in the club's history.

His splendid form continued into the 2016-17 season. In September 2016 he scored the opening goal in the Manchester derby, as well as contributing an assist for the second goal in the 2-1 victory. He was awarded the Man of the Match. A week later another Man of the Match award came his way in a 4-0 drubbing of Bournemouth, in which he scored and assisted in two of the goals, as well as provided key passes in the build-up to the other goals. In a Champions League game in early November against the mighty Barcelona, he scored from a free kick in the 3-1 victory.

This burgeoning footballing talent had the pundits drooling at the mouth. His manager at City, the highly rated Pep Guardiola, who had worked with

Europe's best players at Barcelona and Bayern Munich, said this of him: "I think he is a special, outstanding player. He makes everything. Without the ball he is the first fighter, and with the ball he is clear – he sees absolutely everything." Not only did he score goals and set up opportunities galore for his team-mates, he did it with such technical prowess. His desire to improve his technique was one of his greatest qualities. In his own words, "Playing in different positions helped me to get in the head of the other players; to know what they're thinking, where and how they are going to move. I always try to manage the ball in a way that can help the way my team-mates receive it." Such awareness and ability to read other players' minds goes a long way to explaining the pin-point passing skill we have witnessed from De Bruyne on so many occasions.

Another example of the player's intelligence and desire for technical excellence in terms of the quality of his passing, is summed up in the following comment from him: "If you do an outside spin with the ball, it's more difficult to control it, so I try to pass it in a way that allows them to take the ball quicker in their path." How many players would take the trouble to hone their skill in this way? His obsession with passing the ball well and playing in his team-mates prompted some coaches to insist he shoot more often. Having marvelled at the numerous stunning goals he has scored in the Premier League, this advice has been well and truly taken. Time and again we have witnessed him produce spectacular strikes from distance. His ability to deliver hard, low shots on goal have become his trademark, making it difficult for keepers to get down quickly enough to save them – further testimony to his intelligent approach to his craft.

The 2017-18 season was a productive one for both club and player. With eight goals and 16 assists, De Bruyne continued to impress for Man City, as the team recorded resounding wins over Liverpool (5-0), Watford (6-0), and Stoke (7-2). On December 13th he scored in a 4-0 win over Swansea which took City to a record-breaking 15 consecutive Premier League wins. In January 2018, he was rewarded with a new contract which would keep him at the club until 2023. City progressed to the final of the EFL Cup with De Bruyne having scored the winning goal in the semi-final against Bristol City. They went on to take the trophy, their first under Guardiola, with an emphatic 3-0 victory over Arsenal. More recognition for De Bruyne came when he was awarded the Premier League Playmaker of the Season on its inception. He was also selected in the PFA Team of the Year, as well picking up Manchester City's Player of the Season accolade.

In contrast to the highs of the previous campaign, the following season dealt him an early blow in the shape of a bad knee injury on August 15th, which looked like it might sideline him for several months. The scan revealed ligament damage, but the medics decided that surgery was not required. He returned to action in October 2018 but sustained a further injury during a Carabao Cup match against Fulham. A further three weeks on the treatment table added to his woes. Later in the season, he came on as a substitute in the FA Cup final against Watford, scoring the third goal and assisting in two more, as City won their first ever domestic treble. He received the Man of the Match award for his efforts – you can't keep a good man down! His Premier League stats, at the time of writing, reads 207 matches, 57 goals and 86 assists.

The 2019-20 season was a productive one. He notched up his 50th City goal in all competitions and produced a record-equalling 20 assists. He was awarded the Premier League Player of the Season accolade and also picked up the PFA Player of the Year award to boot, being the first ever City player to claim it.

In April 2021 a trademark De Bruyne free kick was headed home by Laporte to give City a 1-0 victory over Spurs in the EFL Cup Final. The end of the season saw him pick up yet another award, in the shape of the coveted PFA Player's Player of the Year award.

De Bruyne's 2021-22 was no less memorable, featuring a stunning four-goal return in the space of 24 minutes in a 5-1 thrashing of Wolves. The season just got better and better for the amiable Belgian with another PFA Player of the Year award in the bag, and culminating in City pipping arch-rivals Liverpool to win the Premier League for the third time in four seasons. Few will forget the dramatic events of their final match, as City overturned a two-goal deficit against Villa to lift the trophy.

On the international scene, De Bruyne has been capped 88 times by Belgium and his goal tally stands currently at 23. He was an integral member of the national team during the 2014 FIFA World Cup qualifying campaign, during which he scored four goals to help his country reach the finals of a major tournament after a nine-year absence.

Two years later, Belgium qualified for the UEFA Euro 2016 finals with De Bruyne again turning in outstanding performances, notably in games against Ireland and Hungary. He was awarded the Man of the Match in the 4-0 victory over Hungary, having provided assists for two of the goals.

In 2018 he was part of a talented Belgian squad, who were among the favourites to lift the FIFA World Cup Trophy. He picked up yet another Man of the Match award in the 2-1 quarter final victory over Brazil in which he scored the winning goal. Belgium eventually lost in the semi-final against France, but garnered some consolation from convincingly beating England in the third-place play-off.

De Bruyne is a rare talent but also a very unassuming individual. The title of his autobiography perhaps best sums up the persona of the man: 'Keep It Simple'. As a footballer, you need to have supreme ability to make the game look so simple and he certainly has that in spade loads.

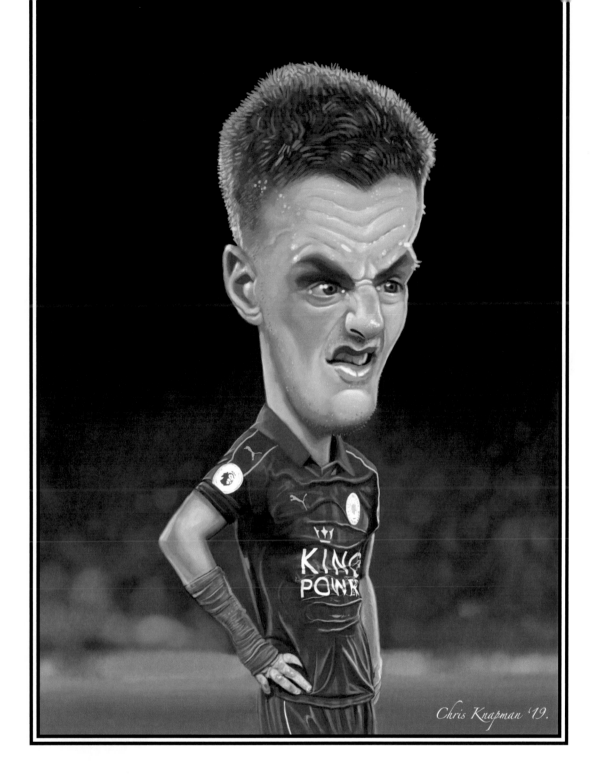

JAMIE VARDY

"The greatest accomplishment is not in never falling, but in rising again after you fall."

(Vince Lombardi)

When reflecting upon the career of Jamie Vardy, journalists and authors usually focus upon his most unorthodox route into the professional game and remarkable rise to the pinnacle of his profession. Whilst one hopes that Hollywood don't butcher his story with a skewed and ill-informed biopic that has us all regurgitating our popcorn, his career to date is undeniably steeped in romance. In fact, it's nigh on impossible to discuss him without charting his emergence from the most humble of circumstances; after a truly inauspicious start.

For some time now, football has been inured to the unpalatable fact that money dictates everything: prices and numbers. It's as much the domain of the accountant and the statistician as it is the avid and uncorrupted lover of football. With this in mind, the analysis of numbers is a good way of making inroads into an evaluation of Vardy's still ongoing career.

Sheffield-born Vardy began his journey – or should I say odyssey – with hometown club Sheffield Wednesday. But, swiftly released in his mid-teens, things did not augur well for the young striker. After a stint on trial at Crewe Alexandra, he rejected a short-term contract offer from Rotherham United. Vardy found himself playing for lowly Stocksbridge Steelers – signing in 2003 and breaking into the first team in 2007. Enjoying three fruitful seasons there, he was still only earning £30 a week. This was a meagre supplement to the poor wages he earned doing low and semi-skilled jobs such as making medical splints and working in a carbon fibre factory. At one point he even returned to education to study sports science. At this point, the giddy heights of what was to follow were barely even a pipe dream. Also, adding insult to injury, Vardy's time at Stocksbridge was marred by his involvement in a fracas outside a pub. He was subsequently convicted for assault and had to play wearing an electronic tag for six months. The tag was for the purpose of monitoring his compliance with a night-time curfew – something which rendered him unavailable for evening fixtures!

In 2010, Vardy was given hope. After three seasons and 66 goals, a move to Northern Premier League FC Halifax Town reawakened Vardy's dream of becoming a professional footballer. For now he dared to abandon his homespun outlook and resignation to a humdrum blue-collar existence. Whilst manual workers obviously provide essential and praiseworthy services, the prospect of life on the shop floor must've seemed rather unprepossessing in comparison to the kudos and glitz of pro football. Vardy seized this opportunity and hammered 28 goals in 37 games – goals which fired the Yorkshiremen to the Northern Premier League title.

Another move quickly followed and Vardy was off to Fleetwood Town. To continue with numbers, Fleetwood paid a then club record £150,000 to secure his services; and, after Stocksbridge barely covering his petrol money and post-match grub, his move to the Fylde came with a comparatively handsome £850-a-week! To a man who'd recently toiled for a paltry £30-per-week, even his Fleetwood wage must've made him feel like Rockefeller! Parallels, here, may be drawn with his time in West Yorkshire; again, he didn't tarry and remained for just one season; and again his goals landed silverware – this time the Conference National title. Across all competitions, Vardy blasted 34 goals in 42 appearances.

Given just how prolific Vardy had been over his two seasons with FC Halifax and Fleetwood, it was perhaps inevitable that clubs from a higher level would take a look at this emerging star. Even in the fifth and sixth tiers of the English football pyramid, 62 goals in just a couple of seasons is bound to command a degree of respect and generate interest.

Not unreasonably, Vardy must've been hankering for a move to the higher echelons. After a solitary season with The Fishermen – one which went stupendously well – Leicester City manager Nigel Pearson homed in on his potential. His belief that Vardy could step up three divisions and prosper at

Championship level was strong enough for him to part with £1m (£1.7m with add-ons). It was a record fee for a non-league player – and to some a huge risk.

Vardy's first season proved to be a struggle. He failed to reproduce the free-scoring form he'd shown playing semi-professional football and drew much criticism. He reportedly contemplated leaving the game, but was persuaded to persevere by Pearson and his assistant, Craig Shakespeare.

Although the following season still didn't see Vardy score with quite the same abandon as he had outside of the league, it certainly marked a significant upturn in his fortunes. He managed 16 goals in all competitions – more than treble the previous year. He went a good way towards winning the supporters' affections by winning and scoring a penalty against promotion contenders and bitter arch-rivals, Derby County. Vardy, now a fixture in the side, was named the club's Players' Player of the Year, as The Foxes romped to the Championship title.

The 2014-15 season saw both Vardy and Leicester City attempt to find their feet at the highest level. The former showcased his potential in September, when he scored one and created four, as Leicester remarkably overturned a 3-1 deficit to beat Manchester United 5-3. This early man-of-the-match performance wasn't to be repeated for some time. The club managed to stave off initial relegation worries by garnering an impressive 22 points between early April and the season end – a run which coincided with Vardy starting to show signs that he could handle the Premier League. Towards the end of what had been a fairly barren debut season, he grabbed crucial winners against Burnley and West Bromwich Albion, and was nominated for Premier League Player of the Month. The club finished a respectable 14th and Vardy's end-of-season form proved to be an omen of things to come.

Leicester now had enough faith in Vardy to put him on a walloping £45,000-a-week ! Bathing in opulence he might well have been – but the trappings and attention that inevitably go hand-in-hand with Premier League stardom did nothing to distract this emerging talent from the task that lay ahead.

Usually, footballers, managers, coaches and supporters alike, begin a new season with renewed hope and a belief (which is sometimes deluded, blinkered and wholly misguided!) that their team will improve upon whatever they did or didn't achieve the previous year. Leicester City and Jamie Vardy were no different in that respect. An air of buoyancy, no doubt, filled the stadium before their opening home game; and Vardy's springtime flourish must've engendered a self-belief. Could he improve upon five goals in 34 Premier League appearances?

The Premier League ranks amongst the most challenging in the world; so Leicester City, therefore, were expected to consolidate their status, perhaps finishing a little higher at best. Twelve points from their opening six games and still undefeated, whilst a very robust start indeed, offered little by way of clues to what was to follow. On a personal level, Vardy eclipsed his goals tally for the previous season with a brace in the club's first loss – 5-2 away to Arsenal. The hungry Yorkshireman continued to trouble the scorers, providing vital finishes in victories over Crystal Palace and West Brom. Before long, he made his entry into the Premier League record books – becoming the first player to score in nine consecutive matches within one season. (Ruud van Nistelrooy had managed ten, but his scoring run had straddled two seasons.) Vardy was rewarded for his sparkling form when he was named Premier League Player of the Month for October 2015. He then equalled the Dutchman's record, when he opened the scoring in a 3-0 victory over Newcastle, before taking it outright when he was on target against Manchester United. He also retained his Player of the Month status with more goals in November. Curiously, he was also presented with a certificate from Guinness World Records in honour of his impressive scoring streak.

By the new year, Vardy's currency in the transfer market had soared dramatically, with manager Claudio Ranieri describing him as "priceless". February came and a Vardy double put paid to Liverpool, on their visit to the East Midlands. His opening strike was a blindingly brilliant long-distance volley. Alive to every opportunity, as every good forward should be, Vardy latched onto a perfectly weighted chip forward from Riyad Mahrez. Then letting the ball bounce once, before any Liverpool defenders could smother him, he lashed the ball on the rise over stranded keeper Mignolet. Although the Belgian was marginally off his line, he wasn't expecting to be punished by this ferocious, dipping volley from approaching 30 yards; plus Vardy was striking on the angle, a touch to the right. Even Liverpool boss Jurgen Klopp was rhapsodic – describing it as "world-class" – as the Merseysiders were dispatched back to Anfield sore and point-less.

The Liverpool volley was a summation of Vardy's attributes. Good positional sense, lurking off the defender's shoulder and having that burst of pace to create sufficient space to pose a threat. Most of his goals come from much closer range, where his composure and ability to finish well with either foot serve him well indeed. Furthermore, his high-octane performances, his relentless running, always yield goalscoring opportunities.

Whilst the taming of Liverpool, English footballing royalty, certainly created waves, the media and footballing community as a whole still weren't couching Leicester in such terms as 'title contenders' or anything similar. They were still portrayed as a bunch of plucky upstarts from the provinces, who would ultimately 'know their place' and accede their lofty position to bigger clubs – more 'befitting' of the status. Leicester and Jamie Vardy, however, simply weren't listening and had no intention of relinquishing their lead at the top. The numbers were looking increasingly favourable for the striker who came from nowhere. Just four days after the momentous victory over Liverpool, he extended his contract to 2019 – increasing his salary to £80,000-a-week in doing so.

The club maintained their form and, as spring arrived, the name 'Leicester City' was now being proffered by journalists and pundits as that of very possible League champions.

April saw Vardy hit both goals in a 2-0 victory over Sunderland, taking him to 21. These goals also saw him become the first Leicester player since Gary Lineker to reach 20 top-flight goals in one season – a record which had stood for more than two decades.

Vardy was actually sent off the following week, for diving against West Ham. The untimely suspension which followed might've proved costly; however, Leicester City and Vardy held out for a gloriously unlikely first League title – having never won the old First Division title. We see the lesser footballing lights wreak havoc in one-off FA Cup ties; whereas Leicester, rather stupendously, did it over a full season. For Vardy's part, he was named in the PFA Team of the Year, Barclays Premier League Player of the Season and, perhaps most pleasingly, as Football Writers Association Footballer of the Year. All of those accolades alongside his Premier League winner's medal. His only significant 'miss' was the Golden Boot – however, finishing joint second scorer on 24 with Sergio Aguero, just one behind Harry Kane, is nothing to be disappointed about! Still a rather plentiful return for a player who teetered on the brink of leaving the game – a true renaissance after all had seemed lost.

With Vardy amongst the goals, his stock had risen immeasurably. From 2015 to 2018, Vardy featured regularly in the England squad. Winning 26 caps and scoring seven times, Vardy played and scored at UEFA Euro 2016 (with a vital leveller in the 2-1 victory over Wales) and also featured at the 2018 FIFA World Cup.

If 2015-16 was a consummate success for Vardy and Leicester, the next few seasons saw the fortunes of both player and club align with old preconceptions of what is expected of them. Leicester have managed three successive finishes amongst the middle order, whilst Vardy – no longer allowed to roam unbridled – hasn't scored quite as freely as during the title-winning campaign. That said, he's still plundered 51 Premier League goals in three middle-of-the-road seasons. He's also done so in a team now shorn of several of its league-winning stars, such as Mahrez and Kante; and there have been some stand-out moments en route.

December 2016 saw Vardy end a ten-match goal drought in rousing fashion, when he blasted a first professional hat-trick in an absorbing 4-2 victory over high-riding Manchester City. The following season, he hit what was to later prove to be the BBC Match of the Day Goal of the Season 2018 winner against West Brom. Pulling off his marker, he allows a flighted forward pass from Mahrez to drop over his left shoulder. Then, before the ball can bounce, he guides a divine, wonderfully controlled left-foot volley into the bottom right-hand corner, from just inside the penalty area. He saw the ball late, had limited time to react, yet steered the ball beautifully into the goal. The goalkeeper had advanced to narrow the angle, but Vardy left him stranded and almost irrelevant. Although Vardy often utilises his pace to great effect, this demonstrates that grace and subtlety are also within his repertoire.

March 2019 heralded his 100th goal for Leicester. In October of the same year, he scored a memorable hat-trick in an astonishing 9-0 drubbing of Southampton. The 2019-20 season proved to be a vintage one for Vardy as he surpassed the 100 Premier League goals milestone, as well picking up the Golden Boot award for his 23 goal tally at the ripe old age of 33 – the oldest player to achieve this feat at the time.

An FA Cup winners' medal came his way in the 2021 defeat of Chelsea. It also marked Leicester's first ever success in the competition.

Jamie Vardy continues to enjoy playing football at the highest level. His boundless energy, awesome work rate and unadulterated enthusiasm can actually induce fatigue in those watching him! His reported preparatory 'regime' involves drinking port to get himself to sleep on the eve of a game; conversely followed by Red Bull for stimulus on match days. These practices might not sit comfortably with Leicester's club doctor or dietician, but who was going to argue with a player who did as much as anyone to bring the club unprecedented success, an uncharted journey into the UEFA Champions League to boot?

A tremendous example to all those footballers who think they're just foundering in the lower leagues.

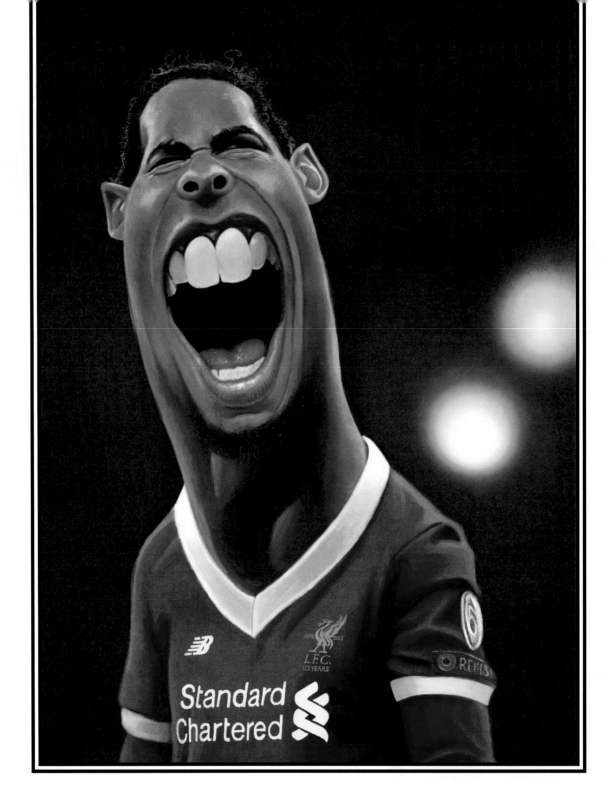

VIRGIL VAN DIJK

"They can conquer who believe they can"

(Virgil (70 BC – 19 BC)

The English Premier League has been enhanced by the presence of several great Dutch players over the years; the names Bergkamp, van Nistelrooy, van Persie, Gullit and Robben immediately spring to mind. Amongst the current crop of Dutchmen in our midst, however, the stand-out performer is a centre back, not a striker as you might expect. Virgil van Dijk has developed into one of the most reliable defenders in the Premier League. A veritable colossus at the heart of the Liverpool defence, his commanding and calm presence has helped to underpin the re-emergence of the Merseyside giants since his arrival at Anfield in January 2018.

The son of a Dutch father and a Surinamese mother, he grew up in the city of Breda in the southern part of the Netherlands. From an early age he was obsessed with playing football and could be seen kicking a ball around his neighbourhood at all times of the day. He joined the Willem II academy as a youngster, starting initially as a full-back but later converting to centre back when he grew a staggering seven inches in height in a short space of time. Despite his best efforts to make the grade, the club felt he had too many limitations and decided to part company with him, so he left on a free transfer to join FC Groningen in 2010.

He made his professional debut for Groningen in May 2011. His first outing was as a substitute and proved largely uneventful. Later the same month, however, he was in the starting line-up for a Europa League play-off match against ADO Den Haag, scoring twice in a resounding 5-1 victory; his first professional goals. In the 2011-12 season van Dijk made 23 appearances for the club, registering his first goal for the Eredivisie team in a 6-0 thrashing of Feyenoord, no less. A serious illness thwarted any further playing time for him in the season, when he was admitted to hospital suffering from peritonitis and kidney poisoning. Such was the severity of his condition that for a time it was touch and go whether he would survive from it. Survive he did and he was back in harness the following season, continuing his impressive form to the extent that top-flight clubs such as Ajax began to show an interest in the big defender. However, no approaches from Eredivisie clubs transpired and he subsequently joined Scottish giants Celtic in June 2013.

Although van Dijk saw his move to Celtic as a stepping stone to greater things, he knuckled down to the task in hand and made his presence felt at the heart of the defence as he continued to work hard to improve his game. In 76 appearances for Celtic, he scored an impressive 15 goals, helping the club to lift back-to-back Scottish League titles as well as the League Cup. Many pundits expressed their surprise that he was not selected for Louis van Gaal's squad for the 2014 FIFA World Cup, with van Dijk himself citing the Scottish Premier League as perhaps being viewed as of a lower standard than other leagues – try saying that in a pub on Sauchiehall Street if you dare!

Van Gaal and his coaching staff at the time felt there was a flaw in his game, namely his tendency to sit back and wait to challenge oncoming attackers too close to his own goal. What was needed was a centre back who would move forward and thwart strikers further up the pitch, thus allowing him to initiate counter attacks against the opposition. A lack of top coaching in his early career was perhaps the reason for this flaw in his technique, but once this missing ingredient had been added to his repertoire, he started to look like the real deal.

Inevitably, when Celtic were knocked out of the 2015-16 Champions League at the qualifying stage by Swedish side Malmö, the fiercely ambitious van Dijk began to think it was time to move on to further his career. It was not long before another Dutch master, Ronald Koeman, who was then managing Southampton, clearly saw the potential in his fellow countryman and brought him into the Premier League for the first time, for a fee of £13m. The Saints have always been a club with a reputation for nurturing young talent, so although he only graced their presence for two seasons, his game was to improve significantly as he started to show the composure and leadership qualities he undoubtedly possessed.

He debuted for his new club on September 1st, 2015 in a goalless draw against West Brom at The Hawthorns. At 6' 4" in height, van Dijk is a persistent goal threat at set pieces, so no surprise when he headed his first goal for Saints from a Ward-Prowse cross against Swansea. So impressed were the Southampton board with their new recruit that they handed him a new six-year contract in May 2016. An international call-up followed soon after, as the then 24-year-old's career began to take off. He became club captain in January 2017 following the departure of José Fonte; however, he soon came on the radar of the mighty Liverpool, who after an initial, albeit illegal approach, got their man after van Dijk submitted a formal transfer request to the Southampton board. The £75m transfer fee no doubt mitigated some of the pain of losing their prize asset, generating a handsome profit of £62m for the club's coffers.

Arriving at a club like Liverpool, with its proud heritage and demanding fans, can be a daunting prospect for any player. In van Dijk's case it was doubly so, since he was also carrying the burden of being the most expensive defender in world football at the time. The words 'squeaky' and 'bum' spring to mind! The solution was simple. All you have to do on debut is to score the winning goal in a Merseyside derby. Van Dijk managed to do just that in a 2-1 FA Cup triumph over the 'Toffies', a feat which hadn't been emulated since Bill White in 1901, giving him the perfect start at his new club and immediately endearing him to the Liverpool fans.

After such an impressive start, great things were expected of the new Anfield hero, and van Dijk didn't disappoint. He formed a strong partnership with fellow centre-back Dejan Louvren and, like the little boy in Dutch folklore who stuck his finger in the dyke to prevent his community being flooded, the appropriately named van Dijk began to plug the Liverpool defensive holes to great effect. His influence at the back was clearly evident in Liverpool's progression to the final of the Champions League. He played the full 90 minutes of the Kiev encounter, but his team lost out 3-1 to the defending champions Real Madrid.

In 2018-19, his first full season in Liverpool colours, his outstanding performances earned him consecutive PFA Player of the Month awards in November and December. He also scored his first Premier League goal for the club in a 2-0 away win against Wolves. More accolades were to follow when he was named PFA Player of the Year in April 2019 and two months later he received the Man of the Match award after Liverpool's 2-0 victory over Spurs in the Champions League final.

The following season got off to a flying start for the Dutchman when he picked up the UEFA Player of the Year award. He was later short-listed for the prestigious Ballon d'Or, for which he narrowly missed out to – who else? – the great Lionel Messi. Having missed out on the semi-final of the FIFA Club World Championship through illness, he was back in the side for the final against the strong Brazilian side Flamengo, and helped Liverpool win the trophy for the first time in the club's history.

Van Dijk's 2020-21 season was decimated by an ACL injury, sustained in a collision with Everton goalkeeper Jordan Pickford. He returned to action on July 29, 2021 in a pre-season friendly and was a key player in Liverpool's quest for honours in a successful season for the Merseysiders, which saw them lift both domestic cups and finish runners-up to Man City in the Premier League. They also reached the Champions League final, but were narrowly defeated by Real Madrid 1-0.

Van Dijk's international career started relatively late at the age of 24. His first outing in the famous orange jersey came against Kazakhstan in a Euro 2016 qualifier with his side achieving a 2-1 away victory. Fast forward to March 2018 when he was handed the captain's armband by manager Ronald Koeman. Less than a week later he registered his first international goal in a 3-0 win over Portugal. In October the same year his second goal came in the shape of a stunning volley against Germany. A cross from the right reached him on the left of the opposition penalty area and, with the technique any top-class striker would be proud of, he powered a crisp right foot strike into the German net – pure class! In a total of 46 games for his country he has contributed five goals. Not a bad return for a defender. Furthermore, at club level with 442 games under his belt, he has chipped in a highly impressive 45 goals.

The van Dijk goal tally is commendable but allied to his undoubted defensive ability makes him a truly formidable all-round player. He has received many plaudits from players, fans and pundits alike. Perhaps this description from Lionel Messi sums up the attributes of the Dutch maestro: "He is a defender who knows how to judge his timing, and wait for the right moment to challenge or jockey [the attacker]. He is very fast and big, but he has a lot of agility for his height. He is fast because of his great stride, and he is impressive both in defence and attack because he scores lots of goals."

One highly lauded example of van Dijk's defensive shrewdness came in a match against Spurs. With the score at one apiece and only a few minutes left, the big defender found himself isolated just outside his own penalty area with both Sissoko and Son bearing down on him, having launched a lightning counter attack which left the rest of Liverpool's back four stranded up-field. In a master class of decision making, with Sissoko in possession of the ball, van Dijk decided that Son would be the biggest goal threat of the two. He calmly positioned himself between the two attackers, forcing Sissoko on to his weaker left foot and preventing him passing the ball to his team-mate. He held his nerve in a very difficult situation, and eventually Sissoko was forced to take the shot on, which he obligingly ballooned over the Liverpool bar. Van Dijk had single-handedly snuffed out the Tottenham threat without even needing to make a tackle!

Defending of the very highest quality; I rest my case.

Chris Knapman '20.

SON HEUNG-MIN

"Pleasure in the job puts perfection in the work."

(Aristotle)

Son Heung-min is a rare individual in the serious business of Premier League football. Not only is he one of a small minority of South Korean players to succeed in the high intensity atmosphere of the English game, he manages to achieve this with a ready smile on his face. This is summed up in his own words – "In every country I've gone to, if you smile at people they are going to be happy. This is my attitude." This philosophy, coupled with his undoubted talent, has made Son an extremely popular player amongst Spurs supporters and football lovers in general.

Born in Chuncheon, Gangwon province, he is the son of ex-footballer Son Woong-jung. He attended the football academy at FC Seoul, the same club that also produced Lee Young-pyo who played 70 times for Tottenham between 2005 and 2008. In August 2008, keen to further his career, Son moved to the Hamburger SV's youth academy at the age of 16, as part of a youth project. He returned to South Korea a year later to participate in the FIFA U-17 World Cup and formally joined the German club's youth academy in November 2009.

He jokes that when he went to Germany, all he knew of the language were German swear words. It has also been reported that he was so anxious to improve his German, he watched numerous episodes of Spongebob Squarepants on TV to help achieve his aim – there's determination for you!

Son signed professionally for Hamburg in 2010 at the age of 18. After scoring his first goal for the club against Chelsea, he sustained a foot injury and was out of action for a couple of months. He was back in harness by October 30th, scoring his first league goal against FC Koln. He was the youngest Hamburg player to score in the Bundesliga at the time. The club rewarded him with a new contract which would potentially keep him in their ranks until 2014. In his early days at Hamburg, the club had signed Ruud van Nistelrooy, and Son has praised the encouragement he received from the Dutchman saying, "He helped me a lot. He saw my first training session, and he talked to me. He told me I was a good player. He gave me confidence, and I want to thank him for that."

The South Korean made a blistering start to the 2011-2012 campaign, scoring 18 times in only nine matches in the pre-season fixtures. The season proper saw him pick up a few niggling injuries but he still featured in 30 matches. He netted on five occasions, two of which came at the climax of the season against Hanover and Nürnberg, helping Hamburg to maintain their Bundesliga status. The following season, he established himself in the starting line-up. In a match against Dortmund in February 2013, he scored twice in the team's 4-1 victory and deservedly picked up the Man of the Match award. He finished the season with 12 goals and became the first South Korean player to score ten or more times in European football.

In June 2013, Son was transferred to Bayer Leverkusen on a five-year deal for a reported €10 million, then a club record fee. He was quickly up and running for his new club and had the satisfaction of scoring a hat-trick in a 5-3 victory against his old club Hamburg. His impressive first season continued as he scored vital goals to help the club clinch a top four spot and qualify for the lucrative Champions League. He finished the season with 12 goals from 43 appearances, a creditable return from a player who was predominantly a winger. The 2014-15 season proved even better with a 17-goal return from this emerging star. Not surprisingly, the English Premier League soon beckoned, and Son became the most expensive Asian player in football history when he signed for Tottenham Hotspur for £22 million in August 2015.

Son made his debut for Spurs on September 13th in an away game against Sunderland and was substituted after 63 minutes of the match. A few days later, in the first match of the Europa League campaign, he bagged a brace of goals, his first for the club, in a 3-1 win against Azerbaijan club Quarabag. His maiden Premier League goal came in Spurs' first home win of the season against Palace, when he scored the winner in the 68th minute. Another Son goal came in the 89th minute of a match against Watford, having come on as a late substitute for Tom Carroll. In May of that season, he scored the second goal in a vital match against Chelsea, a victory which would have given Spurs an outside chance of winning the Premier League title. Alas, it was not to be, as Chelsea equalised in the second half, the draw effectively killing off Spurs' title hopes. Leicester City subsequently clinched the title, with Spurs finishing in a disappointing third spot behind arch-rivals Arsenal.

Prior to the start of the 2016-17 season, Son had reportedly asked for a transfer in the hope of securing more playing time at a new club. He had played few games the previous season, most of which were from the subs bench and he felt he needed to make more progress. He was, however, persuaded by manager Mauricio Pochettino to stay on at Spurs and fight for his place, which he duly did with typical hard work and determination. His patience was rewarded when he, firstly, scored two goals and created a third in a 4-0 win against Stoke on September 16th and then followed this up with a double against Middlesbrough a fortnight later, earning his club a 2-1 victory at the Riverside Stadium. He continued his improved run of form when he scored his fifth goal in five games in a Champions League match against CSKA Moscow giving Spurs a 1-0 victory. For his efforts, Son was named September Player of the Month, making him the first Asian player to achieve the award.

March 2017 saw the likeable South Korean score his first Spurs hat-trick in a 6-0 FA Cup win against Millwall. Regrettably, the lad was racially abused by a section of the visiting fans, with chants of "DVD" whenever he touched the ball, in a pathetic and unkind reference to a certain East Asian stereotype. His good form continued over the season and by the end of April his goals tally of 18 in all competitions, including 11 in the Premier League, earned him a second Player of the Month award. He was the season's only dual winner of the accolade. His full season's tally of 21 goals in all competitions enabled him to emulate his more illustrious team-mates Harry Kane and Dele Alli, with the trio all scoring more than 20 goals apiece.

In November 2017, Son reached a significant milestone when, having notched up his 20th goal for Spurs, he became the top Asian goalscorer in Premier

League history. In January 2018 he had the distinction of scoring five times in consecutive home matches, a feat only previously achieved by Jermaine Defoe in 2004. More records followed as he ended the season in the top ten goalscorers, making him the first Asian player to accomplish this achievement.

At the start of the 2018-19 season, Son was rewarded with a contract extension which would keep him at Spurs until 2023. In February 2019, he was named Premier League Player of the Year at the London Football Awards. In the following April, Son scored three goals over the two Champions League quarter final legs against the mighty Manchester City. A 4-4 aggregate score enabled Spurs to triumph on the away goals rule and reach the semi-finals for only the second time in their history.

In October 2019, Son was named in the 20-man shortlist for the Ballon d'Or. His euphoria, however, was short-lived when, less than a fortnight later, after a collision with Everton's Andre Gomes, he was red-carded for dangerous play. Many who saw the incident felt the tackle was accidental, and that Son had been harshly treated. He was highly traumatised by the sending-off and his anguish was there for all to see. Happily, the club appealed against the three-match ban that was meted out to Son, and the FA upheld the appeal and the red card was finally rescinded. Three days after the incident, after Son had scored two goals in a Champions League match against Red Star Belgrade, in true character, he apologised on camera for what had happened against Everton.

In November 2019 Son scored his first goal under new manager José Mourinho in a 3-2 victory which earned him the Man of the Match. A month later Son scored a wonder goal against Burnley, when he ran virtually the full length of the pitch, leaving seven opposition players in his wake, before calmly slotting the ball into the net. Mourinho was so impressed by the feat that he compared him to the great Christian Ronaldo. Fine praise from a manager who doesn't dish out too many compliments! The goal was rightly chosen as the December goal of the month. It was also chosen by FIFA for the Puskas Award as the best goal in the prevailing 12-month period.

In February 2020, a two-goal haul against Villa thrust him once more into the spotlight, when he became the Premier League's first Asian player to score 50 goals. By the start of the 2020-21 season, Son's striking partnership with captain Harry Kane was taking on formidable proportions, with the duo rattling in the goals and providing numerous assists for each other. Early in the season Son scored four goals in a 5-2 victory over Southampton, with Kane providing assists for them all. He also scored two goals in a surprising 6-1 win against Man United at Old Trafford, picking up his third Player of the Month award in the process.

January 2021 saw the South Korean reach a century of goals for Spurs. As mentioned earlier, Son's highly productive partnership with Kane continued to flourish. Following a Son goal against Leeds in February 2022 assisted by Kane, the pair had astonishingly racked up 37 goals where either player had assisted the other – a new Premier League record. Just for good measure, Son also won the Premier League Golden Boot along with Mo Salah, both scoring 23 goals.

After seven seasons, his 93 goals from 232 appearances, along with his numerous assists, has been a significant contribution to the Tottenham cause. He can look forward to Champions League football in 2022-23 with supreme confidence.

On the International scene, Son has represented South Korea on 98 occasions, registering 31 goals for his country. His first appearance at senior level was prior to the 2011 AFC Asian Cup on December 30th in a friendly match against Syria. He scored his first international goal against India in the group stage of the tournament. He missed the first two matches of the 2014 World Cup qualifying phase with an ankle injury, but featured in later qualifiers against the UAE, Lebanon and Iran. He came on as a late substitute in a match against Qatar and scored the winning goal late into stoppage time. He was selected for the South Korea squad for the 2014 FIFA World Cup.

In June 2018, Son was selected in the squad for the World Cup. In the final group stage of the competition, he had the distinction of scoring in a 2-0 defeat of world champions Germany, which saw the Germans eliminated from the tournament. In the Asian Games of the same year, South Korea reached the final. After a goalless 90 minutes, they scored two goals in extra time and defeated Japan 2-1 to win the coveted gold medal, with Son playing a role in both goals. This was a significant victory for the South Korean players and not just in football terms. Normally, all able-bodied South Koreans must complete 21 months of military service as a deterrent against the North, but exemptions are offered to athletes who win gold at the Asian Games or a medal of any colour at the Olympics.

Son captained the national side in the 2019 Asian Cup, but the team were knocked out at the quarter-final stage against eventual winners Qatar.

Regarded as an icon in his native South Korea, Son's presence in the Premier League has been like a breath of fresh air. His exceptional pace, tireless work rate, goalscoring capability and generally pleasant approach to the game have made him one of football's most popular and admired players.

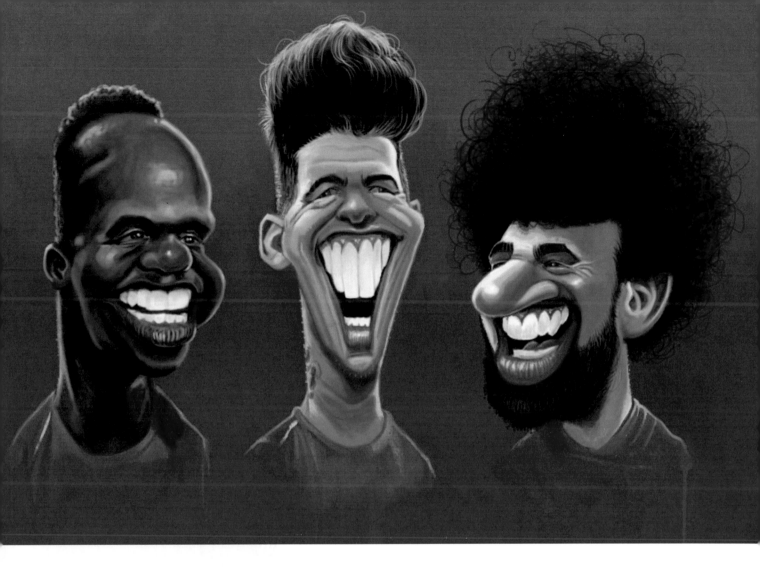

*"All for one and one for all, united
we stand divided we fall"*

(Alexandre Dumas, The Three Musketeers)

MOHAMMED SALAH

Mo Salah didn't arrive in Europe heralded as football's latest prodigy. His four or so seasons (two in Egypt and two in Switzerland with Basel) didn't at all serve warning of what was to eventually follow. Across north Africa and central Europe, 32 goals in 123 hardly had the scouts flocking to see the young Egyptian. Furthermore, given that he was playing in rather modest domestic leagues, it's difficult to cite age by way of mitigation.

One man who perhaps foresaw the player Salah was to become, was Egypt's American coach, Bob Bradley. He noted his explosive speed and intelligent play. Salah is also one of the game's great dribblers. Players who can meander in and out of opponents, particularly with the great influx of exotic foreign stars, are almost two a penny. What is very rare, is a player who can execute this skill at a rate of knots. The intricacy of Salah's footwork – the shoulder feints and stepovers – are in no way to the detriment of his speed; and close control is maintained throughout. This combination immediately puts defenders in a nightmarish predicament. If he doesn't leave them for dead, they're often foxed by the footwork and concede a penalty. Nothing beyond succinct description is required as regards his finishing. It's clinical and this is corroborated by his statistics.

One highlight of his Basel career was in the 2-1 away victory at Stamford Bridge during the Group Stage of the Champions League. Salah also scored the winning goal in the return leg, beating Chelsea 1-0. For the Chelsea management, this must undoubtedly have brought the superb winger into sharp focus. In January 2014, Chelsea announced they had signed Mohammed Salah for a reported £11 million. Salah was to wait more than six weeks for his first goal, as he scored in the 6-0 victory over London rivals Arsenal. Two weeks later, the Egyptian netted against Stoke City, also providing a goal assist and winning a penalty in the same game.

Premier League success had been a long time in coming for Salah, but his first experience of English football with Chelsea saw him enjoy precious little time on the pitch and he was well down the pecking order in the Stamford Bridge set-up.

Already dismayed at being overlooked for a berth in the Chelsea team, more disconcerting news came from Salah's homeland. He'd registered for an education scheme, but this was rescinded by the Minister of Higher Education. This meant that he faced the most unwelcome prospect of being drafted for military service. After meeting with then Egyptian Prime Minister Ibrahim Mahlab, he was spared this ordeal. It would've been a most damaging hiatus in the career of a young footballer yet to bloom.

The following season, things didn't auger well for the Egyptian, as he was criticised by manager José Mourinho. After two and a half years on the payroll at Chelsea, he had made a mere 13 appearances and scored only three league goals. It was no surprise that in January 2015, Salah joined Fiorentina on an 18-month loan deal. Salah's spell at Fiorentina was short and brief, making just 16 league appearances, scoring six goals. Fiorentina wanted to make the loan deal permanent; however, Salah rejected their offer. In the 2015-16 season, Salah joined fellow Italian club Roma on a season-long loan, with an option to make the deal permanent. The Egyptian started well in Italy, scoring against Sassuolo, Sampdoria and Carpi. He then added to his impressive early start with a goal against his former club Fiorentina.

Mo Salah, the 'Egyptian King', according to many around the world, has captured the attention of millions with his deadly pace and finishing. Having started his career with Egyptian club El Mokawloon, he'd certainly come an awful long way.

A year after his loan move to Roma, Salah agreed a permanent deal with the Italians. He scored some vital goals in wins over Sampdoria and Napoli, as well as scoring a hat-trick in the 3-0 victory over Bologna. Salah helped guide Roma to a very creditable 2nd in the Serie A.

In June 2017, he agreed a return to the English Premier League, joining Liverpool for a club record initial £36.5 million, with incremental rises taking it to £43 million. It's worth noting that Salah's initial fee exceeded the fee the club had paid for Andy Carroll by just £1.5 million. In terms of value for money, Salah was – almost immeasurably – better value for money.

Salah started with a bang, scoring on debut in the 3-3 draw against Watford. He also scored in their Champions League qualifier against Hoffenheim. Salah enjoyed a productive first month at Liverpool, with goals against Watford and Arsenal, before winning a player of the month award, as voted by Liverpool fans. Salah began scoring regularly, with goals against Chelsea, a double at Stoke, with him also netting against Bournemouth. He reached 20 goals in the top-flight in only 26 matches, second only to George Allen, who took just 19 matches. Salah scored 36 goals in the 2017-18 season.

Mo Salah's sublime strike in the Merseyside derby, at Anfield in 2017, saw him scoop the Puskas Award for the best goal in Europe for the calendar year. If his co-workers were the hod-carriers (admittedly rather good ones), then Salah showed himself to be master builder. Four players, four slick passes and then, well, just Mo Salah. Taking the final pass in his stride, he showed the strength and balance to withstand the interference of an Everton defender. Then, when approached by another, came a split-second of Egyptian twinkle-toes – as the blessed striker spun 180 degrees, rendering his Evertonian challenger instantly redundant. As a third defender contemplated a challenge, Salah had no time for bystanders and wasted no time in curling the ball into the top left of the Everton net, bringing the home crowd rapturously to its feet. Salah was beginning to garner quite a collection of accolades – winning the PFA Players' Player of the Year award, The Football Writers' Association Footballer of the Year Award, as well as being in the Premier League Team of the year. Similar approval was voiced by the paying public, as Salah added the PFA Fans Player of the Year Award – a prize he was to win again in 2021. The list goes on: Liverpool Players Player of the Year (2018, 2021); Liverpool Fans' Player of the Year (again, 2018, 2021) and African Footballer of the Year (2017, 2018).

Including his scorching form for Egypt, Salah posted a total of 44 goals for the season. Breaking these figures down to analyse his league form, his 32 goals in a 38-match season remains a Premier League record. Only Alan Shearer (34) can boast scoring more – but he did so in a 42-game season.

Not only did the Egyptian fly high in England, he also helped guide Liverpool past Manchester City in the Champions League quarter-final; followed by a brace against his former club Roma, on the path to the Champions League Final. However, the final didn't go according to plan as he got a shoulder injury and was forced off after 30 minutes. Liverpool ended up losing 3-1, unable to add to the five Champions League/European Cup titles.

Salah was less prolific the following season, conversely so – given Liverpool's march towards both domestic and European success. Despite a comparative lull in the scoring stakes, he was still very much at the core of Liverpool's international success. He provided a number of vital goal assists and was still, inexorably, reaching stardom. Being crowned champions of Europe, before winning the 2019 FIFA Club World Cup later that year, beating Brazilian champions Flamengo 1-0, was surely this team's apotheosis? Triumph in this curiously ignored game, to decide which team are the world's best, should not be dismissed. The Liverpool team of 1984, containing Kenny Dalglish and Ian Rush, could not overcome Argentina's Independiente.

Having conquered the world, 2019-20 saw Liverpool's gaze switch to winning the Premier League title. Liverpool didn't just win the Premier title, they roared towards the finishing line like a spanking new Bugatti – and then some! Like potassium hydroxide to animal tissue, any perception that Liverpool were involved in a title 'race' was dissolved lickety-split. By matchday nineteen, the midpoint of the season, Liverpool and Salah were already way in front of second-placed Leicester City, with their challengers facing an insuperable 13-point chasm.

As the club pulled away from their rivals, Salah and Liverpool hit significant milestones in a 2-1 victory over Bournemouth, on March 7th. This set a top-flight record of 22 consecutive home wins; and for the Egyptian himself, his 70th goal in 100 Premier League appearances. Not only is this an estimable goalscoring feat, it surpasses Fernando Torres's record (63) of the most goals scored in one's first 100 league games. Add to this information 31 goal-assists in his first three Premier League seasons, and you have a colossus of a footballer, one of incalculable value to his manager: the complete striker.

When Salah bears down on opponents, as he homes in on goal, serious and immediate danger also emanates from his partners-in-crime, Mane and Firmino. When the three combine, converging in front of goal, defenders must sense imminent peril – the surfer stricken by a Californian riptide.

In a season extended due to problems arising from the Covid pandemic, Liverpool edged close to claiming the title. On the 24th June, Salah was on target in a 4-0 routing of Crystal Palace. After the Premier League title was confirmed, Salah was to score a further two goals against Brighton.

Finally, after a humdinger of a win against Chelsea (5-3), he swelled the ranks of African footballers to hold aloft the Premier League Trophy. A list which now stands at 22 – reflecting the thoroughly cosmopolitan makeup of English football.

Liverpool opened the following season with another thrilling encounter. In a 4-3 win over Leeds United, Salah bagged a hat-trick, with two penalties and a goal from open play. October saw him reach 100 goals across all competitions, in a drawn (2-2) Merseyside derby. Although the club were unable to add to the previous season's silverware, Salah produced 22 Premier League goals and ably assisted his team-mates in scoring their goals.

In October 2021, both the BBC and the Premier League itself, voted Mo Salah's strike, scored in a 2-2 draw with Manchester City at Anfield, as their respective goal of the month winners. Let's be honest, there was absolutely no contest. Just because he isn't right in front of goal, it doesn't mean that there's no threat. Entering the fray just outside the right-hand corner of the box, Salah shimmied past four dumbfounded opponents, before slamming a low right-foot shot in off the left-hand post. This was only made more impressive by the fact that he finished from an acute angle – and with his weaker right foot. Oh, and I should mention the ability to maintain exquisite close control, whilst swiftly covering ground. At the time of writing, the season is two months from completion – but we're unlikely to witness a better goal than this one.

When it comes to individual awards, Mo Salah doesn't so much need a medal drawer as a French dresser. Collectively, he's both a European champion and a world champion. Throw in a League Cup and a UEFA Super Cup and he's doing better than most.

SADIO MANÉ

It would be lazy and, frankly, dull-as-ditchwater to describe Sadio Mané as a 'jack-of-all-trades'. Yes, he certainly has, pretty much, the whole spectrum of attributes a fan hopes to see in his or her team's players. Mane, however, is a veritable potpourri of footballing qualities – and is deserving of the description to match the joy with which he plays the game. This Senegalese wide man follows his brief with a passion and certainly seems to relish being out on the pitch.

As a young boy, his football prospects look rather inauspicious. His tyrannical father, who was an iman, forbid him from playing the sport. Once his father died, he was then able to pursue his dream of becoming a footballer. He left his home village at 15 and headed for the Senegalese capital of Dakar. Thankfully, his remaining family members were far more supportive of his ambitions.

If the name 'Sadio Mané' wasn't being lofted by media's aeolian already, it certainly gusted leeward towards the big clubs in May 2015. Playing for Southampton, Mané grabbed the Premier League's fastest ever hat-trick, as the Saints crushed Aston Villa 6-1. This eclipsed Robbie Fowler's record, which had stood for some 21 years.

Playing primarily as a wide-man (though frequently cutting into the middle) Mané has been a true marvel for Liverpool Football Club. He's essentially on the field of play to create chances for Mo Salah and Roberto Firmino, plus chip in with the odd goal himself. In that respect, he certainly hasn't disappointed. Aside from a slew of goal assists (50+), the former Southampton player has smashed 192 career goals, that's all competitions, in 454 matches; which is a capital return for a player who doesn't play as principal striker. An interesting Mané statistic concerns his physical stature. In the Premier League alone, 14 headed goals is impressively anomalous with his height – 5'9" (175 cm). Peter Crouch he definitely isn't. What's more unusual, is a record he holds to the great alarm of Crystal Palace supporters. In 2021, slightly bizarrely, he became the first Premier League player to score against the same opponents in nine consecutive matches.

The mere sight of him taking to the field must set Eagles' hearts aflutter!

Mané had to wait unit 2020 to be a Premier League winner – with the year before proving every bit as memorable. After the chastening Champions League defeat to Real Madrid in 2018 (in which he scored), he savoured victory in the following year's final. In a 2-0 victory over Spurs, Mané won a penalty – from which Mo Salah put the Reds in front. Back at home, he sparkled in the Premier League: 22 goals in 36 matches saw him share the Premier League Golden Boot 2019 with Salah and Arsenal's Pierre-Emerick Aubameyang. To reiterate, these figures from a player who mostly patrols the flank, must've been a real boon for manager Jurgen Klopp.

His efforts on the international stage are equally commendable – 29 goals in 89 internationals. Also, he recently struck his country's winning penalty, as they claimed their first ever African Cup of Nations crown. And in a competition bursting with Premier League talent and beyond, he was officially named player of the tournament.

Sadio Mané is someone who can leave you gasping for air merely seated in the stands. His whip-smart reading of the game, combined with his double-quick movement, enables him to dart past opponents and take up the most dangerous of positions. If that's not enough, his touch is usually immaculate and his trickery with the ball at his feet, dazzles the crowd and mystifies defenders. If you're propping up the rearguard, you better be on your mettle, as this player will fizz by you in an instant and probably destroy you.

Whether it be the sacrifice of lesser mortals before the Anfield altar, or the 5-0 Champions League blitzkrieg of Porto (where he helped himself to a blistering hat-trick) Mané is usually in the thick of it.

ROBERTO FIRMINO

Completing Liverpool's deadly alliance in attack is Brazilian international Roberto Firmino. Firmino first caught the eye playing for 1899 Hoffenheim (38 goals in 140 games) in Bundesliga 1. Having grown his reputation in one of Europe's toughest leagues, a move to Premier League Liverpool was a natural progression.

His first season was only moderately successful, and he finished as the club's top league scorer on ten goals. It was, without doubt, the arrival of Sadio Mané and Mo Salah, in 2016 and 2017 respectively, which enabled Firmino to elevate his game from the rather good to the outstanding. Individually, Firmino, Salah and Mané are proven in their own right – superior goods to those purchased by rival clubs; however, this irresistible trio didn't take long to coalesce. Playing in unison, they've proved to be the most potent attacking force the Premier League has seen in years.

Not dissimilar to Mané, Firmino must be applauded for the high quality of his all-round game. Like a full-bodied red, straight from the Aquitaine, Firmino is one of the most complete number 9s in Europe. Deployed as a centre-forward, he's found his natural home – after being tried as a 'false 9', out wide or breaking from the midfield.

There isn't anything lacking here. Technically proficient, Firmino's adroitness and vision enable him to tear defences apart, with an intelligent pass. At the heart of a threefold threat, Firmino is often the architect of a goalscoring opportunity for his colleagues.

This triple entente of Egypt, Brazil and Senegal aren't merely the scourge of Premier League defenders – they're an international terror and rightly feared across the continent. Woe betide any team who thinks otherwise. When swarming in on goal, they're pretty much unplayable. Surely that's how we prefer it? A strike force who can't simply be snuffed by the archetypal no-nonsense, burly centre-half, or your ever so reliable fullback. Normally dependable defenders, even venerated internationals no less, have been made to look like a bunch of ill-equipped clodhoppers, dredged from the foulest sediment of Sunday morning park football. But there's no shame to be had – for this is the best forward-line of three to have played in the English Premier League.

This superb trio's attacking flair and inherent understanding of each other's game, propelled Liverpool to the verge of a possible quadruple in the 2021-22 season. Having snapped up both domestic cups, their assault on the Premier League title was only thwarted by Man City in the final match of the season. In the Champions League final they succumbed 1-0 to a very strong Real Madrid team, who secured the club's 14th European League title – no less. Oh, what might have been for the Three Musketeers!

OTHER NOTABLE PLAYERS

The Premier League, unsparing, ruthless and sometimes heartless, in the way that it floods the imagination; it deluges our senses, phones, diaries and every conceivable place that we can possibly accrue knowledge of, possibly, the greatest league in the world. The very mention of the Premier League ignites passion – and rightly so. Every lifelong fan, every season-ticket holder, can name the best game they've ever seen; those words might come from the portly 52-year-old who bears his chest to the *Match of the Day* cameras **on** bleakest Teesside; maybe someone who's worked for £7.00 an hour putting aspirins in a blister-pack; it could be someone whose first game was only slightly post-war. As football fans, we need to come together and savour the things which brought us into the stadiums in the first place. The finest players we've seen trip off the tongue and the memory banks are stirred. Given five minutes, every self-respecting footie fan can name you the next England team. But players from abroad dominate every team-sheet. This shouldn't herald gloom; no pregnant clouds poised; there's no expectant catastrophe; we've seen some extravagantly talented players from every nation shower us – spoil us in fact – with their wares. Let us celebrate some of those players. From Chipping Sodbury in Gloucestershire, to the arid plains of Mozambique, we've embraced players who can thrill, tantalise and sometimes disappoint – welcome to the English Premier League.

A player who never failed to surprise was **Jay-Jay Okocha**. He seemed to have the low centre of gravity for which we remember Tom Finney. He could simply leave defenders and create opportunities when he'd appeared to be running into a cul-de-sac. He shimmied from defenders' clutches and, more often than not, provided a goalscoring opportunity. A sprightly bundle of energy who could illuminate any game. People want to pay money to see their team win. If they're entertained in the process, everyone is satisfied. Okocha didn't disappoint.

It's difficult to downsize the breadth of talent to play in our league. The one thing I can attempt to achieve as a writer is cross-section the players who've starred. There will, without question, be players missing from the compilation – such is the enormity of the task. So, with apologies in advance, here are some of the influential players we think deserve a mention. In no running order:

Peter Beardsley was the scourge of defences throughout his career. He played just behind a modern-day centre-forward and that made him incredibly difficult to mark. He found the room to press a back four already wrong-footed by his slightly unconventional positional play. He pressed, teased and downright tormented defenders. He was neither forward nor midfielder. He occupied spaces that defenders weren't trained to mark. The benefit of his nuisance play was to leave Gary Lineker unattended. Beardsley sometimes played Lineker in – but his chief purpose was to bombilate just outside the penalty-area.

Before he played with distinction for Newcastle United, Liverpool and Everton, he exemplified something which all would-be professional footballers undoubtedly need if they're to succeed: tenacity. Incredulously, he was rejected at trial stage by Cambridge United, Gillingham and Burnley. Even an apprenticeship in his native north-east, with Newcastle United, came to nothing. (He ironically returned to the club who'd rejected him in his youth, eventually becoming an idol of the Gallowgate End.) Even Manchester United – a club renowned for nurturing raw talent – didn't see fit to give him a crack in the first team. Still, Beardsley remained undeterred; his desire to play football saw him doggedly chase this dream. Maybe it was inevitable that a player brimming with ability would eventually be recognised? By the time he was winning his 59th England cap, the one-time coaches of Gillingham et al must've been kicking themselves! His perseverance was more than vindicated, insofar as he made 816 career appearances, scoring 237 goals.

He will, of course, be remembered as a player who could do just about everything – and do it with sheer class; and in his case, it emanated from innate natural ability, more than it did coaching. From his zestful play, it was clear that he loved his job; though it's doubtful defenders loved him. Dynamic and irrepressible – he was harder to get rid of than a bad dose of nits!

Beardsley's story is one of the happiest the English game has seen. Quite simply, he worshipped the game and saw his determination handsomely rewarded. Winston Churchill famously made the following observation: "Success is not final, failure is not fatal, it is the courage to continue that counts." That's Peter Beardsley.

In our recollections of those who've made the Premier League the eye-catching extravaganza that it is, we are understandably drawn to the creative forces, the goalscorers. We should also give consideration to those performing the less glamorous – but equally vital – roles. I can think of fewer better examples than **Henning Berg**. Strong and dependable, his mistakes were rendered more noticeable by their extreme rarity. His reading of the game was reflected in his astute positional play. If you were saddled with him as your marker, you were likely to be in for a quiet afternoon, thanks to this most reliable of chaperones. Whilst this type of player may not have you on the edge of your seat, aquiver and open-mouthed, he did his job effectively. His qualities didn't go unnoticed. In 1993, Kenny Dalglish shrewdly installed him at right-back for Blackburn Rovers, in the side which went on to claim the Premier League title in 1995; nor did it escape the attention of Alex Ferguson either, and the wily Scot signed him for Manchester United two years later. Ferguson wasn't an easy man to impress. A phone call from Fergie is the footballing equivalent of receiving Royal Assent.

The English Premier League has attracted many overseas players since its inception and Australia has provided some notable footballers over the years, **Mark Viduka** being a prime example. Viduka started his professional career down under with Melbourne Knights, a club which had strong ties to Croatia, having been called Melbourne Croatia up until the 1993 season. In his two seasons with the club, he was top scorer in the league and was twice awarded National Soccer League Player of the Year, known as the Johnny Warren Medal. His goal tally of 40 goals from 48 appearances is testimony to the goalscoring prowess of the big Aussie.

Although his time with the Knights was relatively brief, Viduka was greatly lauded by club and fans alike, to the extent that the club's main stand was renamed The Mark Viduka Stand in his honour. From there he moved to Croatia and spent three and a half seasons at the club now known as Dinamo Zagreb, helping them achieve a treble of league and cup doubles between 1996 and 1998. His contribution of 40 goals in 84 appearances added to his growing reputation as an effective striker.

In December 1998, Celtic paid £3.5m for his services and he scored a staggering 27 goals in his first full season at the club, picking up the Scottish Player of the Year in the process. He also helped Celtic to win the 1999-2000 Scottish League Cup.

After only one full season at Celtic Park, Viduka finally made it into the English Premier League, when he was signed prior to the start of the 2000-01 season by Leeds manager David O'Leary for £6m. A consistent goalscorer throughout his career, Viduka continued in that vein for his new club with a creditable 59 goals from 130 appearances during his four seasons at Leeds. In 2004, amidst the Yorkshire club's deepening financial crisis, he was sold to Middlesbrough, where he stayed until 2007 before moving on to Sam Allardyce's Newcastle United. His final season at Newcastle saw the club relegated from the Premiership, as the curtain also came down on Viduka's football career.

Viduka had the distinction of captaining the Australia national side to the Round of 16 at the 2006 FIFA World Cup, which remains their best-ever performance to date. For a big man with little pace, he was an extremely effective player. His strength and touch enabled him to score many goals, 202 in 409 league/cup matches and 11 in 43 international appearances. He was excellent at holding the ball up with defenders at his back and his ability to play in his team-mates produced many assists to add to his outstanding goal tally.

Since retiring from football, the player affectionately known as the V-Bomber by Australian fans, now runs a café in Croatia, the country of his heritage.

Another notable Aussie, **Tim Cahill**, proved to be the bargain of the season for David Moyes's Everton, when he joined the 'Toffees' from Millwall in 2004 for the modest sum of £1.45million. Although he had enjoyed a useful career at The Den, contributing 52 goals in 217 appearances, his finest moments were yet to come at Goodison in the Premier League.

A native of Sydney who, despite growing up in a largely Rugby League playing family, chose to play football instead and joined a local boys team to pursue his footballing ambitions. It was in 2007 that he made the move to England, joining Championship club Millwall on a free transfer. He subsequently made his debut against Bournemouth in May 1998. He was an integral part of the side which reached the 2004 FA Cup Final, scoring the winning goal against Sunderland in the semi-final. Although Millwall lost the final 3-0 to Manchester United, they had the consolation of securing a place in the UEFA Cup, now the Europa League.

At the start of the 2004-05 season, Cahill made the move to Everton and what a dream start the Aussie had at his new club. He ended the season as the club's leading goalscorer, and was also voted as the Player of the Season by the Everton fans, who incidentally had given him the nickname of Tiny Tim after the Dickens character. Actually, Cahill is 5'10" in height which is by no means tiny, and he certainly showed a strong presence in opposition penalty areas despite his physique. In a 226-match career with Everton, which spanned eight years, he scored 56 goals – no mean return for a midfield player. Many of his goals came from headers due to his prodigious ability to leap high, leaving opposing defenders aghast at being out-jumped by the smaller man. He often treated fans to his trademark goal celebration, in which he hilariously shadow-boxes with the corner flag, whilst holding his Everton shirt badge between his teeth.

Finally, the likeable Aussie has the distinction of being the all-time leading goalscorer for his country, having notched up 50 goals in his 108-match international career – a remarkable achievement and a fitting accolade for a truly great player.

Another popular import, **Willian** couldn't be described as a mercenary who breezed through the Premier League, picked up a hefty pay cheque or two and then swanned off to the Chinese Super League. He's ensconced himself at Stamford Bridge for the best years of his career. He managed a short spell with Arsenal in the 20-21 campaign, before making a nostalgic return to

Corinthians the following season where his footballing career began. Not a formidable physical presence, this Brazilian has other qualities. No issues with ball control, this sylph-like attacking midfielder will habitually dart into the spaces not occupied defensively. If you surrender possession just inside your own half, the last person you want to sweep up the ball is Willian. Affording this shock-haired waif the ball in such a position is as close to footballing suicide as you can get. Not a prolific scorer (though he has contributed) he's ever likely to open things up for a colleague. He's also been called upon by his country on 70 occasions to date; that statistic alone is testament to a bristling talent. The Brazilian national football team don't employ the feeble.

To conclude: a player with the physical prowess of a damaged swing, Willian compensated with a capricious flair and demonstrated the ability to overturn proceedings in seconds; his dynamic has undoubtedly contributed to many Chelsea successes.

Not all Premier League players are drafted in from abroad, for preposterous transfer fees – matched only in absurdity by their wages. Not all of them are romanced by big clubs at an age when they're still wearing short pants off the pitch as well as on it. For some footballers, stepping out onto the pitch at top-level, is the joyful culmination of an epic journey. Starting in the lower leagues – including those outside the football league – there are players who've trekked all the way up the English football pyramid to the land of milk and honey that is the Premier League. Unrelenting belief, punctilious professionalism and noticeable ability means such players are sometimes afforded the opportunity to try their hand at the highest level. Being a big noise in a small room and accustomed to small-scale localised celebrity is one thing, handling the international media glare of the Premier League is quite another. Equally, facing AFC Barrow on a Tuesday night, at a Holker Street cloaked in freezing fog – in front of a paltry 2000 people – is not what boyhood dreams are made of. So the chance to trot out before a pulsating full-house at Old Trafford, after years of stoic toil down the leagues, is just-reward for some stalwarts of the English Football League.

Brett Ormerod found himself in football oblivion after a failed apprenticeship with his hometown Blackburn Rovers. He then joined Accrington Stanley, playing semi-professionally. As this was well before Stanley's elevation to League Two, he had to take a job in a textile factory, reportedly earning a miserly £130 a week, to keep himself afloat. When he first netted for Southampton, he joined a small band of players who've scored goals in all of the top four English divisions.

Another member of this select group is Sheffield United's **Billy Sharp.** By the time Sharp reached his late twenties, he'd rattled in 110 career goals. Some of these goals came for Southampton, vitally helping the Saints return to the Premier League. At his peak, the free-scoring Yorkshireman must've felt that he'd made the best case he possibly could for a break at the higher level.

So when the south coast club began to farm him out on loan stints with Football League clubs, before eventually selling him to Leeds United, he would've felt aghast, dismayed and profoundly disappointed. The best possible response? – simply carry on doing your job with the same commitment and trademark proficiency; and that he certainly did. Brand Billy Sharp continued to be one of the best on the EFL market. When he returned to his home city for a third stint with Sheffield United, a glut of goals followed. This proved to be the platform for a second opportunity in the Premier League, but for a sustained period this time. He continues to play at this level at the time of writing.

The list of players who've worked the EFL, before being given a go in the Premier League, include **Dean Windass**. Windass started as a non-leaguer with North Ferriby United, before touring the EFL with a miscellany of clubs, interrupted only by a spell with Aberdeen in the Scottish Premier League. Any player who exceeds 200 career goals in the Football League and/or the Premier League must have some ability and Windass managed a commendable 225. He also holds the distinction of being the Premier League's second oldest ever goalscorer, behind Teddy Sheringham. When he equalised for Hull City to snatch a 2-2 draw at Portsmouth, he was the tender age of 39 years, seven months and 21 days old: a real testament to his professionalism and commitment; and playing second fiddle to Teddy Sheringham hardly carries shame!

He'll always meet with affection from Hull City fans. In their 104-year history the Humberside club had never hosted top-flight football. Windass changed all that when he lit up Wembley with a majestic volley from the edge of the Bristol City penalty area. Whilst the goal made it a red-letter day for The Tigers, it was also acclaimed for its superlative execution. With technique one might have thought to be beyond Windass, the Hull-born striker whacked a ball dropping from the heavens into the west country side's goal. A goal Cristiano Ronaldo would've been proud of.

Hull City Council have talked about a permanent tribute to Windass, responding to his cult status amongst fans and epithet 'club legend'. The player modestly played this down: "Nah, I'm not a legend. I don't like that word. People fight for their country, there are soldiers in Iraq. I'm just a footballer who gets paid a lot of money to do what I enjoy."

For someone who looks more like a builder or your on-call plumber, he's acquitted himself most creditably. Some might describe him as a 'journeyman'; maybe so, but a pretty decent one at that. 'Everyman' personified, it's hardly surprising that fans warmed to him.

It's hard to think of a successful team who haven't had a first-rate goalkeeper. Latterly Arsenal, but Chelsea for the most part, have been very well catered for in this respect. They don't, perhaps, get the attention that they deserve and are likely to remain in the shadow of their outfield comrades. One of the most accomplished goalkeepers to grace the Premier League is **Petr Cech**. In detailing the Czech international's qualities it's impossible to be concise and any attempt to be so would be disrespectful to him and his contribution to the Premier League. It's hard to know where to begin with his sundry attributes. At 6' 5", Cech towered above almost everyone else. He was also athletic and strong. His merits, though, certainly extended way beyond the purely physical. He also showed great leadership in marshalling the defenders before him. His concentration never seemed to waver and he usually handled crosses – aided by his stature – with little fuss. Great agility and excellent decision-making were also notable features of his play, and his reflexes were seldom found wanting. He also possessed a powerful kick and a strong distributive throw; the latter being a useful tool in precipitating swift Chelsea counter-attacks.

Of Cech's many attributes, surely the awesome courage he showed in the wake of serious, life-threatening injury stands out. When the knee of Reading's Stephen Hunt connected with his head in 2006, he suffered a depressed fracture of the skull. Disturbingly, doctors later confirmed that the collision almost cost him his life. He's since stated that he's no memory of the incident at all. The aftermath of such a shockingly dangerous incident would've seen some people crumble, quit their profession and follow a less hazardous career path. Undaunted, Cech played on – but with the precautionary measure of a rugby-style headguard. Refusing to be overwhelmed by trauma, he played on until 2019, finishing with 443 Premier League games under his belt.

Early in his Chelsea career, Blues fans were still very much enamoured with Carlo Cudicini – so the man brought in from Ligue 1's Rennes had it all to do, if he was to win the affection of Stamford Bridge's regulars. His blinding save at home to Tottenham certainly helped matters. Meeting a Simon Davies cross, Robbie Keane planted a firm header goalwards in what appeared to be a formality for the Spurs striker; not so. Cech's response was almost superhuman, leaping to tip the point-blank header over the crossbar. Expecting to see the ball flash past the goalkeeper, the Irishman could only look on with incredulity. This was an acute test of Cech's goalkeeping reactions, and he passed it with the utmost distinction. Although fans can recall singular moments of brilliance from the players they admire, consistency is surely the best way to cultivate veneration. Chelsea romped to their first Premier League title, amassing a then record 95 points. The aforementioned couldn't possibly have been achieved without the reliable and commanding role played by Petr Cech; and his record 24 clean sheets that season is a record which still stands 15 years later. In terms of sheer attainment at the highest possible level, Chelsea's UEFA Champions League title in 2012 is surely it. When evoking Chelsea's greatest games, their followers always reference their penalty shootout win over Bayern Munich. To have the destination of the European crown resting on a series of spot-kicks, is the most unpalatable scenario for any player. With tension reaching almost insufferable levels, Cech saved memorably from Ivica Olic and Bastian Schweinsteiger, before Didier Drogba sealed victory. As always, there when it mattered.

Cech's stable performances, peppered with moments of brilliance were deservedly rewarded. Multiple titles in the Premier League, FA and League cups underscore his English career; in Europe, he won both the UEFA Champions League and the UEFA Europa League.

Although there are even more decorated players in Premier League history, no player has broken more records than the Bohemian goalkeeper – which in itself is a record 27! This body of information is best abridged; highlights, though, include minutes played without conceding a league goal. He didn't wait until he came to England to start setting records. Whilst still in his homeland with Sparta Prague, he went a record 855 minutes without conceding. He eclipsed Peter Schmeichel's Premier League record by going 1,025 minutes with his goal intact. (Later to be beaten by Edwin van der Sar.) Along with Joe Hart, he's the only player to be awarded the FA Golden Glove on four occasions. He also boasts an unrivalled career total of 202 Premier League clean sheets. It's no wonder the Czech Republic capped him 124 times – another record, of course!

When England's King Edward I subjugated Wales in the 13th century, he buttressed his position by dotting the Welsh landscape with a series of fortified castles. At each one, every gateway was barred to the enemy by a sturdy portcullis; in other words, nothing or nobody was getting past it. This undoubtedly bred confidence amongst the king's minions therein. The Welsh weren't going to lie down and proved difficult to subdue. One generation passed to the next and, still there was considerable resistance. This metaphor can be extended to homage one of the best players we've seen. Whether you were manning a defensive line, or José Mourinho watching from the sidelines, Petr Cech was every bit as trustworthy.

He was the portcullis – and arguably the best the Premier League has ever seen.

Two players who have been at the very heart of the Premier League story are the **Neville brothers, Phil and Gary.** In terms of both players' chronologies, their development as players and success with Manchester United, runs parallel with the rise of the Premier League itself. Both are regarded as being part of the 'Class of 92' – a reference to the cornucopia of talent to emerge from the Manchester United stable at the start of the decade.

Right-back Gary was not in the same class as Roberto Carlos, Dani Alves or Javier Zanetti; nor was he as technically adept as his England left-back counterpart, Ashley Cole. His list of shortcomings continues, in that he wasn't well-built and powerful, or particularly quick either. He did, however, embody many of the attributes traditionally associated with a good full-back. He was supremely fit and had the stamina to endure 90 minutes and beyond. His judgement was rarely amiss and he didn't tend to get caught out of position. He was robust in the tackle and would remain toe-to-toe with his opponent throughout. He also had an important attacking dimension to his game and would, crucially, feed the ball to David Beckham further up the same flank. On occasions, he would overlap for a return pass, where he'd ably cross the ball in the danger areas. His tireless play reflected his strong work ethic – a principle he'd frequently – rather vociferously – share with team-mates. The sight of Gary Neville clapping and shouting – issuing a rallying cry to his colleagues – is an abiding Premier League image. His willingness to express an opinion did, on occasions, lead to contretemps with the opposing team. Above all, he was the proverbial 'safe pair of hands' and one of the most consistent performers the league has ever seen. He must also have been one of the first names on the England team – 85 times no less; in addition to a sterling 602 matches, in all competitions, for the Red Devils.

Younger brother Phil shared much of Gary's success and is also ascribed membership of the 'Class of 92'. In terms of his style, like his brother, he wasn't blessed with extraordinary pace or skill; however, again like Gary, he was a reliable 8/9 out of 10 in most other areas of play. In terms of his usefulness to a manager, he was rather useful indeed. He could be deployed at either right-back or in midfield and function most efficiently in both – though he did mainly feature at full-back. A succession of England managers also recognised his worth as a utility player – giving rise to an impressive 59 England caps.

Though Phil Neville's Premier League career was almost equally divided between Manchester United and Everton, he was in Manchester long enough to amass an enviable collection of trophies and medals; though Gary's tenure was much longer and he garnered even more! Including both domestic cup competitions, the Champions League and the Premier League itself, the Neville brothers have a staggering 34 titles between them. Gary leads with 20, whilst Phil still has an admirable 14. If you happen to drop by for a cuppa with either brother, and hear the words "let me show you my medals", notify loved ones that you'll be home a little late – because you'll be in for the long haul and several more cups of tea!

Although we marvel at stars from afar, commentators often bemoan the fact that the Premier League is top-heavy with a surfeit of non-Brits. The Nevilles are clear proof that we can – and should – encourage the development of home-grown talent.

Jermain Defoe is a great example of how British talent can flourish in the Premier League. Aside from his obvious talent, it appears that his 'upbringing' as a young footballer has had a positive bearing on his development. He began by simply playing five-a-side football, before joining a well-respected London Sunday league side called Senrab. Senrab have a reputation for providing a springboard for players to go on to greater things. Former players include Lee Bowyer, Ledley King, John Terry and Ashley Cole. Clearly not a bad place to cut your teeth! At the age of 14, he spent valuable time

at the FA National School of Excellence at Lilleshall in Shropshire. This was supplemented by a youth career at Charlton Athletic and West Ham United. At West Ham, his prospects were further aided by the excellent football management of Harry Redknapp. Redknapp knew that Defoe had real potential, but didn't think he was quite ready for the febrile cauldron that is Premier League football. Instead, he prudently sent him on a near season-long loan to third tier AFC Bournemouth, to gain some experience of first team football. This decision proved to be most judicious and inspired, with Defoe plundering 19 goals in 31 matches for The Cherries. In so doing, he equalled a post-war record of scoring ten goals in ten consecutive matches, which he now holds jointly with Clarrie Jordan and John Aldridge. To do this at just 18 is supercalifragilisticexpialidocious!!

When he returned to West Ham, he demonstrated that he was well capable of scoring at the highest level. Whilst never as prolific as someone such as Alan Shearer, he was never far away from the goals either. West Ham, Portsmouth, Tottenham Hotspur thrice, Sunderland and Bournemouth again, have all been beneficiaries of Defoe's prowess in front of goal; 298 goals in 735 league and cup appearances is some achievement. Perhaps more praiseworthy, this includes 162 Premier League goals – placing him 8th on the all-time Premier League goalscorers list. He's also one of only five players to score five goals in one game in this league. This came about in Tottenham's remarkable 9-1 dismantling of Wigan Athletic at White Hart Lane in 2009. As Spurs cut the Latics to ribbons, Defoe smashed the second fastest hat-trick in the league's history – requiring just seven minutes to complete this stunning feat.

Defoe's game is based upon his pace, technique and composure in front of goal. A key constituent to good forward players is having the right temperament; to remain unflustered at the vital moment – namely one-on-one with the goalkeeper. Defoe certainly possessed this quality. At times, he finished with a nonchalance more akin to a training ground exercise. Like all strikers some of his goals were clinical and unadorned – bearing down on goal, before the sliding of the ball past the advancing keeper. Sometimes, however, he would surprise the goalkeeper by striking the ball early, finishing with an audacious flick or chip. He was a team player, and this is illustrated by the good number of assists that he has to his name. Defoe has also won 57 England caps, scoring for his country on 20 occasions. This record alone attests to his talent.

Defoe retired in 2022 at the ripe old age of 37. Having seen many of his generation hang up their boots at an earlier age, Defoe's longevity appears to owe much to his salubrious living. A devout and practising Roman Catholic, he follows a vegan diet and is teetotal. Still running into the channels as though he's ten years younger, there can be little doubt that his measured lifestyle has enabled him to extend his career beyond that of his peers.

Whilst at Sunderland, he became friends with six-year-old fan Bradley Lowery, who was terminally ill. When Bradley was named 'Child of Courage' at Pride of North East Awards, Defoe attended with him. He has since been awarded the Order of the British Empire (OBE), for his work with vulnerable children, through the Jermain Defoe Foundation.

The Premier League has both shaped and rewarded Jermain Defoe. He reciprocates this benevolence by entertaining fans on the pitch, and serving his community off it.

"Why should I subdue the world, if I can enchant it." These profound words can be found on the website of **Mesut Ozil**; they neatly sum up the philosophy of this gifted footballer's attitude to life in general and football in particular.

Ozil is a third generation Turkish-German born player who started his

senior career in 2006 at his hometown club Schalke 04 in the Bundesliga. His supreme technical ability, creative skill and stylish qualities quickly became evident and, after a two-season stint at the club, he moved on to join Werder Bremen for a fee of €5m. His sublime ball control and passing ability enabled him to create numerous goal assists for his team, and his record 25 assists in European and domestic games during his final season with Bremen was testimony to these qualities.

European giants Real Madrid were next to acquire the services of the attacking midfielder for a fee of €15m. He was soon rubbing shoulders with the likes of Kaka, Ronaldo and Benzema. He clearly relished playing in such exalted company and settled instantly at his new Bernabeu home. His first season saw him collect a Copa del Rey winners' medal, and the following season he contributed 17 assists, as Real collected the La Liga title. Ozil was fast becoming the club's main playmaker under then manager José Mourinho and his outstanding performances were recognised in his inclusion on that season's short-list for the coveted FIFA Ballon d'Or.

Undaunted by the arrival of Luka Modric at the start of the 2012-13 season, he continued his good form with a staggering 26 assists, more than any other La Liga player.

Arsène Wenger had been coveting Ozil's play-making qualities for some time and eventually persuaded the German to sign for The Gunners in September 2013. The fee of €50m made him the most expensive-ever German player at the time. In his time with Arsenal he has picked up three FA Cup winners' medals but the Premier League title has eluded him, with United, City and Chelsea largely dominating proceedings.

In recent seasons with Arsenal, a few of his harshest critics have suggested that he occasionally "goes missing" in key matches and appears to be disinterested in proceedings. His reluctance to chase back to help his under-pressure defensive colleagues has long been an issue for Gunners' managers.

As mentioned earlier, his supreme technical ability has impressed football fans of all persuasions. One feature of his repertoire has been regularly highlighted by football pundits, namely, in one-to-ones with opposing keepers, he has become adept at 'dinking' the ball over them and into the net. It appears at first glance that he chips the on-rushing keeper, yet he actually hits the ball into the turf making it bounce up and over the keeper into the empty net. Notable instances where he has done this were against Burnley, Bournemouth and Liverpool. This feature of his technique is much easier to spot on action replays.

Granted he may have a few critics, but this truly gifted footballer has enhanced the Premier League for many years now. He is not about to let us forget his career statistics either! His website includes a running count of all his stats under a 'My Facts' section. At the time of writing his latest tally reads as follows:

Games 537   **Assists 209**   **Goals 96**

Passes 23846   **Passing accuracy 86%**   **Minutes played 40584**

Res ipsa loquitur, the facts speak for themselves!

Michael Owen sits proudly in the Premier League's top 10 all-time leading scorers – 150 goals in 326 league games is what every manager looks for in his centre-forward. He had pretty much the full complement of required assets. Firstly, he was quick to sense an opportunity, secondly he had the swiftness and agility to simply take him away from defences. The Argentine defence circa France '98 will certainly testify to this! Thirdly, his ability to crash the ball home with accuracy – and power when needed – was there for all to see. And, most surprisingly, his heading ability was completely at odds with his diminutive stature. He also had the vision to link up with others in building an attack.

Although he scored freely in the league, in the minds of English football lovers, he's ultimately defined by his iconic goal against Argentina in the French World Cup of 1998. With the score at 1-1, David Beckham knocks the ball into Owen's path. Still lying pretty deep, he skips past the first opponent. Already, the Argentine defence begin to retreat, terrified by his electrifying pace and movement. He then effortlessly slalomed past another defender and, from just inside the penalty area, lashes the ball into the top left-hand corner. What makes this goal all the more remarkable is that he was 18 years-old – barely a man – and up against seasoned world-class defenders. He made them look like both dummies as fools, and dummies as manikins; statuesque and powerless to intervene. After the World Cup, he went on to score with pleasing abandon in the Premier League; however, despite this, the goal against the nation's Argentine nemesis is, immutably, 'Michael Owen'.

Having set the bar so high in the spectacle of a World Cup, he'd quite a bit to live up to. He didn't disappoint. His wicked speed and ice-cool finishing proved to be the undoing of many a defence. The bane of every centre-half, Owen's masterly performances saw him become the first British player to win the Ballon d'Or award (European Footballer of the Year) since Kevin Keegan, way back in 1979. Furthermore, the expert clinician was much coveted and Real Madrid made him an offer which he evidently couldn't refuse. It should also be noted that Owen's breathtaking bow on the world stage was no one-off. He went on to score 40 international goals in 89 games. Like his impressive Premier League record, this statistic underlines his standing as one of the world's best centre-forwards of his generation; say no more.

As Premier League strikers go, there was only one name on everyone's lips at the dawn of the new millennium: Sunderland's **Kevin Phillips**. Having blasted 60 goals in two Championship seasons, as The Black Cats romped to promotion, he then had to prove that he could cope in the big league. Oh he coped alright – it was the opposition defenders who couldn't. For the duration of the 1999-2000 season, he was absolutely lethal and almost unplayable. Thirty goals in 36 Premier League matches was almost beyond belief – especially in his debut season at top-level and for a side with, at best, distinctly middling prospects. This unlikely profusion of

goals saw Phillips land the prestigious European Golden Boot. He still remains the only Brit to achieve this in the Premier League era and the first to do so in the English top division since Ian Rush in 1984. Deadly though he was, his success owed something to his foil, Niall Quinn. This symbiotic relationship saw Quinn occupy centre-halves with his considerable frame and all-round awkwardness, with Phillips snapping up his knockdowns and lay-offs with aplomb, before unerringly dispatching them. It also gave Quinn an Indian summer to a flagging top-flight career. Recognised at international level eight times, Phillips might well have been given more opportunities, if it weren't for the pre-eminence of Alan Shearer. A goalscorers' goalscorer, he ended his career with a highly commendable 282 goals in 660 games. And it's always pleasing to see a player bridge the sizeable gulf in class between the English Football League and the Premier League.

Joe Cole was a joy to watch when he was on song. He was often the sunbeam to brighten the drabbest of English afternoons, due to his abundant skill and mercurial influence on a game. He was a product of the highly regarded West Ham United youth system which, in roughly the same era, brought us

Michael Carrick and Frank Lampard. By the time he reached his mid-teens, he was already considered to be the most exciting prospect of his generation. The media's rumourmongers even talked of Manchester United being willing to part with ten million pounds to whisk him north. In the late 1990s, that would've been a fee of cosmic proportions for a boy just 16 years of age. Cole reinforced his reputation, playing a central role in the Hammers' 1999 FA Youth Cup triumph.

After more than a century of Premier League matches in claret and blue, it was clear that his sparkling talent demanded a bigger stage – certainly if he was to scoop any of the game's honours. Any dream of trophies and medals was realized aplenty at Chelsea: three Premier League titles, two FA Cups, one League Cup and an FA Community Shield amount to a haul few players can match. Cole moved to Liverpool in 2010 – a move which proved to be less than inspired. In two-and-a-half years, he managed just 26 league games for the Merseysiders and won absolutely no silverware as his career effectively flatlined. His career waned to such an extent that he was even allowed to go on a season-long loan to French champions Lille. His career petered out with low-key spells at Aston Villa, West Ham again, Coventry City and across the Atlantic with Tampa Bay Rowdies.

Joe Cole had the ability to change a game in a flash. He could vacillate between sitting on the fringes of a game and then, most suddenly, skilfully dribble past opponents to provide a team-mate with opportunity to score. He was strong, fleet of foot and had the football intelligence to cleverly unpick a defence with the cleverest of passes. Whilst his vision and passing made him a creative force, his technical ability gave him versatility. Whether as an attacking midfielder, second striker or a winger, this gifted central Londoner was always able to affect play and win games. Steven Gerrard is alleged to have said that he felt Cole's technical ability was equal to that of Lionel Messi, and Pele has gone on record saying that Cole was blessed with the dribbling skills of a Brazilian; you can't be given stronger references than that!

Joe Cole's career was effectively over not long after he signed for Liverpool; everything thereafter was largely inconsequential. It's been suggested by some that the bloom of youth remained unfulfilled potential here. That seems rather harsh – given that his career was bedevilled by injury.

He represented his country on 56 occasions and has a raft of medals from his time at Chelsea. That is not, by definition, failure.

In a career spanning the former Second Division, old First Division and the newly configured Premier League, **Ian Wright** was on the scoresheet no fewer than 324 times in 626 matches. This includes 113 goals in 213 Premier League games. Whichever way the figures are broken down, they tell us, unequivocally so, that Wright enjoyed a very distinguished career as a centre-forward.

His start in start in life was unpropitious to say the least. He endured a troubled childhood and lived in poverty right through to early married life. He even spent a fortnight in Chelmsford Prison for non-payment of fines for driving offences. It was during his incarceration that he steeled himself and vowed to make the grade as a professional footballer.

Failed trials at Southend United and Brighton and Hove Albion did nothing to dampen Wright's enthusiasm. After playing Sunday league football, he joined Greenwich Borough as a semi-pro. His £30 match fees did little to alleviate his financial hardship. After being scouted by Crystal Palace, he impressed manager Steve Coppell and signed for the South London club. Despite his late entry into the professional game at nearly 22, his career quickly accelerated. His goals propelled

Palace into the First Division. His star was rising and he further enhanced his reputation in the 1990 FA Cup Final. He came off the substitutes' bench to equalize impressively. A meandering run saw him skilfully take out two United defenders and coolly slot past Jim Leighton – 2-2. Although he then volleyed Palace ahead, it was not to be for Wright and Palace. United grabbed a late leveller and took the subsequent replay 1-0. After just over two seasons at Palace, Arsenal forked out a club-record £2.25 million to take him over the Thames.

At Highbury Wright was obviously in the midst of better quality players and his goalscoring potential came to fruition. The sight of him bursting beyond defenders, to crown Arsenal's intricate approach-play, became happily familiar to Gunners' fans. After exchanging umpteen passes, such florid build-up required a marksman who could unceremoniously bang the ball home; and that was Ian Wright all over.

In the same team as Viera, Petit and Bergkamp, Wright was part of Arsène Wenger's emerging force in the late 1990s, playing his part when Arsenal seized the Premier League and FA cup double in 1998. Equally effervescent both on the pitch and off it as a BBC Sport regular, 'Wrighty' remains a popular figure to this day.

Although Liverpool took until 2019-20 to collect their first Premier League title, playing for the Anfield club is still regarded as very prestigious indeed. You don't get to play for the six-times European champions if you're not at a certain benchmark; Liverpool supporters will only suffer fools for a finite period. **Sami Hyppia**, captain of Finland, earned the privilege of donning the Liverpool shirt a distinguished 464 times – surely the hallmark of excellence.

Hyppia was strong, a very good reader of play and more than competent on the ball as a defender. Known to be a quiet and controlled man off the field, his calm and temperate nature also served him well on it – yet he still showed real authority.

He formed a sure-footed partnership with Stephane Henchoz in the early 2000s. The duo laid the foundation for Liverpool's treble of the FA Cup, League Cup and the UEFA Cup in 2001. Their presence was also a major factor in Liverpool's second-placed finish the following season. Towards the middle of the decade, Hyppia was to form another winning partnership – this time in tandem with Jamie Carragher. Without them, it's highly unlikely that they would've lifted the Champions League trophy in 2005. It's also no coincidence that Liverpool conceded a niggardly 25 goals the following season. This still stands as a club record in the Premier League era.

His final Liverpool game came in a 3-1 victory. When he came on as a late substitute for Steven Gerrard, the Liverpool skipper passed him the captain's armband – though it was by no means the first time he'd worn it. At the end of the match, he received a standing ovation as the players held him aloft. It wouldn't be overly magnanimous to describe him as a 'club legend', not at all.

One of the most respected figures of the Premier League years thus far is **Edward 'Teddy' Sheringham**; in fact, he's respected throughout football full-stop. Anyone with a penchant for statistics can't fail to be impressed by those of Teddy Sheringham. Playing in three different decades, he delighted in a career which lasted a quarter of a century. So for those who feel a frisson in the presence of numbers, Teddy's career statistics will make their bow-ties spin and spin. In a prodigious 926 league and cup games, Sheringham made the scoresheet 361 times – and very few players make the '300 club' – irrespective of which division they play in. Crunching the numbers, this included 146 goals in 418 Premier League matches. Over his career, he played in all of the top four English divisions and even experienced the anonymity of Swedish football's fourth tier – not altogether promising!

He rose to prominence at Millwall, where his formidable partnership with Tony Cascarino was simply too much for Second Division defences. Although Millwall's 1988 title and promotion gave him top-flight football, Millwall's team wasn't good enough overall and they were back in the Second Division after two seasons. The 1990-91 season saw Sheringham thrash 33 goals in 46 games. With goals aplenty, it was obvious that Sheringham was far too good for second tier football; Brian Clough thought so and took him to Nottingham Forest. After little more than a year in the East Midlands, the London-born forward was headed back to his home city to join Tottenham Hotspur. It was now that he entered his heyday. His debut season at White Hart Lane saw a sudden blooming of his talents and he scooped the Premier League Golden Boot. Seventy-five goals later, 'Sherry' was invited to the very top table when he signed for Manchester United. Unusually, he'd reached his early thirties without winning any major honours. His decision to move north proved most astute. Domestically, he won three Premier League titles, an FA Cup and the FA Charity Shield. In the Champions League Final, his injury time equaliser as United pipped Bayern Munich at the death, is forever seared into the Manchester United psyche.

Although Sheringham and United won the treble that season, his pinnacle as an individual came in the 2000-01 season. To be voted PFA Players' Player of the Year alone is kudos indeed; but to be named Football Writers' Association Footballer of the Year in the very same season is some endorsement.

Internationally, Sheringham linked up superbly with Alan Shearer. This pairing is well remembered for a brace apiece, when England thrashed highly-rated Holland 4-1 at Euro '96.

It's often noted that Sheringham thrived at the highest level in spite of an alarming lack of pace. It wasn't merely a case of him not being as quick as the quickest – he was distinctly slower than the majority. However, playing mostly as a second striker, his many-faceted game did more than just keep him afloat. With a real football intelligence, his vision allowed him to be a prolific creative influence. With appreciable core strength, Sheringham often stood his ground, back to goal, feeding his co-striker with clever, short passes. As support striker, his perspicacious play resulted in an impressive 76 goal-assists. He was also very proficient in the air. His raft of skills gave him the versatility to play both as an out-and-out centre forward, or sit behind the main striker and orchestrate support play.

His later career saw him revisit Spurs and also represent Portsmouth, West Ham United and Colchester United. Whilst at West Ham, he became the Premier League's oldest ever outfield player. At 41 years and five months old, it's a distinction he holds to this day.

Setting aside his sluggardly movement, Sheringham had every other attribute one could wish for and that is why he could affect matches. Not many players could match his razor-sharp thinking; every team needs a Teddy Sheringham.

Though ephemeral, the 2015-16 season saw a thoroughly unexpected and absolutely seismic shift in hierarchy, as Leicester City drove a coach and horses through the Premier League power base. Along with Jamie Vardy and N'Golo Kante, **Riyad Mahrez** was at the very epicentre of a truly cataclysmic season.

The arrival of Algerian playmaker Mahrez was somewhat fortuitous. Leicester City scout Steve Walsh travelled to France to watch Ryan Mendes play for Ligue 2 outfit Le Havre. Instead, he was mightily impressed by Mahrez. Before he was whisked to the King Power, Mahrez had never heard of Leicester City and presumed them to be a rugby club! Fortune favoured Leicester for a second time, when Mahrez resisted pressure from both family and friends to opt for a club in Spain. They were concerned that the physicality of the Premier League would stymie his particular style of play. This proved to be wildly inaccurate as Mahrez gradually grew into English football. It may have helped that he was able to settle into English life out of the main spotlight, in the Championship.

As Leicester clinched promotion he then had to acclimatize to the rarefied atmosphere of the English Premier League.

But he only needed one season; in 2015-16, Riyad Mahrez simply caught fire.

All of his countless attributes made him the scourge of Premier League defenders. Mahrez is really the proverbial box of tricks; and like many players of that ilk, he's not particularly noted for his defensive abilities or work-rate and he is no tactician. Going forward, though, Mahrez is truly menacing. Naturally left-footed, he tends to play on the right, enabling him to cut inside and strike with his stronger foot. Good balance and flawless technique are pretty good foundations for any player's game – and Mahrez boasts both. Playing purely on instinct, his precipitous bursts of pace would often leave defenders trailing, or rooted to the spot and wondering what the hell had just happened. If that's not sounding dangerous enough already, throw in his mesmerising ball skills; his trickery and flair bewilders opponents – either taking him past them or inviting a desperate foul. And opponents aren't helped by the fact that he can dribble with both feet! He's also well capable of pinching a goal, from both open play and set-pieces. On his day, this sprightly, nimble-witted Algerian can take out an entire defence with one killer ball.

Of his own strikes, his goal in Leicester City's 2-1 victory over Chelsea, at the King Power, is more than noteworthy. As a lofted through-ball sailed into the Chelsea penalty area, Mahrez took up his position on the far right-hand side, level with the six-yard box. Cesar Azpilicueta, arguably one of the best defenders in the world, was on to deal with the situation. I don't think he'd reckoned for the Leicester man's exquisite touch. The way he controlled the flighted pass with his right foot was truly delicious. A lightning shimmy as Mahrez moved the ball to his left – and the Spaniard didn't know what day it was. With Azpilicueta turned well and truly inside out, Mahrez crashed his shot into the left-hand corner.

This goal typifies the Algerian's style of play and was a salient feature of Leicester's season as a whole. Though not the only stellar Foxes performer in 2015-16, their unlikely title triumph could not have been achieved without his abundant creative flair and 17 goals to boot. At the end of the season, he was deservedly named PFA Players' Player of the Year.

Having won the title in England's top two divisions, he needed to move to a bigger club if his acquisition of honours was to become habitual. A move to Manchester City has provided exactly that. Thus far, his appearances in sky blue have landed him another three Premier League titles, an FA Cup, three League Cups and the FA Community Shield. Internationally, he also helped Algeria win the African Cup of Nations in 2019.

When people pay sizeable sums of money to watch football, they want to be enthralled – and this is an emotion which Riyad Mahrez can most definitely pique.

In a country obsessed with cuisine, 'build your own sandwich' shops are up-to-the-minute and trendy. Though abstract and hypothetical, imagine if you could take the very same principle and apply it to footballers. Imagine if you wanted to build the complete centre-forward. In constructing your composite striker, you would want to incorporate a range of integral qualities. Alternatively, however, you could save yourself the bother, and just buy **Ruud van Nistelrooy**. That's what Alex Ferguson did, when he took him from PSV Eindhoven (where he'd averaged virtually a goal a game) to Manchester United.

Firstly, the Dutchman showed excellent positional sense – whether that be in escaping his marker, beating the offside trap or finding space in the box when there was none. His ability to be in the right place at the right moment was furthered by pace as well as intelligence. He was almost invariably on hand to capitalise on an opportunity; and his ability to head the ball and strike with both feet rendered him the most deadly of clinicians in front of goal. As a player of considerable strength, he would usually convert chances most forcibly. Whilst scoring goals was his stock-in-trade, his physical prowess enabled him to retain possession and create opportunities for others.

When van Nistelrooy crossed the English Channel, sighs of relief must've swept through the Dutch Eredivisie and its centre-halves. But could he replicate his prolific strike-rate in the harsher environs of the English Premier League? Well, although not quite matching his slew of goals in the Netherlands, 95 goals in 150 Premier League games is no mean feat; defenders had every reason to fear the man from the curiously named Dutch city of Oss.

Of course, if you played for Manchester United under Alex Ferguson, you found yourself quickly wreathed with honours. In just five seasons van Nistelrooy collected the Premier League title, the FA Cup, the Football League Cup and the FA Community Shield. In 2002, he was named PFA Players' Player of the Year, and 25 goals gave him the Premier League Golden Boot a year later. It's also worth noting that, in United colours, he was Champions League top scorer on three occasions. He was even Sir Matt Busby Player of the Year twice and similarly recognised with the fans' award. So much was achieved in only half a decade. Sadly for the club, they were unable to prevent him leaving for Real Madrid.

Ruud van Nistelrooy had the complete skillset, lacked absolutely nothing and was the bane of many a central defender.

All great teams need a watertight defence and a potent forward line; but in between the two must be a source of creative flair – one which can unhinge the tightest of defensive lines. A player who did this – and repeatedly so – was **Cesc Fabregas**. Ryan Giggs holds the record for the most assists leading to a goal in Premier League history, with 162. Fabregas is placed second with 111. Most tellingly, it should be noted that Giggs required a whopping 672 matches to achieve his record, whereas Fabregas took just 350. Mathematical gymnastics aren't needed to see that Fabregas's assists to games ratio is actually superior to that of the Welsh superstar. Just for the statistically minded, Giggs provided an assist every 4.14 games; Fabregas every 3.15. This statistic alone places the Spanish playmaker in the very upper echelons of Premier League players since its birth in 1992 – never mind just midfielders.

To be classed in the very top bracket of Premier League superstars, one must possess a raft of qualities. Fabregas most certainly didn't have the full gamut. An absence of pace, stamina and athleticism was noted at the very outset of his Arsenal career – and defensive duty was his bête noire. In reference to his lightweight frame, team-mate Ashley Cole even described him as an 'unproven featherweight'.

Fabregas was, however, in certain respects, simply better than pretty much everybody else. Flawless technique, occasioning faultless ball control, gave him the platform to menace opponents with his bewildering vision and passing. With a natural ability in finding time and space, he was frequently the architect of successful offensives. He was also proficient in taking corners, free-kicks and penalties.

The only slight disappointment to his time in England, with Arsenal and Chelsea (punctuated by a spell with Barcelona), is that there are lesser gifted players who are decorated with more honours. These two spells saw him win two Premier League titles, two FA Cups, one League Cup and one FA Community Shield. He was also part of the Arsenal team who reached the

2005 Champions League Final – coming distressingly close to winning it. On the individual front, he was named PFA Young Player of the Year in 2008. He also holds the distinction of being Arsenal's youngest ever goalscorer. In October 2003, he struck against Rotherham United in the League Cup, a still adolescent 16 years and 177 days old.

If the Spaniard underachieved a little at club level, he assuaged this disappointment playing for his country, during a period of dizzying success. Twice winning the European Championships, this was bettered only by them reaching the glorious apex of winning the 2010 World Cup. And for Fabregas to win 110 Spanish caps, at a time when the nation's squad was bursting with the world's finest players, is as great a testament to his talents as any of his winners' medals.

Cesc Fabregas: one of the most accomplished players ever to grace the Premier League.

Every football supporter, of course, wants to be captivated and bewitched by mind-boggling skill and remarkable goalscoring feats et cetera. Whether it be David Beckham or Zinedine Zidane, it's inevitable that we latch onto players with the greatest ability and a swagger and exuberance to match. Though sometimes bordering on the vainglorious, these are the players who hold court with fans and are equally alluring to the media. When eulogising about certain figures – Tom Finney, George Best or Lionel Messi – it's often said that the player in question can win a game all on their own. This, upon closer inspection, is a cliché; and not literally true. A player can be head-and-shoulders above every other player on the pitch, but their skills can only come to bear if they've a decent platform to build on – both defensively and in the middle of the park.

On a steam train, the driver is the person who receives the most attention and adulation; but the train can't operate without the largely unnoticed fireman, who regulates steam pressure in the boiler by putting the right amount of coal into the firebox. Football's a bit like that – somebody has to run, tackle, fetch and carry.

Two players who've done just that – and done so for many years – are **Gareth Barry and James Milner.** Not only that, they've both demonstrated admirable versatility. Barry has performed adeptly in a variety of defensive and midfield roles – and even as a left winger, whilst Milner has done likewise as a full-back, in defensive, central and attacking midfield roles and also on either wing. Neither of them would leave onlookers drooling or star-struck, but the necessity for such players is borne out by the sheer number of times they stepped out onto Premier League turf. Their combined appearances are millennial (Barry a Premier League record of 653; Milner 538). Unlike the recently retired Barry, Milner is still playing at the top level, so surpassing his former England colleague is a strong possibility. The value of reliable utility players is also reflected by the fact that Barry and Milner have garnered 53 and 61 England caps respectively; both valued by several England managers and selected for a number of international tournaments between them.

Chris Kaupman '20.

Gareth Barry's game is marked by a rare level of consistency, and he would sometimes make the scoresheet, with 57 domestic and international goals in all competitions. A player capable of crossing the ball when played wide and also the occasional goal-assist, his most commendable statistic is one of 1,668 accurate long passes. (At least that's what the official Premier League statisticians, Opta, are telling us!) A vigorous competitor, he was no stranger to a referee's notebook (as documented elsewhere in this book). Similarly, James Milner is a reliable, multifunctional footballer who reads the game just as intelligently; and again, like Barry, also admired for his courage and single-mindedness; and also in the same bracket as an occasional goalscorer, with a total of 59 in all spheres of the senior game. He's also proved that you can succeed at the highest level without the mercurial trickery of a player like Cristiano Ronaldo being part of your game. An abiding feature of Milner's game is his fitness and energy – which enable him to maintain a feisty presence wherever he plays in a team; without this, he wouldn't be the calibre of player that he has become.

If you want to differentiate between these two stalwarts, then the obvious place to look is their respective medal hauls. Barry has three: a Premier League title and FA Cup success with Manchester City; plus the often belittled and now defunct UEFA Intertoto Cup with Aston Villa. His England buddy, by comparison, has fared rather better. At the time of writing, Milner boasts ten: three Premier League titles and one of each of the following: the FA Cup, Football League Cup and FA Community Shield. Beyond domestic football, again one of each: the UEFA Intertoto Cup, UEFA Super Cup, The UEFA Champions League and the FIFA World Club Championship. Named PFA Player of the Year for 2009-10, nearly all of Milner's titles have come mid-to-late career. This upsurge owes to a transition from playing for middle-ranking clubs to the ranks of Premier League nobility with Manchester City and, notably, Liverpool. Barry's major successes also came with an elevation to English football's top table – again by relocating to silk-stocking South Manchester. He, too, was well into his senior career before he savoured major honours.

Aside from the Premier League's A-listers, the more we think about those on the B-list, the more that list grows. There are numerous players, not necessarily record-breakers, nor players ascribed rock star status by the press, who've made a telling contribution. Players who've perhaps been loyal or steadfastly and quietly set about their business, playing a crucial role. **Michael Carrick** gave Manchester United and Alex Ferguson 12 years of unstinting service. He didn't court the media, or seek out a film star bride; his demeanour and presence was far more reserved. He almost silently performed his role, perhaps mirroring what some fans see in their own lives. He wasn't noted for his stamina or agility. Instead, Carrick would hover just behind the more attacking midfielders, namely Scholes and Keane, protecting the defensive line with vital interceptions. The fact that he wasn't terribly mobile was absolutely no impediment – such was his vision, his range of passing and crossing ability. With more than 300 Premier League appearances for United (plus 136 for his boyhood club, West Ham), Carrick was his team's metronome, dictating both the rhythm and tempo of the Manchester United team. As games ebbed and flowed, Carrick's reassuring presence helped regulate United's pattern and pace of play. In short, Carrick was more queen than worker bee. He mastered the art of running a game, but without getting drawn into the abrasive cut and thrust of a midfield rumpus – he left that to the battle-hardened Roy Keane. Though heavily decorated, winning every possible trophy at home (several Premier League titles therein) and in Europe too, many onlookers were surprised at his relatively modest tally of 34 England caps. Manchester City manager Pep Guardiola, whose native Spain celebrate the more measured approach to the game, identified Carrick as one of the best holding midfielders he's ever seen. High praise indeed.

Fans of my own club, Blackburn Rovers, don't just point to Alan Shearer and his title-winning team-mates. Another figure remembered with huge fondness is **Tugay Kerimoglu**, known simply as 'Tugay', who was essential to the club prolonging their Premier League stay and often qualifying for European competition. Very similar to his English counterpart Carrick, Tugay exuded all of the same attributes. Etched into the memory of every Ewood Park regular of the early noughties, was his seemingly endless time on the ball, allowing him to select the most apposite ball, then execute the pass with devastating accuracy. Supporters of Galatasaray, and those who saw him play 94 times for Turkey, will attest to these qualities.

Any attempt to document the careers of even the top 5% best of those who've played in the Premier League would demand a tome of gargantuan proportions and represent a nigh-on impossible task. On that note, apologies to the admirers of players who don't feature in the book. But there's still time and space to pay homage to one or two more, before I sign off.

Fans of Tottenham Hotspur will fondly recall the subtle delights of **Luka Modric**. Not dissimilar to Tugay, his pristine touch gave him a few extra seconds on the ball – which he used most tellingly. Whether crossing the ball, or making a shorter slide-rule pass to open up a defence, Modric delivered time and again. His intelligent reading of the game also enabled him to find pockets of space and hurt the opposition with the sheer accuracy of his passing. Deft, disguised and defence-splitting, Modric the playmaker could precipitate his opponent's downfall when there'd been no obvious cause for alarm. Sadly, their respective paths never crossed – but Brian Clough's astute observation that "it only takes a second to score a goal" is never better illustrated than by the quick-thinking and craft of Luka Modric. Whilst noted for guile and artistry, and despite being waif-like in stature, Modric always attended to his defensive responsibilities. This mercurial butterfly of a midfielder was gone all too soon (making just 127 Spurs appearances) – but it would be wholly

remiss not to mention, arguably, the most gifted, elegant footballer the Balkans have ever produced.

Messi and Cristiano Ronaldo. The only player to smash this duopoly – Luka Modric. This was an achievement of some magnitude – and the kudos which comes with it, befitting his utterly prodigious talent.

The term 'right-back' in no way does justice to the strengths of **Seamus Coleman**. 'Leader' and 'marauding full-back' – and we're getting a bit nearer. Both Everton fans and those of the Premiership per se, should appreciate the full-blooded performances of this committed Irishman. Never found wanting for pace and stamina, the man from Donegal is frequently the instigator of an Everton sally. His dashing raids leave opponents looking like they're running through an Irish peat bog, or some other handicapping quagmire. He's served his club more than 300 times and represented his country on 61 occasions – thus far. His leadership qualities have seen him captain both club and country; and he proudly led out the Republic of Ireland at UEFA Euro 2016. The 2013-14 season culminated in the popular defender being named in the PFA Team of the Year. This was one third of a treble celebration, which saw Coleman scoop the Everton Players' Player of the Year and Everton Supporters' Player of the Year awards to boot. Loyal and dependable – every team needs a 'Seamus Coleman.

Another meritorious mainstay at Goodison Park was **Leighton Baines**. Dependable, rarely injured and an excellent team player, Baines could effectively link play down the left flank. He was probably most influential when he combined with the South African midfielder, Steven Pienaar. Taking penalties was a salient feature of Baines's career. In the Premier League alone, he netted 20 out of a possible 22. Only Trevor Steven (20) converted more in the top-flight for Everton.

Unsurprisingly then, Baines was also very adept with free-kicks and whipped in many a sterling cross for onrushing forwards. Arguably, his finest goal for Everton came from a direct free-kick at Newcastle United, in 2013; a game which Everton were to win 2-1. Thirty yards from goal, this was just about within his range – though Newcastle goalkeeper Tim Krul, and his defensive wall, were still expected to keep Baines at bay. Admittedly, the home side's woeful attempt to construct a wall would've left Emperor Hadrian apoplectic with his foot soldiers, but that in no way detracted from the quality of the strike. Bisecting Newcastle's leaping 'wall', this brutal blast seared into the far left-hand corner. If utter ferocity wasn't enough, a late swerve cruelly put paid to any hope for keeper Tim. Hadrian, his minions, limestone and earthworks – nothing could've kept this one out!

His team-mates saw fit to vote him their best player on three occasions, the club's fans twice and he also made PFA Team of the Year twice. Like his colleague Seamus Coleman, he proved to be a model of consistency.

Baines showed enough ability to win 30 England caps and played at the 2014 FIFA World Cup in Brazil.

This guitar-loving Merseysider retired in 2020 and immediately joined Everton's coaching ranks. A truly wholesome career – and one which continues mentoring the young.

Back to Manchester, **Joe Hart** was an enduring feature in the Premier League for a number of seasons. This Salop-born goalkeeper began his professional career with his hometown club, Shrewsbury Town. Standing at 6'5", his height was always going to provide him with incredible reach and make him warden of his own penalty area. This confident young keeper had only played 54 matches and still a teenager, when he was quickly snapped up by Manchester City.

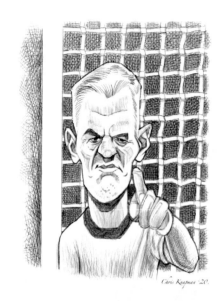

In February 2015, Hart excelled himself against Barcelona in the Champions League. Though City were eventually overcome by the Catalan aristocrats and eventual European champions, Joe Hart made every attempt to thwart them. Losing 2-1 at home (3-1 on aggregate), Hart produced ten saves at the Etihad – a competition record for an English keeper. This included a penalty from Lionel Messi, who was simply peerless at the time. The multiple Ballon d'Or winner later described Hart as a "phenomenon". Endorsements don't come much better than that!

Many players will envy the contents of Hart's medal drawer – two Premier League titles, one FA cup win and two more triumphs in the Football League Cup. The not-to-be-sniffed-at haul would have been further augmented, had it not been for two key reasons. Firstly, he suffered a dip in form – for both club and country. Secondly, new Spanish gaffer Pep Guardiola strongly favoured a goalkeeper more adept with his feet. His preferred game plan was to play out from the goalkeeper, with the ball very much on terra firma. Though undoubtedly a very good goalkeeper, Hart wasn't altogether comfortable with this method of play.

Post Manchester City, Hart became a serial loanee, which included a season with Torino in Italy's Serie A, followed by a permanent (if brief) stay at Burnley, before settling at Celtic – where he's presently incumbent.

Despite the downturn in his fortunes, Joe Hart will, time immemorial, be regarded as one of the finest goalkeepers we've seen. You don't play 266 Premier League games for one of the country's eminent football clubs and reach the estimable figure of 75 England caps if you aren't blessed with considerable ability. A loss of confidence may have affected his form latterly – but he'd already proven to be a master of his craft.

Manchester City fans will long remember his gobsmacking save at home to their arch-rivals, Manchester United, in 2008. With City losing 1-0 and the game drawing to a close, Hart ran up-field for a City corner, hoping to add extra firepower in their moment of need. Unfortunately for City and Hart, things quickly broke down and United began to counter. This required him to hightail it back to his own goal. As he made his way back, Wayne Rooney (himself some distance from City's goal) lofted the ball goalwards, hoping to land the ball home before the keeper could complete his hasty retreat. Showing a brisk turn of pace, Hart was simply too quick. He made it just in time and spectacularly tipped the ball over the crossbar whilst still moving apace – which is not an easy thing to do.

Frequent overseas imports have been a facet of the Premier League for decades now – and this has come to include many goalkeepers. Joe Hart, though, has reminded us that that our long-standing tradition of England producing accomplished goalkeepers is certainly not consigned to history and are ever-present in our top flight.

Elsewhere in this book, I've referenced West Ham's noteworthy youth system. Bobby Moore, Rio Ferdinand, Chelsea's John Terry and Frank Lampard all germinated at the Upton Park club. Amongst the latest to be nurtured there is **Declan Rice**. In the modern game, he really benchmarks what a holding or defensive midfield player should be.

If we were discussing the monarchy, we might talk about royal lineage. When it comes to defensive midfield players, Rice shares ancestry with Billy Bonds and a more recent bloodline with former Hammer Michael Carrick.

At the tender age of 23 this talented footballer is already the captain of his club and has 28 England caps under his belt. Although born in South London, his parental grandparents hailed from Ireland's County Cork, thus giving him the eligibility to represent Ireland at international level. Indeed, he represented the Emerald Isle at every youth level and went on to play at senior level in three friendly matches in 2018.

Jamaican-born **Raheem Sterling** first came to the notice of Premier League aficionados in 2010, when he was plucked from the relative obscurity of the QPR academy by Liverpool for a modest fee of £450k plus add-ons. He was heralded as a young player of great potential, with phrases such as 'Wonder Kid' being bandied about in some quarters at the time. Indeed, in 2014 his talent was duly recognised by sporting journalists who bestowed on him their prestigious Golden Boy award.

Having made his senior Liverpool debut in March 2012, he continued to impress the fans with his lightning pace and dribbling skills. His most natural role is as a winger, but he has great adaptability and can also perform well in a more central midfield position, no doubt endearing him to his then manager Brendan Rodgers. For a relatively small man (1.7m) he is very strong on the ball and extremely adept at out-muscling bigger defenders to retain possession.

Although his Liverpool career was progressing well, with the PFA Young Player of the Year now under his belt, he opted for pastures new with a £44m + move to the ambitious Manchester City. There was some controversy surrounding the transfer, with Liverpool having offered him improved terms to stay at Anfield. It is fair to say he didn't part on the best of terms.

A tally of 23 goals from 129 Liverpool appearances was a modest return for a player of Sterling's quality. It's fair to say though that his move to City catapulted Sterling to a different level. Whether it was his own desire to succeed, coupled with the top-class coaching skills of Pep Guardiola is open to debate, but his career certainly took off following the transfer – 130 goals from 337 appearances certainly bears testimony to the improvement, not to mention the four League titles, four EFL Cups and FA Cup achieved during his time at The Etihad. Nineteen goals from 74 appearances for his country is also a decent return for a player deployed in an attacking wing position.

Outside of football, Sterling has been a significant advocate of racial equality in sport. His contribution in this area was rightly recognised with the award of an MBE in 2021.

Documenting the careers of those players who've graced the Premier League with distinction is, manifestly, a colossal undertaking. Whilst some players merit a full chapter all of their own, others have been mentioned in dispatches. These are the players who, whilst not quite deemed worthy of an entire chapter to themselves, have played very well and cannot be ignored altogether. Even so, there are still innumerable figures who haven't been covered, as to do so would effectively render the book an encyclopaedia. Fans may bemoan the absence of Gilberto Silva, Stuart Pearce, Matthew Upson, Les Ferdinand or even Niall Quinn. Scope remains to pay a homage to such stars in a future publication; and along with rising stars yet to reach their apogee (the supremely gifted Phil Foden being the perfect example) and fledgling footballers yet to step out in front of the cameras. Almost like a living and breathing organism, the Premier League will continue to evolve; meaning that the list of candidates worthy of a writer's 'ink' will grow – as some existing players dramatically improve and brand new names emerge.

MAVERICKS AND DELINQUENTS

'Thou art a traitor, and a miscreant; Too good to be so, and too bad to live.'

From Tybalt to King Claudius to Lady Macbeth – Shakespeare gave us a veritable profusion of characters who, in some cases, just didn't want to toe the line, and others who simply perpetrated unadulterated wickedness. Quite what the Bard would've made of the English Premier League and the unseemly behaviour therein, one can only speculate; doubtless to say, it would've surely met with strong and floridly worded disapproval. Yes, from the rash to the downright unscrupulous, England's top division has seen a plethora of individuals who've flouted the rules. Some of these players have been repeat offenders and some have transgressed in the most novel of ways.

Perhaps it's apt to begin with Manchester United's 'King Eric' **Cantona**. Like some of the other characters who feature in this chapter, he'll be covered elsewhere in this book – owing to his considerable ability and influence. Equal only to his undisputed talent, was his tendency to do and say the unexpected.

On a cold January night at Selhurst Park, Cantona committed what might be considered the ultimate sin for a professional sports person – by reacting to crowd hostility. Cantona had been well-shackled by Crystal Palace defender Richard Shaw. His frustration at being so closely marshalled got the better of him and he responded by kicking his opponent. Unsurprisingly, he was instantly dismissed. As he trudged despondently towards the tunnel, Palace fan Matthew Simmons began to holler abuse towards the Frenchman. At this point, Cantona was supposed to keep his professional cool: cue the complete opposite. Cantona – astonishingly to this day – launched himself wildly at Simmons with a 'kung-fu' style kick. Not content with his initial lunge, the boy from one of Marseille's toughest neighbourhoods followed up his initial sortie with a flurry of punches – much like a heavyweight boxer seeking to finish someone off. He apparently grew up in a cave in the Les Caillols Hills on the city's outskirts – made habitable by his stonemason grandfather. Well, it would seem that he'd taken his neanderthal living arrangements rather too seriously with an outburst befitting a barbarian! After serving an eight-month ban, Cantona was accepted back into the fold, whereupon he resumed his role of tormenting the opposition. Had he not been such an integral part of manager Alex Ferguson's plans, one wonders whether the club would've got rid of him.

There are different breeds of footballing offenders. What footballers do in their spare time has often proved to be their undoing. A prime example of this particular species is former Everton and Glasgow Rangers frontman **Duncan Ferguson**. Whilst extremely competent at needling defenders and irking referees, Ferguson presented just as great a danger off the field. He was known (some might say affectionately in the 'lovable rogue' sense) as 'Duncan Disorderly' amongst Scottish journalists. A litany of offences demonstrates that he

didn't acquire this sobriquet for nothing. Make no mistake here, affectionate or not, this particular nickname was well-earned: an epithet suitable for a man who struggled to curb his temper when befuddled by excess alcohol. It wasn't advisable to stand in his way when he'd had too much liquor. He garnered four convictions for assault: two arising from taxi-rank melees, one involving an altercation with a fisherman at a pub in Fife and, notoriously, for headbutting Raith Rovers defender John McStay. Whilst the first three of these crimes resulted in either a fine or probation, the McStay incident resulted in him being handed down a three-month prison sentence. It's extremely rare for a professional footballer to receive a criminal conviction for an on-the-field offence – let alone to be sent to jail. Word of 'Duncan Disorderly's' shameful track record clearly spread far and wide, as Finnish composer Osmo Tapio Raihala was inspired to pen a symphonic poem as a 'musical portrait' of this Scottish felon, titled *Barlinnie Nine* – presumably a reference to the infamous HMP Barlinnie, where he was incarcerated. Another black mark on his record is his eight Premier League red cards – a record he shares with Patrick Viera and Richard Dunne. Ferguson was born in Stirling; unlike the town's most famous associate, William Wallace, it's doubtful that they'll be building a monument to him!

Another 'type' is the recidivist. Whereas Cantona is remembered for a moment of unexpected ultra-violence, some players quietly go about the business of consistent low-level offending. Appearing with the fresh-faced innocence of a choir boy, **Gareth Barry** isn't known for out-and-out bellicose thuggery; but he has kept the statisticians busy. Whilst Barry holds the record for the most yellow cards in the Premier League to date, one has to compute the data in terms of a cards-to-games ratio. Although Barry has received a whopping 123 yellow cards and counting, one has to bear in mind that it's taken him 678 matches to achieve this dreadful record. Lee Cattermole, who performed for Middlesbrough, Wigan Athletic and mainly Sunderland collected 88 yellows and seven red cards in 271 appearances – significantly worse a record than Barry, when one takes into account that he's played far fewer Premier League matches.

One cannot conduct a conversation on the subject of ill-disciplined footballers without the name '**Joey Barton**' being mentioned at some point in proceedings. If his tendency to nark referees is evidenced by his 78 yellow and six red cards isn't bad enough on its own (it places him well up the Premier League's poor discipline charts), behaviour outside of actual matches has been truly abominable. In May 2008, Barton was involved in a 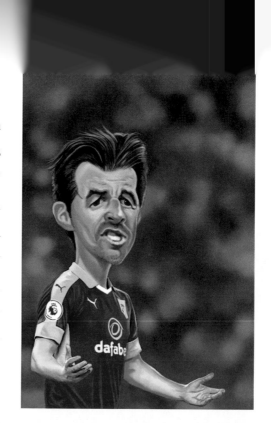 fracas in Liverpool city centre, resulting in him receiving a six-month prison sentence for common assault and affray. He was released after serving 74 days. And, three weeks before this release, he was given a four-month suspended prison sentence for assault occasioning actual bodily harm, as a result of a bust-up with 'team-mate' Ousame Dabo on the training ground. Additionally, the fact that the Football Association have thrice charged Barton with violent conduct provides further evidence that this pugnacious Merseysider appears to be on rather a short fuse! This resulted in Barton being banned for the longest period in Premier League history – an incredibly punitive 12 matches!

It's often the case that the most indecorous of behaviour is born out of intense rivalry. This was certainly the case with Arsenal's French hero, **Patrick Viera**. Whilst he was capable of transgressing in any given game, it was his bitter midfield rivalry with Manchester United's **Roy Keane** that brought out the best – and worst – in this Senegal-born player. Quite simply, Roy Keane was his nemesis and vice-versa. This poisonous relationships was exacerbated by its sheer longevity. Both players were dominant presences in the Premier League for the latter half of the 1990s and well into the 2000s. Both wanting to be the Premier League's alpha male in the centre of the park, this animosity bubbled away, season after season – sometimes reaching boiling point. Asked to articulate his thoughts on Arsenal in interview, Keane bluntly cuts to the word 'hatred'; his assessment of competing with Viera does nothing to play down their reciprocal hostility. Keane, remaining succinct, talked about "going into battle" against Arsenal. He didn't mention Viera by name – but in the mind of the Irishman, it's surely fair to say that the words 'Viera' and 'Arsenal' were – and maybe still are – interchangably synonymous. Viera, a little more balanced, said "he is my favourite enemy. I don't know if that makes sense to you, but it makes sense to me – because I loved every aspect of his game".

The pair had a good 19 opportunities to leer menacingly at one another – sometimes seeking to maim their foe for good measure. Additionally, the pervasive media coverage of Premier League provided ample opportunity for both of them to aggravate the situation, with the odd barbed interview. This enabled both of them to intensify their rivalry, and in doing so, raise the bar when they both next took to the same field; and so it rolled on.

Then there is **Paulo Di Canio**. The word 'maverick' doesn't do justice to the emotional extremity and oddball behaviour of this capricious Roman. Once described by his manager, David Pleat, as having "a mind like a blast furnace",

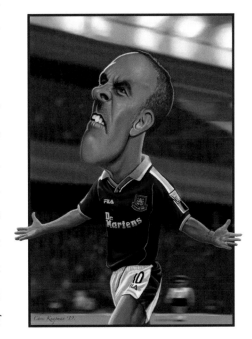

Di Canio functions on a different intellectual level to many of those he played with and against.

Expressing sympathies for the leader of the National Fascist Party, Benito Mussolini, Di Canio's controversial opinions are matched only by his wayward responses to fellow players, managers and boardroom figures. He has gone on record saying that he believes that Mussolini was a principled individual and deeply misunderstood. Di Canio himself added weight to the claims that he's a fascist by making a fascist-style salute to his beloved Lazio fans – a club who are considered to align with the political far right-wing. In a country such as Italy, where football clubs have closer ties with political parties, it was no surprise when this provoked an incendiary response from both the media and football fans. Likewise, the Italian FA concurred with the view that this was a political statement and duly banned and fined him. Di Canio has claimed that this gesture was merely to show his affinity with adoring *I Biancocelesti* supporters; however, the ambivalence continues – his body is floridly tattooed with imagery synonymous with fascism. On his right bicep he sports the letters 'DUX', which means 'Il Duce' in Italian and translates as 'The Leader' – an epithet commonly attributed to Mussolini. There are other symbols amongst his tattoos (of which there are known to be at least 14) allied to fascism, covering his back: an imperial eagle holding the fasces (a bound bundle of wood indicating power over life and death) and even one of Mussolini wearing a military helmet ! Quite how his extensive and seemingly fascist body art squares with his repeated claims that he rejects fascism is a source of continued debate. And all of this from a man who claims to have a deep interest in Japanese culture – which espouses notions of calmness and pacifism!

Unfortunately for Di Canio, the defining moment of his time on English soil came whilst at Sheffield Wednesday. He caused a sensation when he floored match referee Paul Alcock, against Arsenal at Hillsborough. It all started with a foul by Di Canio's Wednesday team-mate Wim Jonk, on Patrick Viera. Viera reacted by shoving the Dutchman; then enter rapscallion Di Canio. Angered by this, the Italian pushes Viera, who is chased by Richie Humphreys. Several players become involved, including Gunner Martin Keown, who tries to quell this growing

affray. He, apparently by accident, catches Di Canio in the mouth. His response was not the most gentlemanly – he responds by kicking the Arsenal centre-half, then attempts to gouge his eye. Alcock then wades in, brandishing a red card towards Di Canio; and this sends the already maddened midfielder into apoplexy. He firmly pushes the referee, who stumbles backwards as though someone's quickly whipped away a chair as he motions to sit down. Alcock – probably trying vainly to remain upright – back pedals and goes down in stages. Di Canio's assessment is spot-on:

"It wasn't a violent gesture, it was a gesture of disappointment. I could push my eight-year-old daughter Ludovica that way and she wouldn't fall over."

He also likened it to slapstick comedy. He later asked Sky Sport's Andy Hinchcliffe if he was likely to be banned. The pundit's reply: "Paolo, nobody has ever done this in the history of the English game." The Football Association took the dimmest possible view of this and duly banned him for a hefty 11 matches and fined him £10,000. The repercussions of this moment were long-lasting. When he was appointed manager of Swindon Town, backers GMB Union withdrew their support. It was a similar story when he became Sunderland boss. Labour Party one-time bigwig David Miliband resigned from the board – referencing Di Canio's "past political statements". In addition to numerous contretemps, his explosive temper was already known in Italy. In one incident his Lazio chairman, Claudio Lotito, said something that didn't sit right with Di Canio and his boiling rage saw him overturn a buffet table. One might question why Premier League and Scottish clubs even considered bringing him to British shores. But Di Canio, who could play as a deep-lying forward, winger or midfielder, possessed the ability to dribble and other ball-skills that rend spectators speechless and agog. His ability was such that the revered Alex Ferguson twice tried to sign him for Manchester United. Despite this talent (his West Ham manager Harry Redknapp said "he can do things with the ball that people can only dream of"), he never played for Italy. In the light of his many ludicrous moments – not to mention his outlandish ideas – is it any wonder that several coaches of Italy's national team overlooked him?

Though outrageous, Di Canio doesn't have a monopoly when it comes to wacky and outrageous behaviour. Manchester City and Liverpool striker **Mario Ballotelli** perplexed colleagues and onlookers alike. His career at Inter Milan had been marred by disciplinary issues – souring his relationship with manager José Mourinho. This came to a head when he was suspended from the first team. Fellow Italian Roberto Mancini gave him a new beginning at Manchester City. His performances were somewhat inconsistent and his off-field buffoonery did nothing to enhance his reputation.

On the eve of the Manchester derby in 2011, his more level-headed team-mates might have been reclining on the sofa, perhaps watching a film with a camomile tea, or focusing their minds on the task that lay ahead. Ballotelli's preparation, however, was different – very different. No yoga, no session booked with a masseur; nor was he in a sequestered place musing over the poetry of Byron or Keats, or listening to the soothing dulcet tones of Chopin or Brahms. Instead, to the dismay of his employer, Manchester City, not to mention Greater Manchester Fire Rescue Service, he thought it apposite to have a firework display – in his bathroom! Two fire crews, four breathing apparatus and two hose reels were deployed to the smoke and fire-damaged property. Apparently, he'd been launching fireworks from a bathroom window when his towels caught fire. Thoroughly unpredictable, enigmatic and downright unruly, Ballotelli's crackpot behaviour doesn't end there. With Mancini already on the warpath after his recent European dismissal against Dynamo Kiev, the striker provided yet another turn of the screw. This time it was throwing darts at City youth team players from a first-floor window at their training ground. Unless a dartboard is a feature of this facility, one can only assume that he saw fit to take his darts with him that morning. This being the case, it appears that this offence was possibly aggravated by premeditation! Fortunately, his aim wasn't as good as in front of goal and nobody was hurt – but that's not entirely the point. He said that he did it to relieve boredom. This action alone speaks volumes about the Italian's mentality and lack of maturity. Although he scored 20 goals at the Etihad, ongoing disciplinary problems led to him being fined and eventually sold to AC Milan.

Premier League players are handsomely paid and this, in some cases, feeds an inflated sense of self-importance. **Carlos Tevez** perhaps illustrates this point better than any other. In 2011, he allegedly (according to Roberto Mancini) refused to take to the field during a Champions League match with Bayern Munich. What actually happened was never truly established, with Tevez claiming that a language barrier led to a misunderstanding and that he was actually prepared to play.

Tevez had reportedly done the same at Brazilian club Corinthians and the City hierarchy chose to believe Mancini's claim. The Argentinian forward was, at the time, the Premier League's highest earner and City fined him £500,000 – the biggest fine ever meted out in English football history. He was also placed on garden leave for two weeks and wasn't even permitted to train with his team-mates. After initially being told by his manager that he would never play for City again, he remained at the club until 2013. It seems that Mancini simply couldn't ignore him as City pushed for the league title.

If Tevez was guilty of refusing to play, it certainly wasn't his first indiscretion. In a career littered with petulant transfer requests and tantrums, he'd previously upset fellow players at his former club, West Ham. When he was substituted against Sheffield United, he preceded to have a hissy fit upon leaving the pitch and marched out of the ground in a huff. The West Ham squad weren't impressed and were allowed to choose a fitting punishment. They decided that he should donate half a week's wages to charity and train in a Brazil shirt; he assented to the former, but refused to comply with the latter.

Despite many bumps in the road, Tevez has never struggled to attract the attention of big clubs – his work-rate (when on the field), skill and very healthy goalscoring record being his saving graces.

Other troublesome individuals were Dennis Wise, Robbie Savage and Stan Collymore. **Dennis Wise** was booked on 70 occasions – a not inconsiderable number for a player who managed 278 Premier League games. Some players have more than doubled his number of appearances before getting anywhere near a figure even approaching that number of yellow cards; and to that you can add three reds. Despite managing more than 300 games in just over a decade at Chelsea, the England midfielder was constantly beleaguered by disciplinary issues. In the 1998-99 season, he missed just over a third of the season, when a slew of cards saw him sidelined for a preposterous 15 matches.

Wise's worst delinquent acts didn't occur during matches. In 1995, he was convicted of assaulting a taxi driver. He received a three-month custodial sentence, which was overturned upon appeal. He did, however, still have to pay £965 for damage to the cab, £169 for damaging the driver's spectacles and £100 compensation for causing him shock and distress. Even worse was to follow during his transient stay at Leicester City. He was sent home from Finland for breaking the jaw of Foxes defender Callum Davidson. He was sacked by the club and his appeal, on this occasion, was summarily rejected.

A different type of offender was **Robbie Savage**. His admirers might describe him as 'competitive' or 'tenacious', whereas others may employ less complimentary adjectives. In his 346 Premier League appearances, he amassed 89 yellow cards. For a time, this was a Premier League record – but has since been surpassed by Paul Scholes, Lee Bowyer and Kevin Davies. Interestingly, many people have expressed amazement that he only ever received one red! Whether it's the fact that he was quite tall for a central midfielder – together with his lambent locks of blond being ruffled by English squall – but something made his foul play seem that bit more egregious than it perhaps actually was. This was compounded by his habit of verbalising his thoughts to opponents and referees for most of the 90 or so minutes. During his time at Blackburn, the Sunderland manager, Roy Keane, was supposedly poised to sign him. It is said that Keane received a rather puerile "wazzupp" voicemail from the Welshman – to which Keane responded "I can't be f***ing signing that".

Frequently accused of simulation, Tottenham Hostspur fans are said to hold a long-standing grudge towards Savage. Savage scythed down Justin Edinburgh in the 1999 League Cup Final, resulting in the Spurs player raising his arms. Though the retaliation was minimal, Savage feigned injury and Edinburgh was dismissed.

Darting back and forth between defence and attack, Savage was an irrepressible nuisance to other players and officials. In retirement, he's still very much in the consciousness of the footballing public. Just as charismatic off the field as he was on it, he's very engaging in his work as a match pundit; and when he co-hosts post-match radio phone-ins, he can be entertaining and insightful in equal measure

No tour of the Premier League's mavericks and delinquents would be complete without a look at the career of **Stan Collymore**. A winner of just three England caps, one of his former managers, John Gregory, said of him "he had everything Thierry Henry has got and more". Bearing in mind the considerable abilities and colossal achievements of the French forward, that's some statement! Gregory wasn't the only one to eulogize about Collymore. *The Daily Telegraph* wrote in 2004: "until Wayne Rooney came along, Collymore was as naturally talented an individual as British football has produced in forty years." It is certainly true that he possessed staggering innate talent; unfortunately, this wasn't allied to a temperament to match. Furthermore, Collymore is, perhaps, the ultimate personification of the 'maverick' concept – in that he'd absolutely no conception of the fact that football is a team game and was far too self-absorbed to entertain such a notion.

From disgracefully punching his then girlfriend, television personality Ulrika Jonsson, to being sent home early from Leicester City's Spanish break (for discharging a fire extinguisher, amongst other things), he was always liable to do the unexpected. It's also worth noting that he totalled just 163 Premier League appearances, and 64 (at Liverpool) was the most he ever managed at one club; facts which surely say something about his inability to integrate. In his autobiography, he states that he's been treated for clinical depression and has supported the *Depression Alliance* charity. He goes on to state that he's been diagnosed with borderline personality disorder – which may go some way to explaining his conduct as a footballer.

He sometimes works as a football pundit – which is not unusual in retirement. What is more unusual is his support for *The Scottish National Party* (despite being born and raised in Staffordshire) and his appearance as 'Kevin Franks' in the film *Basic Instinct 2*, co-starring with Sharon Stone. But, by now, we should've learnt to expect the unlikely – something which is likely to continue.

Lee Bowyer, in his heyday with Leeds United, was unquestionably a fine player – well-remembered for a string of scoring appearances in the club's Champions League campaigns and run to the semi-final. Most regrettably though, fans are just as likely to recall him for a career tainted by a woeful disciplinary record and a series of most unsavoury incidents, both on and off the football field.

Bowyer's first brush with authority, though a technical breach of criminal law and FA code of conduct, was relatively inoffensive, compared to what was to follow. It occurred in his early days at Charlton Athletic, when he failed an FA drugs test for cannabis use. He was subsequently dropped from the England Under-18s squad and suspended for eight weeks whilst he attended the Football Association's own rehabilitation course. Only a few months later he was up before the beak again – a panel with which he was to become far too well-acquainted. This time, however, it was for an offence that some might deem more reprehensible morally. He was convicted of affray and fined £4,500 for an incident in a fast food outlet. CCTV footage corroborated allegations that he'd hurled chairs about the restaurant and racially abused a staff member of Asian origin. Then, after his transfer to Leeds, he was involved in a most serious incident in a nightclub. He and a fellow Leeds player, Jonathan

Woodgate, were charged with causing grievous bodily harm with intent and affray. Again, the victim (who was severely injured) was Asian. After two trials, the first of which collapsed, Bowyer was acquitted. This episode didn't end there. Some five years later, Bowyer agreed an out-of-court settlement, paying £170,000 in damages to the victim and his less severely injured brother. Clearly, despite his acquittal at the second trial, this is tantamount to accepting some level of culpability. Also – rather amazingly – Bowyer took exception to being fined four weeks' wages for breaching the club's code of conduct. This is rendered even more appalling by the fact that the club had met his extensive legal fees and supported him throughout. They reacted by transfer-listing the midfielder. The dispute was settled and Bowyer was removed from the list; however, this proved to be temporary – as he was returned to it when he rejected a five-year contract at the season's end. Bowyer proved to be a rather contradictory team figure. An impressive career with the West Yorkshire club was interspersed with moments of recklessness.

In 2003, after the briefest of stints at West Ham United, he moved to Newcastle – where his unruly behaviour showed no sign of abating. His continued to enter referees' notebooks on an alarmingly regular basis – one wonders why the FA didn't provide them with a library-style stamp bearing his name! 2005 saw a spike in his aggression, when he was involved in a pitch brawl with one of his own team, Kieron Dyer.

His initial punishment was the statutory three-match ban but, being perceived as the instigator, the FA doubled his ban and imposed a £30,000 fine. Newcastle added to his woes by fining him six weeks' wages. The repercussions also reached into the domain of criminal law, when Northumbria Police charged him under section four of The Public Order Act. He pleaded guilty to using threatening behaviour, was fined £600 and ordered to pay £1000 costs.

In 2006 a return to his boyhood team, West Ham United, got off to a somewhat inauspicious of start. Many of the Hammers faithful were unhappy with the signing of Bowyer, due to his perceived racist attitude and behaviour – so much so that they staged a protest outside Upton Park, when he was introduced to the fans.

Bowyer rounded off his career with spells at Birmingham City and Ipswich Town. The cards continued to flow and, whilst with Brum, he was forced to make a public apology for issuing a verbal tirade to a West Bromwich Albion supporter.

A career characterized by a mixture of fine play and abject behaviour is strangely at odds with his presentation as the Charlton Athletic manager. A series of candid media interviews have shown him to be a thoughtful and balanced individual, who's seemingly matured in retirement.

Then we have **Luis Suarez**, once of Liverpool. Before moving to Merseyside, he plied his trade in the Dutch Erdivisie for Ajax. It was here that he began to cultivate a reputation for cheating and, specifically, biting opponents. His first victim was PSV's Otman Bakkal. This caused immediate waves in the media, with national newspaper *De Telegraaf* branding him the "the Cannibal of Ajax". Although Ajax had imposed a two-match suspension, the Dutch FA deemed this insufficient and increased it to seven matches. He was also fined. The one carnal act wasn't, of course, enough to satiate a simmering vampiric need. It was more than two years before he was apprehended for this again. In 2013 he sunk his teeth into Chelsea's Branislav Ivanovic. It was missed by officials, but video evidence confirmed the offence.

Even then Prime Minister David Cameron saw fit to proffer an opinion, calling for the FA to take a hard line with the Uruguayan. Maybe they were listening; following careful consideration, the Football Association hit Suarez with a ten-match ban.

Suarez also tarnished his reputation by racially abusing Manchester United's Patrice Evra. Supported by his club, but found guilty by the FA (after a 'not guilty' plea), he was banned for eight matches and fined £40,000. He maintained his innocence and avoided shaking hands with Evra when the clubs next met. He later apologized for this act of churlishness.

Despite playing in an advanced role, Suarez collected a fair number of yellow cards and also the occasional red. This, together with a propensity for trying to deceive officials and harming opponents, could be viewed as the epitome of how Premier League football has developed; the financial stakes of each and every match being so high that some players will do anything to eke out an advantage – even if it's illegal and unpalatable to the spectator.

'Humans, so easily electrified by the snap, crackle, pop of blood, brutality, and butchery.' (Artemis Crow)

Vinnie Jones stands alone amongst those to have graced the English Premier League. Making 446 career appearances in all, with 184 falling in the Premier League era, his curriculum vitae bears a number of entries not to be found on anyone else's in English football per se.

Playing as a defensive midfielder, he was best known for combative and somewhat pugnacious approach to the role, as opposed to any kind of grace, finesse or creativity. In addition to an abundance of yellow cards, the brutal Jones was sent off on a shameful 12 occasions. Only Leicester City centre half Steve Walsh (who also graced the Premier League many times) and Roy

McDonough in the lower divisions, have outdone him with 13 red cards. He's tied in third place with Mark Dennis, whose top-flight career predates the inception of Premier League. Let's put it this way, if Attila The Hun had played football, his incarnation on the pitch would've been much like Vinnie Jones.

The indignity of holding the record for quickest ever yellow card also rests with Vinnie Jones. Playing for Chelsea in a 1992 FA Cup tie with Sheffield United, he managed to find his way into the referee's notebook after just 3 shocking seconds. One is not quite sure whether to stand aghast at this outrage, or marvel at the tremendousness of it as a feat.

Capped 9 times by Wales, Jones did experience some success. In 1988, he was part of the Wimbledon team, dubbed 'The Crazy Gang' by the media, who stole the FA Cup from odds-on favourites Liverpool.

But on or off the field of play, Jones and strife were never far apart; and it wasn't just football referees with whom Jones has been at loggerheads. This gritty, warmongering midfield man has oft incurred the wrath of the law. Convictions for actual bodily harm and criminal damage appear on his rap sheet. In 2003, an 'air rage' incident saw Jones convicted of assault and threatening behaviour, when he slapped a fellow passenger and threatened to murder the cabin crew !?! An £11,100 fine and 80 hours community service were to follow; as was the revocation of his firearms licence and seizure of his weaponry.

Finally, if his existence wasn't sufficiently vivid already, Vinnie Jones embarked on a now lengthy acting career. A veteran of more than fifty film credits, he rose to acting fame when he appeared in Guy Ritchie's hit crime caper, Lock, Stock and Two Smoking Barrels. Since then, he's also appeared alongside John

Travolta. He's now so entrenched in the acting profession, many publications list him as an English actor before they even mention football. The American public know him simply as an English actor and nothing more. Football fans, however, know him well as a belligerent midfield enforcer. One might say that things have come full circle, as he's very much typecast as someone who can play the brooding, criminal hardman – much the same as when he took to a football pitch.

Not the poster boy for the Premier League, or indeed 'the beautiful game' at all, but Vinnie Jones, football would be poorer for your absence.

EPILOGUE

The 2020-21 season, already besieged by the Covid-19 and its enormous complications therein, was further destabilised by an attempt to create a new European super league. It was the 'brainchild' of Juventus chairman Andrea Agnelli, Real Madrid president Florentino Perez and the Glazers at Manchester United.

This would involve 12 clubs breaking away and completely severing ties with the rest of the football community – with no promotion or relegation at all. Structurally, most European countries adhere to the pyramid system – meaning that a relatively modest club can aspire to reach the pinnacle of domestic or European club football. A super league would've completely put the kibosh on any club who dared to dream.

Though marketed as a coming together of the cream of the crop, this was quickly seen for what it really was: namely a cynical ploy to make money. It wasn't long before this unholy cabal faced staunch opposition from fans, players, managers, club owners, journalists, politicians - and beyond.

Such was the strength of opposition to the proposal, fierce rivals suspended hostilities to unite against what they collectively perceived to be a monstrous threat. For example, online communication between fans of Liverpool and Manchester United was shorn of its usual antipathy; instead, they were practically at the point of entente cordiale – becoming one voice in their condemnation of any European super league.

Within football, the reach of commerce is far and wide – and inevitably so. Indeed, some clubs would go to the wall without financial backing. A European super league, however, was more than the football could bear. Fierce opposition came from all quarters; the proposal was castigated by all and quickly expunged from UEFA's agenda – if it was ever really on it in the first place.

Those who tabled the suggestion of a new European league presented the biggest threat to the English Premier League in nearly three decades. The way in which we railed against this threat says a great deal about our affection for the Premier League as a format. Thankfully, as a result, our league systems retain their structural integrity; and those who run the game, their moral integrity.

If you're a club occupying the middle ranks, even outside the Premier League, a trip to the Allianz Arena in Munich remains ever the possibility.

COMING SOON

We've shone a light on the lives and careers of the Premier League players who set the gold standard. Next we'll be delving into the world of the football manager. We'll examine their quotes, anecdotes and sometimes eccentricities. From the old-fashioned taskmasters who ruled by fear, to the 21st century thinkers who see football as a science. From 'Cloughie' to 'The Professor' Wenger, plus many more, we'll reflect upon the managers who made a big impression. And we will, of course, pay homage to the real luminaries of football management and their monumental achievements. Both in triumph and disaster, we ruminate over the relative merits of the men on the touchline. Stepping into the realm of the football manager should pique the interest of every football fan.

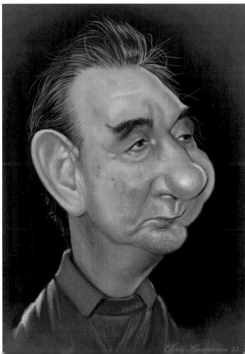